Creative Drama
for
the Classroom Teacher

SECOND EDITION

Creative Drama
for
the Classroom Teacher

RUTH BEALL HEINIG
Department of Communication Arts and Sciences

LYDA STILLWELL
Department of Theatre

Western Michigan University

Prentice-Hall, Inc., Englewood Cliffs, New Jersey 07632

Library of Congress Cataloging in Publication Data

Heinig, Ruth Beall
    Creative drama for the classroom teacher.

    (Prentice-Hall series in theatre and drama)
    Edition for 1974 published under title: Creative
dramatics for the classroom teacher.
    Bibliography: p.
    1. Drama in education.   I. Stillwell, Lyda
        joint author. II. Title.
PN3171.H33   1981   372.6'6   80-21275
ISBN 0-13-189415-3

Printed in the United States of America

10 9 8 7 6 5 4 3 2 1

Editorial/production supervision
and interior design by Virginia Cavanagh Neri
Cover design by Jorge Hernandez
Manufacturing buyer: Edmund W. Leone

PRENTICE-HALL INTERNATIONAL, INC., *London*
PRENTICE-HALL OF AUSTRALIA PTY. LIMITED, *Sydney*
PRENTICE-HALL OF CANADA, LTD., *Toronto*
PRENTICE-HALL OF INDIA PRIVATE LIMITED, *New Delhi*
PRENTICE-HALL OF JAPAN, INC., *Tokyo*
PRENTICE-HALL OF SOUTHEAST ASIA PTE. LTD., *Singapore*
WHITEHALL BOOKS LIMITED, *Wellington, New Zealand*

Contents

Contents

three

STORIES AND POEMS
FOR NARRATIVE PANTOMIME 46

four

DEVELOPING
NARRATIVE PANTOMIMES 70

five

STRENGTHENING CONCENTRATION
AND INVOLVEMENT 92

six
DEVELOPING
CREATIVE PANTOMIMES 110

seven
CREATIVE
STORY-BUILDING 125

eight
PANTOMIMES FOR GUESSING 139

nine
BEGINNING VERBAL ACTIVITIES 155

Contents

ten

CREATING DIALOGUE 170

eleven

STORY DRAMATIZATION 192

twelve

PLANNING DRAMA LESSONS 215

thirteen

THE LEADER AND THE GROUP 222

BIBLIOGRAPHY OF STORY AND POETRY ANTHOLOGIES AND BOOKS FOR DRAMATIZATION 241

INDEX 251

Preface

As I finish this second edition, I realize that there are two important risks I have taken. First, I have written alone this time. My coauthor, Lyda Stillwell, who is no longer involved in the field of child drama, chose not to participate in this second venture. I have missed being able to interact with a partner, and particularly with a good friend. At the outset it should be made clear that I am solely responsible for all the changes in this second edition and that she cannot be blamed for any errors in judgment I may have made.

The second risk is in thoroughly revising what was a successful first edition. As we indicated in the first edition, the book grew out of our creative drama classes at Western Michigan University. For over fifteen years, we have had demonstration classes from local elementary schools bused to our campus so that our college students can observe our work with children. At the end of the semester course, students are placed in teaching pairs in classrooms or other settings for a practicum. Both pre-service and in-service teachers, as well as students from a variety of other fields, including special education, theatre, psychology, and recreation, are able to take the course. Participation usually takes place in elementary classrooms of all types including regular, open, alternative, special education, mainstreamed, and bilingual. In addition, nursery schools, day care centers, libraries, churches, and recreational centers have also been utilized. My constant interaction with children, teachers, and college students in the field has resulted in a continuing modification of our original ideas, which I hope are still as useful as they were in their earlier stages.

This book is directed at the novice from any field who is interested in teaching creative drama and who needs practical advice on how to begin. Its aim is to guide the student through a step-by-step explanation of a number of activities, ranging from the simple to the more complex. This does not mean that the leader must try each type of activity before proceeding to the next. If the leader feels ready to try some of the more challenging material in the later chapters, he or she should do so. Ultimately, leaders are encouraged to develop a personal approach and to create activities geared to meet the needs and interests of their own groups.

Because space is limited, I have purposely continued to focus on materials and methods for teaching drama rather than on theories, other teaching approaches, history of the field, and so forth. I have found over the years that students and teachers have become increasingly aware of creative drama from a variety of sources, often have their own particular goals and objectives in mind, and are most concerned about being able to start on their own with techniques and ideas that work. It is with this purpose in mind that we began the book, and it is this purpose that I have continued to carry out.

Readers of the first edition will notice changes in chapter titles and numbers. Chapter Four of the first edition has been reworked and incorporated into other chapters. Chapter Twelve, "Planning a Drama Lesson," is a new chapter. The entire book, however, has been so thoroughly revised and reorganized with some new sections added, some deleted, new bibliographies, and new pictures, that it is impossible to detail them all. The basic approach has remained the same. I hope that rather than confusing our old readers, this new edition will be easier to understand and follow and will present many additional ideas and techniques. The words *Creative Dramatics* in the title of the first edition of this book have been changed to *Creative Drama* in keeping with the term preferred by the Children's Theatre Association of America.

As before, I have relied heavily on children's literature. This is not to suggest that teachers and children will not have ideas of their own. Good literature, however, can be an excellent stimulus for original ideas. In addition, children's literature has broadened in recent years to include an even wider variety of excellent materials to enhance many areas of the school curriculum. For these reasons, I feel that children's literature continues to be particularly helpful to the beginning leader.

I would like to thank the many people who have helped make this book possible: former teachers, colleagues, classroom teachers, college students, and children. The influences of all are evident on each page.

Thanks is also expressed to the wonderful people at Prentice-Hall, particularly to production editor Ginny Neri, who helped lessen the trauma of authorship.

Most of all, I wish to thank my husband, Ed, who always gives me encouragement and support, even when I'm ready to give up on myself.

Ruth Beall Heinig

TO LOOK AT ANY THING

To look at any thing,
If you would know that thing,
You must look at it long:
To look at this green and say
'I have seen spring in these
Woods,' will not do—you must
Be the thing you see:
You must be the dark snakes of
Stems and ferny plumes of leaves,
You must enter in
To the small silences between
The leaves,
You must take your time
And touch the very peace
They issue from.

John Moffitt

Creative Drama
for
the Classroom Teacher

Chapter One

Introduction

We are looking in on three classrooms during creative drama sessions:

"The Three Little Pigs" is being dramatized in a first-grade classroom. The teacher has divided the class into groups of four. Each group has its specified area to work in. The teacher narrates the story, pausing for the children to act out the appropriate action.

In the background a recording of Henry Mancini's "Baby Elephant Walk" is being played softly. Its lilting beat obviously influences the movements of the children as they play the story.

When the first and second little pigs are eaten, they sit on the sidelines and become the sound effects for the rest of the story. They help the Wolf huff and puff; they rumble for the butter churn rolling down the hill; and they make the noise of the crackling fire under the pot of boiling water.

After the story is played once, there is spontaneous applause from everyone for everyone. The children ask to repeat the story, and some decide they want to switch parts in their group. After reorganizing themselves, the second playing begins.

We move to a third-grade classroom where we learn that the teacher has been dealing with the subject of slavery and freedom. The children have been interested in the story of Harriet Tubman and her work with the Underground Railroad, so the teacher has decided to guide the children in exploring what it would be like to be a slave seeking freedom. Some of the activities the children have already experienced are writing secret messages of escape plans using code systems; learning the song "Follow the Drinking Gourd" and the significance of

"Little Pig, Little Pig, let me come in . . ."

the gourd as symbolizing the Big Dipper or northward direction; discussions of situations encountered by slaves and the feelings they generate—separation from family, traveling by night under cover, and being assisted by sympathetic people. Today, the children will experience the trip to freedom.

The classroom has been rearranged, and chairs have been pushed back against the walls. The children are sitting on the floor in the center of the room. The teacher specifies that one side of the room is a roadway, the adjacent side is designated as a marshland, the third is a woods, and the fourth side is a clearing and free territory. The window shades are pulled just enough to darken the room and to simulate night. A freedom song is being played softly on the record player. The children are just finishing group discussions about who they are planning to be in their drama and what they think will be their biggest difficulty on the trip. Some of the children are in groups of three and four; some are planning to work in pairs; and a few have preferred to make their freedom flight alone.

The teacher asks the children to decide the order in which they will progress around the room, and they organize themselves accordingly. They begin the experience by pretending to be asleep, waiting until it is dark enough to start the journey. One child, who has suggested that a hooting owl should be the signal for the action to begin, hoots softly on a cue from the teacher. The children, still in the center of the room, silently make their preparations to depart. The first few children start along the "roadway."

The teacher speaks softly as the action begins. She describes the surroundings and suggests the feelings that they might be having as they begin their adventure. She reminds them of the possible dangers that could happen and how they must be cautious. Suddenly she pops a blown-up paper bag, and there is no doubt that it is a gun shot. Everyone huddles closer to the floor, and they proceed even more cautiously than before, continuing on their trip. Some appear to have been wounded and are assisted by others.

Now most of them have reached the "marshland" area, and again the teacher quietly describes what this environment is like and suggests the problems it offers. As before, some of the children listen to her descriptions, while others are engrossed enough in their own ideas that they need no assistance.

As most of the children approach the end of the trip, the teacher turns up the music and reminds them that they have almost reached freedom—it is only a short way off—within grasp at any moment. The children's faces bear encouraged looks; the walking wounded who are being aided by friends smile faintly. As they pass by the record player, the teacher turns up the volume and begins to sing, encouraging the children to join in. As they sing they return to their original places on the floor. They continue singing until everyone is seated and the teacher fades out the music.

The entire experience has lasted only about three minutes. The teacher now leads a brief discussion about what happened to whom. The children ask to repeat the experience; some have new plans, and the process begins again.

Our third and final visit is in a sixth-grade classroom where we observe the following:

The children are listening to two records, "Alley-Oop"[1] and "I'm Bugged At My Ol' Man,"[2] brought in by the student teacher. He tells them that the records were favorites of his when he was their age and that the songs deal with strong feelings. They talk about the songs for a few minutes, and he suggests that they might want to make up some skits based on the songs or ideas suggested by them. The children seem anxious to try this. They break up into small groups of their own choosing to prepare their skits. After about ten minutes of preparation, the following skits are enacted:

Four boys, standing in a row, are each a head taller than the one next in line. The tallest chants, in a deep voice, "I'm Alley-Oop and I'm the tallest and the strongest." The second repeats the chant in a somewhat deep voice. The third repeats on a higher pitch. The fourth, in the highest-pitched voice, chants, "I'm Alley-Oop and I'm the shortest and the weakest." Mock fighting for a few seconds between the boys is followed by the collapse of the three tallest. The little one remains, quietly smiling.

In another group there are three boys. One plays the father, one the son, and a third the policeman. The son talks for a long time on the phone. The irate father rips out the telephone. The son goes out to steal and is caught by the policeman and taken to the police station. The policeman calls the father (apparently the phone has been

---

[1]   Words and music by Dallas Frazier. Recorded by The Hollywood Argyles, ERA Records, 45 r.p.m.
[2]   Words and music by Brian Wilson. Recorded by The Beach Boys on the album *Summer Days* (Capitol Records).

miraculously reconnected) and the father goes to the station and asks how much the bail is. He is told there is no bail allowed for adolescents, but that he must stay in jail in place of the son. The son leaves and the father closes the scene with a "That's life!" gesture of hopelessness.

Four girls in another group pantomime to the accompaniment of the "Alley-Oop" record. The lead singer holds a ruler for a microphone. The backup singers have worked out a dance step they perform on the chorus of the song.

A fourth group chooses not to show its skit, even though their classmates encourage them. No reason is given, and the teacher accepts the group's decision.

Another group of boys also chooses to work on the record, "I'm Bugged At My Ol' Man." They, too, select the reference to the father yanking the phone from the son. The boys engage in a verbal argument that seems to have no end. The teacher asks, "Are you finished?" They agree that they are and return to their seats.

After each of the skits the audience applauds appreciatively. As we leave, the student teacher is about to play a record that he says will be "mushy," but that they might like. As the children listen to the first strains of romantic music, they begin to whisper excitedly to each other about their ideas.

WHAT IS CREATIVE DRAMA?

What has been described in the above examples is usually called *creative drama,* although other terms such as "informal drama," "creative play acting," "developmental drama," "educational drama," and "improvisational drama" have sometimes been used interchangeably.

The Children's Threatre Association of America, the largest national organization of child drama professionals in this country, uses the term "creative drama"[3] and defines it, in part, as

> an improvisational, nonexhibitional, process-centered form of drama in which participants are guided by a leader to imagine, enact, and reflect upon human experiences. . . . The creative drama process is dynamic. The leader guides the group to explore, develop, express and communicate ideas, concepts, and feelings through dramatic enactment. In creative drama the group improvises action and dialogue appropriate to the content it is exploring, using elements of drama to give form and meaning to the experience.[4]

WHAT ACTIVITIES ARE INCLUDED IN CREATIVE DRAMA?

Because creative drama stresses spontaneity and improvisation, a multitude of activities and approaches to those activities can fall under the rubric of creative

---

[3]   "Creative Drama" is preferred over "creative dramatics." While the organization acknowledges some ambiguity in the term, it is considered to be the most frequently used and generally understood label.

[4]   For a more complete discussion of this definition, see Jed H. Davis and Tom Behm, "Terminology of Drama/Theatre With and For Children: A Redefinition," *Children's Theatre Review,* 27, no. 1 (1978), 10–11.

drama. Among these activities might be movement exercises and exploration, pantomime, theatre games, improvised story dramatization, group improvisations, and so forth. An activity might be as simple as a game of "Statues," or as sophisticated as improvised group dramatizations on the topic of nuclear energy.

Most drama leaders, particularly as they gain experience, develop their own activities and their own approaches to stimulating children's creative expression, taking into account their own personalities and styles of leadership. And, while their materials and methods may differ, most leaders would subscribe to the use of the drama medium as one of the most effective ways of guiding children to grow and learn.

DO CHILDREN IN CREATIVE DRAMA EVER PERFORM?

The purpose of creative drama is to promote personal growth and educational development of the players, not to entertain an audience or to train actors. Children do, however, share their ideas in the classroom and thus serve as an audience for each other.

There may also be times when the children have a collective desire to share a particular activity with other groups outside the classroom society. If a project has so captured the attention and interest of the children that they have spent a great deal of time with it, the activity may appear to have been rehearsed and polished as a formal production.

In some cases, plays may even be created by children, but the action and dialogue are improvised rather than memorized from written scripts. Sometimes scripts are written *after* a scene is improvised, as a record of what has been created.

WHAT ARE THE GOALS
OF CREATIVE DRAMA?

Referring again to the Children's Theatre Association of America's definition of creative drama, "Participation in creative drama has the potential to develop language and communication abilities, problem solving skills, and creativity; to promote a positive self-concept, social awareness, empathy, a clarification of values and attitudes, and an understanding of the art of theatre."[5] Although several of these areas overlap each other, we shall look at each more closely.

Language and Communication

Linguists, as well as English and communication educators, have in recent years encouraged the incorporation of both verbal and nonverbal communication into the language arts curriculum. Recognizing oral language as the precursor of

[5] Davis and Behm, "Terminology," p. 10.

reading and writing, they advocate its use as an underlying base for all language learning. Both McIntyre[6] and Stewig[7] have specifically emphasized the language arts in their creative drama texts, focusing on the ways in which drama enhances reading, literature, oral language and vocabulary development, nonverbal communication, listening abilities, and creative writing. English educator Betty Jane Wagner asserts that "drama is nothing less than the 'basic skill' that is the foundation of all language development."[8]

Creative drama also offers numerous kinds of communication experiences. Children's interpersonal relationships depend on their ability to express themselves through movement and speech. This communication serves the numerous purposes of informing and questioning, forming self-concepts, investigating, organizing and sharing ideas, solving problems, and enjoying the knowledge, skills, and companionship of others. Through communication children learn to understand themselves, others, and their culture.

Communication is an integral part of creative drama. When children discuss what their dramas will be about, who will play which parts, how it will all take place, this is communication. They also learn about communication in their character roles, working through the characters' situations verbally and nonverbally. The drama itself encourages them to become more effective in their use of language.

When drama is improvised, children are enacting language situations as they might meet them in everyday life, where there is no predetermined script. They are able to rehearse alternatives and note their consequences. And if mistakes are made, or the scene takes an unexpected, and what might be a disastrous, turn in real life, it does not pose the same threat that a real-life consequence might deal out. Drama thus provides the opportunity for children to broaden their repertoire of verbal and nonverbal interactive behaviors and to evaluate their effectiveness.

Problem Solving Skills

Problem solving goes hand in hand with creativity. When children are presented with problems to solve, with open-endedness that requires a filling in of gaps, with information and ideas to synthesize into new relationships, they are learning creatively, according to Torrance.[9] Although the degree of creativity varies with each situation, in problem solving, children are encouraged to guess, to hypothesize, to test alternatives, and perhaps even redefine the problem.

---

[6]   Barbara M. McIntyre, *Creative Drama in the Elementary School* (Itasca, Ill.: F. E. Peacock, 1974).
[7]   John W. Stewig, *Spontaneous Drama: A Language Art* (Columbus, Oh.: Chas. E. Merrill, 1973).
[8]   Betty Jane Wagner, "Educational Drama and Language Development," in *Educational Drama for Today's Schools*, ed. R. Baird Shuman (Metuchen, N.J.: Scarecrow, 1978), p. 95.
[9]   E. Paul Torrance, *Encouraging Creativity in the Classroom* (Dubuque, Ia.: Wm. C. Brown, 1970), p. 1.

The characters one enacts also face problems which the children must solve. How can one get around the stone that blocks the path in "The Stone in the Road"? (p. 213). How does one pretend not to understand in order to escape a villain's clutches? Or what does a mayor say to appease two opposing factions within the city council?

In all of these situations children are encouraged to search out the many possibilities available, testing their usefulness and evaluating their effectiveness. Pushing for new ideas, exercising imagination, generating solutions, and synthesizing diverse elements are all a part of the problem-solving process, which drama can stimulate.

Creativity

Through the efforts of numerous writers and researchers in the past thirty years, the concept that creative potential exists within every human being, albeit in varying degrees, is generally an accepted one. In order to recognize the full development of each individual and to foster independent thinking in a free society, our educational system has come to include this aspect of learning in its curricula.

The characteristics of *creativity* have been identified by a number of writers. Creative people are innovators, problem solvers, alternative testers, and adventurers. They are fearless, fluent, flexible, curious, unpredictable, constructively discontented, and sometimes even a bit "off center." But creative expression is necessary for the celebration of the individual, the one who will survive in a dehumanizing technological age and in a world that is so complex that its problems, let alone solutions, often elude us.

Although creative potential is present in each child, it needs to be released and given a nurturing environment in which to develop fully. Teachers can encourage creative thinking abilities by providing an accepting climate in which a child can try and fail; in which children are not afraid to take risks and explore. They can also help by sensitizing children to environmental stimuli and by encouraging the spirit of playing with ideas. They can stimulate creative thinking by presenting a variety of problems for children to explore.

Although studies of creative drama's effect on children's creativity are limited both in size and scope, at least three should be noted. A study by Karioth in 1967 showed that creative drama could aid in developing creative thinking abilities in disadvantaged fourth graders as measured by Thorndike tests of creating thinking.[10] In 1971, Prokes reported that creative drama was useful in promoting the imaginative capacities of forty-five gifted junior-high-school stu-

---

[10] Emil Karioth, "Creative Dramatics as an Aid to Developing Creative Thinking Abilities" (Unpublished Ph.D. dissertation, University of Minnesota, 1967). Although problem-solving skills remained unchanged in this study, Torrance's work both with creative drama and with disadvantaged children may present additional insights. See Torrance, *Encouraging Creativity*.

dents.[11] In a more recent experimental study by Schmidt, Goforth, and Drew, thirty-nine kindergarten students were exposed to sixteen half-hour sessions of creative drama and then compared with a control group who continued in the normal classroom routine. The experimental group scored significantly higher on two creativity tests, one verbal and one visual.[12] Although the need for more studies is apparent, the evidence seems to suggest that drama is an important vehicle for releasing and nurturing the creative potential of children.

Positive Self-Concept

Within each individual is a distinct being ready to unfold. Being creative, according to Moustakas, means continually evolving into one's own unique self: growing forward, responding to life, fulfilling one's maximum potential.[13] In order to continue to grow, we must have faith in and value ourselves. When we feel secure about ourselves, we are willing to explore, experiment, and take risks. This self-expression furthers the awareness and growth of the self.

In creative drama, children's *positive self-concept* and self-expression is fostered by the leader who believes in each child's personal worth and creative potential. The leader's attitude produces a climate of psychological security in the classroom so that the children are not afraid to be themselves, growing and searching for new awarenesses. Often the teacher who uses an activity like creative drama is one who already believes in children's need for self-expression and is sensitive to the kind of leadership that encourages it.

One study which suggests the effect of creative drama on personal growth was done by Irwin, who demonstrated that a large group of third graders receiving forty minutes of creative drama each week for fifteen weeks, showed significant improvement in personal and social adjustment when compared with a control group. The testing measurements were the California Test of Personality, sociograms, teacher ratings, and grades.[14]

Among the kinds of anecdotal material most frequently shared by creative drama leaders are those which point to children's improved self-concept. Sometimes children feel better about themselves because of a certain role they have played which appealed to them—a king, a hero, a brave person. Or because self-expression has been encouraged and positive guidance rather than criticism has been the leader's method, the child who might otherwise feel rejected now feels that his or her ideas have importance. The self can stand taller.

[11]   Sister Dorothy Prokes, F.S.P.A., "Exploring the Relationship Between Participation in Creative Dramatics and Development of the Imagination Capacities of Gifted Junior High School Students" (Unpublished Ph.D. dissertation, New York University, 1971).

[12]   Toni Schmidt, Elissa Goforth, and Kathy Drew, "Creative Dramatics and Creativity: An Experimental Study," *Educational Theatre Journal,* 27 (March 1975), 111–14.

[13]   Clark E. Moustakas, *Creative Life* (New York: D. Van Nostrand, 1977). This theme pervades the entire book.

[14]   Eleanor Chima Irwin, "The Effect of a Program of Creative Dramatics Upon Personality as Measured by the California Test of Personality, Sociograms, Teacher Ratings, and Grades" (Unpublished Ph.D. dissertation, University of Pittsburgh, 1963).

Social Awareness

It has often been said that drama is a rehearsal for living. Through creative drama, children can pretend to be the people or things they find interesting and significant. They can relive the experiences of others, of the various people that inhabit their story books, their history and social-studies books, and their everyday life and fantasy world. They can experiment with societal roles, and in the process, identify and empathize with others, learning of their concerns, confronting their problems, and experiencing their successes as well as failures.

Through drama, children can begin to establish a tangible relationship with the human condition. What is it like to experience discrimination of any kind? What is it like to hold a particular political or religious view? What is it like to be a member of another culture or another nation? Through drama, children can discover the common bond of humanness that transcends time, age, and geographical boundaries.

Creative drama also provides learning experiences in social and group interaction. Children plan together, enact ideas together, organize their playing space, and experience a variety of human interactions in their dramatizations. Effective socialization becomes a high priority, and the rewards of cooperative group behaviors are often clearly demonstrated to them.

Empathy

Empathy is the ability to see life from another's perspective and to feel with that person. This "as if" feeling is similar to the one the Russian theatre director Stanislavski attempted to encourage through "emotional memory." Actors were urged to sense and understand the character they were playing by recalling similar situations in their own lives.

Children begin to develop empathy as their thinking matures and they move away from egocentricity. Two studies specifically have demonstrated the effectiveness of using creative drama as an aid to children's empathic or role-taking abilities. Wright, using sixth grade students, discovered that children who had had creative drama classes showed significant improvement in role-taking skills.[15] Lunz also discovered that training in creative drama significantly increased seventh graders' communicative effectiveness by providing practice in role taking through dramatic role playing.[16]

Through creative drama children have the opportunity to see the world from another point of view and respond as that person would respond. If the inner attitudes of another can be identified and understood through creative drama, if

[15] Mary Elin Sommers Wright, "The Effects of Creative Drama on Person Perception" (Unpublished Ph.D. dissertation, University of Minnesota, 1972). See also Lin Wright, "Creative Dramatics and the Development of Role-Taking in the Elementary Classroom," *Elementary English*, 51 (January 1974), 89–93.

[16] Mary E. Lunz, "The Effects of Overt Dramatic Enactment on Communication Effectiveness and Role Taking Ability" (Unpublished Ph.D. dissertation, Northwestern University, 1974).

children can experience "walking in another's shoes," then it could seem that more tolerant understanding and more effective communication would be the result.

Clarification of Values and Attitudes

An area of the curriculum receiving much attention in recent years is that of *values clarification*. Values clarification is the process of helping students find, test, and refine their own belief systems.

In order to deal with life's situations, we make decisions constantly, basing them on the values we hold. Yet if we are not sure of what we believe in, we may find it difficult to make the decisions required of us. In a world in which values are under constant scrutiny and appear to be changing at every turn, it is essential to help students develop the personal values that will affect their ways of behaving.

Creative drama deals with people in action, facing life, making decisions, and then living with the consequences of those decisions. In the dramatization of a story, for example, children are involved in a life situation in which events take a particular turn. Students experience first hand what it is like to be involved in those events. As Charles Duke suggests, "When a person is required to act 'as if' he holds a certain belief, he is more likely to examine the application of that belief to his own life."[17]

In addition, with improvisational dramatizations, alternative patterns of behavior can be explored. What happens when this is said or when that tactic is taken? Students can try out alternatives as well as seeing the choices and the results of the choices others make. Through this process children may be able to find their own personal answers to universal questions.

An Understanding of the Art of Theatre

Because informal drama is based on the various elements of threatre such as action, conflict, plot, mood, and characterization, children will gain an understanding of this art form as they participate in creative drama. Although this goal may not be a main emphasis in many classrooms, particularly with priority given to the other goals just discussed, it is important to note an often overlooked point. As the David Rockefeller, Jr., panel report, *Coming To Our Senses: The Significance of the Arts for American Education* documents so well, we have been remiss as a nation in acknowledging and appreciating the arts as a central part of our cultural heritage.[18] The result is that the arts have been neglected in education as a whole.

---

[17]   Charles R. Duke, "Educational Drama, Role-Taking, and Values Clarification," in *Educational Drama for Today's Schools,* ed. R. Baird Shuman (Metuchen, N.J.: Scarecrow, 1978), p. 95.
[18]   David Rockefeller, Jr., Chairman, *Coming To Our Senses: The Significance of the Arts for American Education, A Panel Report* (New York: McGraw-Hill, 1977).

Recently, however, a number of educators have become aware of the interrelationship of the arts and the traditional disciplines of learning, so that when the cry is heard for "back to basics" in the curriculum, the arts are considered by many to be central to that core. For these educators, participation in the arts not only broadens an individual's understanding of art forms but also develops a variety of intellectual and social skills, and as such, is basic to the education of all children.

WHAT ARE SOME OF THE USES
OF CREATIVE DRAMA?

Creative drama has been used in a variety of educational settings and with persons of all ages, including the senior adult. Many classroom teachers, who have either taken a preservice or in-service introductory course in creative drama or who have read about it in texts and or journals, have tried it out for themselves. Some school districts, either on a temporary or permanent basis, have the luxury of educational drama specialists who work with children in addition to serving as consultants to teachers in providing drama experiences.

Both recreational programs and library programs have long incorporated creative drama into their varied schedule of activities. Religious programs use creative drama as a more meaningful way to teach religious literature and ethical attitudes. In community theatre programs, creative drama is frequently offered to give children experience in informal drama and an understanding of the art of theatre.

Because of the therapeutic aspect of the arts in general, creative drama has been useful in special areas of education. Even when the goals of creative drama are educational or aesthetic (stressing curricular information, encouraging imagination), the psychological well-being of the participants can also be enhanced. Some educators and specialists have found creative drama useful in alleviating emotional tensions that contribute to reading problems, speech and language disorders, and socialization difficulties, to cite only a few examples.[19]

Thus the uses of creative drama continue to expand, reflecting the growing recognition of the power of the drama experience to enrich learning and enhance living for all persons.

---

[19] A distinction is made between "therapeutic" and "therapy." Generally, any activity in which participants feel better about themselves can be termed "therapeutic." "Therapy" is a more restricted term, and is the domain of the highly trained professional whose responsibility it is to bring about behavioral change in a client. For a more complete discussion of this point see Eleanor C. Irwin, "Drama Therapy with the Handicapped," in *Drama, Theatre, and the Handicapped,* ed. Ann M. Shaw and CJ Stevens (Washington, D.C.: American Theatre Association, 1979), pp. 21–30). For more information on drama, theatre, and the handicapped, see Linaya Leaf's review of the literature and annotated bibliography in this same text.

WHAT ARE THE ELEMENTS
OF DRAMA?

In creative drama there are several elements basic to all dramatization with which the leader should be familiar. These elements appear in formal drama, but are also the ingredients in informal drama activities as well.

Conflict

Perhaps the most basic element of drama is *conflict,* or the struggle between opposing forces. This struggle, whether comic or serious, arrests our attention and sustains our interest until it is resolved and the story or problem ends.

Generally there are three kinds of conflict. Characters may struggle against nature, as does the little spider in the action song, "The Itsy Bitsy Spider," who is washed down the drain spout. Characters may struggle against each other, as does Andersen's "Ugly Duckling," who is faced with the dilemma of living in a society that does not accept him. Or characters may struggle against themselves, as does Collodi's *Pinocchio,* whose goal to become human is thwarted by his own internal weakness.

Conflict is also basic in creating the suspense of drama. Suspense keeps us in a state of anticipation over the outcome of a situation as we continue to wonder, "What is going to happen next?"

Characterization

Characters create and carry out the plot, and must be believable in order that we may identify with them. The leader will want children to gain an understanding of what motivates behaviors and why people behave as they do. How do we interpret feelings and behaviors and how do we convey them?

As children pretend to be different characters in creative drama, they must be aware of the physical, mental, and emotional attitudes of another person. How does Cinderella react when her stepsisters taunt her? How does it feel to be a parent saying "no" to a child who wants to stay out late? What reasons does one give, as a twenty-first century pioneer, for wanting to join a space colony?

Action/Movement/Pantomime

Action is basic to drama. It forms the plot of the story; it is the happening of "What's happening?"

Movement is also a part of drama, both creative movement or movement exploration and pantomime. In observing young children, we see that movement is their natural means for exploring and discovering. They integrate themselves physically with whatever interests them; rarely do they passively observe. Movement in drama, in part, continues this mode of learning.

Movement in drama has another goal: to help children express themselves and to achieve mastery over their physical being. The leader will want children to learn to move freely and creatively, yet with disciplined, sustained, and thoughtful movement as well.

Pantomime, or the expression of ideas and feelings through bodily action, is also a part of drama. Facial expressions, posture, and gesture all communicate a variety of messages both by themselves and with the accompaniment of speech. Learning to interpret and to convey these messages with maximum effectiveness is as necessary a part of language as verbal expression.

Sensory Awareness

Sensory awareness is central to drama, as it is to all learning. Our basic knowledge of the world around us is derived from our sensory experiences with it. From our various sensory experiences we make observations, comparisons, discriminations, and form our concepts about the nature of things.

Strengthening sensory awareness leads to a greater understanding of self and the world in which we live. It also strengthens the imagination and our ability to experience all aspects of our being with greater clarity.

Verbal Interaction

In addition to nonverbal communication expressed through movement and pantomime, creative drama is also concerned with *dialogue* or *verbal interaction.* Children need to have opportunities not only to play a variety of roles in a variety of situations but also to experiment with the verbal interactions those situations could produce. They will need to increase their skills in expressing their ideas verbally and to listen and respond to the thoughts expressed by others.

HOW DOES THE TEACHER INCORPORATE CREATIVE DRAMA INTO A FULL CURRICULUM?

Many educators feel that creative drama provides an essential style of learning for children. Since children naturally dramatize, the teacher who uses creative drama is actually capitalizing on what the children already inherently know how to do.

Through dramatization, children are provided an opportunity to use a wealth of information in a more concrete and meaningful way. When children play out an idea, they become an integral part of it. They become kinesthetically involved in experiences that might otherwise remain only words on a printed page.

Creative drama, then, need not be considered a special subject area. Since it incorporates so many desirable educational goals, it can be used in conjunction with many subject areas, whether they be the language arts, science, social studies, or the fine arts. In history, for example, children may enact the conquests of Pizzaro; in literature, the adventures of *Alice in Wonderland*. In music children might dramatize the folk song, "Frog Went A-Courtin' ' "; in science they may enact a day in the life of a kangaroo rat; and in an oral language activity they may be lobbyists advocating their causes.

Creative drama activities can focus on facts and concepts as well as emphasizing the broader goals of problem solving, and evaluative and creative thinking. Children may enact the various facets of work in a logging camp or be members of two warring factions attempting to reach a compromise.

Creative drama can encourage children to discover new information and skills. For example, children may be motivated to do further research on historical figures in order to play the roles with greater accuracy.

Drama experiences can also provide one way to check children's understandings. After studying simple machines, children may pantomime some examples. As the children play, the leader can observe their ideas and note what misconceptions need correcting. Or, as older children take on roles of northern and southern sympathizers during the Civil War period, the leader can assess their understanding of events and attitudes which led to the conflict.

Learning experiences can be previewed or extended through creative drama. For example, before a field trip to a fire department, the leader can guide the children to enact their ideas. Afterward the field trip experience can be replayed, utilizing the information gained.

A classroom teacher may also want to use creative drama as the central activity in an extended project involving a number of curricular areas. For example, the leader may select a story from a specific country the children have studied and integrate music, dance, art, social studies, or science activities into a long-range project.

Finally one of the most important benefits of incorporating creative drama into the curriculum is the enjoyment and feeling of success children gain from it. The effect of this often carries over to other areas of classroom learning. Enjoyment and success lead to self-confidence, a prime requisite for becoming a thinking, feeling, and creative person in any environment.

For both the leader and the children, creative drama may be an adventure and an exploration into a new style of teaching and learning. It may take time to build the confidence needed to explore new activities and new methods of executing them.

Educators know that people can grow and change. They know that experimentation and having the leeway to fail and try again are essential to learning. They will allow their students this right. And just as important, they must allow *themselves* the freedom to experiment, fail, and try again. They must be as patient with themselves as they are with the children.

If creative drama is to serve in the classroom, it should be practical, meaningful, and enjoyable for everyone. We have tried to keep in mind both the children's and the teacher's needs in order to insure maximum success. It is hoped that this approach will assist teachers in providing exciting learning experiences for both the children and themselves.

FOR THE COLLEGE STUDENT

1. Discuss with your classmates your early experiences with drama in school or in other settings. What are your remembrances of them? Are there both pleasant and unpleasant memories? Identify them as specifically as you can. How might you increase the pleasant experiences and diminish the unpleasant ones for your students?

2. Discuss with your classmates your early remembrances of the dramatic play you enjoyed. Speculate on some of the benefits you derived from such play.

3. Using Richard DeMille's book *Put Your Mother on the Ceiling: Children's Imagination Games* (New York: Viking, 1973), begin to stretch your own imagination and recapture the play spirit you may have "misplaced" in the growing up process. You might want to try these games with some children also.

4. Read Albert Cullum's *Push Back the Desks* (New York: Citation Press, 1967). What additional ideas for exciting, dramatic teaching does it inspire in you?

5. Study the current curriculum goals and objectives in your state or local area. Is creative drama mentioned or implied in the teaching of basic skills, the fine arts, or other areas? What specific goals and objectives have been identified? Should others be added? Report on your findings in class.

SUGGESTED READINGS

BOLTON, GAVIN, *Towards a Theory of Drama in Education.* New York: Longman, 1979. Using classroom examples, a well-known British drama educator presents his theories and outlines a drama approach which combines children's play and elements of theatre.

COTTRELL, JUNE, *Teaching with Creative Dramatics.* Skokie, Ill.: National Textbook Company, 1975. Presents a basic overview of creative drama with chapters on play, sensory awareness, pantomime, dialogue, drama in curriculum, and storytelling.

COURTNEY, RICHARD, *Play, Drama and Thought: The Intellectual Background to Drama in Education.* New York: Drama Book Specialists, 1974. A theoretical treatment of the background of drama and education and the relationship of drama to other fields such as anthropology and psychology.

CROSSCUP, RICHARD, *Children and Dramatics.* New York: Scribner's, 1966. An autobiographical account of a gifted teacher's many years of experience working with children and a variety of dramatic forms, including pantomime, improvisation, and original plays.

375.792

372.66

EHRLICH, HARRIET, ed., *Creative Dramatics Handbook*. Philadelphia: School District of Philadelphia, 1974. A handbook prepared by the many drama teachers in the Philadelphia school district. Presents numerous ideas for including drama in the curriculum.

HAAGA, AGNES, AND PATRICIA RANDLES, *Supplementary Materials for Use in Creative Dramatics with Younger Children*. Seattle: University of Washington Press, 1952. A helpful manual, often with detailed narrative, of twenty-seven sessions with five- and six-year-olds.

HAGGERTY, JOAN, *Please Can I Play God?* New York: Bobbs-Merrill, 1966. The amusing and inspirational account of the author's struggle to conduct drama activities with slum children in London in a short-lived program.

HENNINGS, DOROTHY GRANT, *Smiles, Nods, and Pauses, Activities to Enrich Children's Communication Skills*. New York: Citation Press, 1974. A wealth of activities focusing on nonverbal communication. Pantomimes based on a number of topics with many references to children's literature. Also includes listening and speech activities.

372.6044

JENNINGS, COLEMAN A., AND LOLA H. JENNINGS, *Creative Dramatics in the Elementary School*. Austin, Texas: Texas Education Agency, 1978. A practical handbook designed for classroom teachers synthesizing a number of ideas from other sources.

LOWNDES, BETTY, *Movement and Creative Drama for Children*. Boston: Plays, Inc., 1971. A basic text paralleling creative drama and movement with chapters on sensory awareness, self-discovery, creative movement, mime, and verbal improvisations.

372.66

McCASLIN, NELLIE, *Children and Drama*. New York: D. McKay, 1975. A compilation of essays representing contemporary thinking of a number of well-known drama leaders such as Agnes Haaga, Geraldine Siks, Ann Shaw, and Dorothy Heathcote.

792.07

———, *Creative Drama in the Classroom* (3rd ed.). New York: Longman, 1980. An introductory text presenting theory and practical application. Includes exercises in sensory awareness, pantomime, and improvisation. Story dramatization and formal production also covered.

McINTYRE, BARBARA M., *Creative Drama in the Elementary School*. Itasca, Ill.: F. E. Peacock Publishers, Inc., 1974. This text presents the rationale for using creative drama in a language-arts program. Detailed activities are explained in two sections, one for kindergarten through grade three and another for grades four through six.

O'NEILL, CECILY, ALAN LAMBERT, ROSEMARY LINELL, AND JANET WARR-WOOD, *Drama Guidelines*. London: Heinemann Educational Books, 1977. This handbook is a statement of the aims of drama teaching with actual lesson descriptions and an examination of the leader's role. Includes contributions from many practicing teachers.

PEMBERTON-BILLING, R. N., AND J. D. CLEGG, *Teaching Drama* (2nd ed.). London: University of London Press, Ltd., 1968. A very practical, easy-to-follow text presenting both rationale and a wealth of activities for drama in the classroom.

373.1332

SANDERS, SANDRA, *Creating Plays with Children*. New York: Citation Press, 1970. A booklet giving one teacher's approach to creating plays. Includes several short scripts that children recorded *after* their plays were improvised, such as "Hansel and Gretel" and "Julius Caesar."

808.824

SCHER, ANNA, *100+ Ideas for Drama*. London: Heinemann Educational Books, 1975. This little book presents a mixed bag of numerous activities, including games, pantomimes, improvisations, and verbal activities.

SCHWARTZ, DOROTHY THAMES, AND DOROTHY ALDRICH (eds.), *Give Them Roots and Wings*. Washington, D.C.: American Threatre Association, 1972. This manual is the combined work of several creative drama leaders, and is a useful source for the beginning teacher. Covers creative movement and pantomime, characterization, improvisation, dialogue, and story dramatization, with more than fifty sample lessons.

SHUMAN, R. BAIRD (ed.), *Educational Drama for Today's Schools*. Metuchen, N.J.: Scarecrow, 1978. This book presents a variety of essays on some of the uses of drama such as values clarification, language development, and moral development by several authors, including Dorothy Heathcote, Betty Jane Wagner, and Charles R. Duke. Extensive annotated bibliography is also included.

SIKS, GERALDINE BRAIN, *Creative Dramatics: An Art for Children*. New York: Harper & Row, Pub., 1958. A basic and fundamental text on philosophy and practical application of creative drama. Discusses developmental needs of children and presents appropriate drama materials and methods for three age groups. Appendices include extensive bibliography of materials for creative drama.

————, *Children's Literature for Dramatization*. New York: Harper & Row, Pub., 1964. An anthology of stories and poetry for the creative drama leader. Each selection is introduced with suggestions for dramatization.

STEWIG, JOHN W., *Spontaneous Drama: A Language Art*. Columbus, Oh.: Chas. E. Merrill, 1973. In this text the author, a language-arts educator, presents his rationale for the incorporation of creative drama into this area of the curriculum. A number of language-arts activities and references to literature are made throughout.

WAGNER, BETTY JANE, *Dorothy Heathcote: Drama as a Learning Medium*. Washington, D.C.: National Education Association, 1976. This book explains the techniques used in drama by British educator Dorothy Heathcote, whose work has become well known in this country in recent years. Wagner carefully describes Heathcote's philosophy and practice with specific examples. Chapter headings focus on Heathcote's specific terminology such as "edging in" and "dropping to the universal."

WARD, WINIFRED, *Playmaking with Children From Kindergarten Through Junior High School*. New York: Prentice-Hall, 1957. This text is the American classic in the field of creative drama written by "the first lady of child drama" in this country. Discusses drama in elementary and junior high school as well as drama in recreation, religious education, and therapy. Emphasis is on story dramatization.

————, *Stories to Dramatize*. New Orleans: Anchorage Press, 1952. A collection of excellent stories and poems suitable for dramatization with children from five to fourteen.

WAY, BRIAN, *Development Through Drama*. Atlantic Highlands, N.J.: Humanities Press, 1967. Well-known British dramatist presents his philosophy, focusing on development of the whole person. Included are a number of practical exercises and activities in sensory awareness, imagination, speech, and improvisation.

WILDER, ROSILYN, *A Space Where Anything Can Happen: Creative Drama in a Middle School*. Rowayton, Conn.: New Plays, 1977. This guidebook is based on one leader's personal experience in a drama program in a middle school. Many techniques and ideas are presented in the author's description of her procedures.

Chapter Two

Activities
to Begin On

When both the teacher and the children are new to creative drama, it may be helpful to try simple activities first, such as drama games, action songs, and simple pantomimes. These activities can also be used for warm-up activities in longer drama periods. They may involve some skills building or "rehearsing" for more challenging material. Simple materials are also helpful in ending a period, particularly if they have a calming effect on the group.

GOALS OF BEGINNING ACTIVITIES

One goal of beginning activities is to create the appropriate climate for psychological security. Such activities can relax the class, generate good feelings, and promote a sense of group cohesiveness. Often they can unite the children in a common effort, which becomes strong enough that individuals forget themselves and participate freely.

Another important aspect of these beginning materials is that they encourage movement, focus and concentration, imagination, social cooperation, and self-control of the players, necessary skills in other areas of learning as well as in further drama work. While not all of the activities presented in this chapter will achieve each of these goals equally, consider, for example, the intense concentration little children exhibit in mastering and coordinating the movements in a simple finger play, the imagination required in inventing different ways to move about the room to a musical stimulus, or the discipline required to mirror the movements of a partner.

Another value of these materials is that they almost organize themselves. When the children learn the rules of a game or learn how an activity is to be played, they help keep each other "in line." The student teacher who has not had much experience working with groups of children will usually find it easier to teach these beginning activities.

Most experienced teachers know how to conduct classroom activities and games. For the student teacher, however, this may be a new experience. Giving directions, rearranging the classroom, and keeping order and control are tasks that require some thinking ahead and planning. Just one experience with unorganized and chaotic "running around" is enough to discourage any future attempts with creative drama. The new teacher must recognize and accept the responsibility for guiding and controlling even the simplest activity. It does not happen magically or automatically. This chapter is designed to help the inexperienced teacher learn some initial skills in planning simple activities.

PARTICIPATION

In creative drama it is important to involve as many children in the experience as possible while still maintaining order and control. Frequently the children all work individually without interacting with others, which provides privacy and a minimum amount of distraction. It is essential for concentration. Also, when children work alone they have the opportunity to savor their ideas and their uniqueness.

Children may also work in pairs and in groups. Here they have the opportunity to engage in important social interaction. They can stimulate each others' thinking, integrate ideas, lend support, and learn to compromise and cooperate. While group process involves trials in power struggles and personality conflicts, it also provides the opportunity to enmesh the creative thinking of several individuals. Individual efforts become part of the greater whole.

Children may participate in creative drama in several ways. They may participate as observers, discussants, analyzers, or as players. Their participation will vary according to their interest in the topic, their mood, their confidence, and their awareness of their own needs.

Shy Children

Children should be invited rather than forced to participate. Some children will be relieved to hear the teacher say, "*If* you would like to play . . ." Feeling that they *have* to play can cause anxieties. Extending an invitation encourages children to make their own decisions. When they do join in, it is more likely to be because the activity looks like fun and they want to be a part of it.

Reticent children may wish to "sit out" during the first playings of an activity and enter in on replayings. Watching their peers lets them see how the

Forcing shy children to participate only increases their reluctance.

activity is played. The leader's continual acceptance of children's efforts will eventually give reluctant children the courage to try on their own. Forcing shy children to participate only increases their reluctance. For some shy children, participation in itself is a great achievement.

Outgoing Children

On the other hand, there are many children who need and want to be involved in as much of the playing as possible rather than watching their classmates. Although they can appreciate each other's contributions and can work cooperatively together, the fun of the activities is so compelling that they usually want immediate and continuous involvement.

These children may need frequent reminding of the limitations and rules in playing. Sometimes, such children need to be cajoled and pushed toward higher achievements. This can be done good naturedly, but then with quiet seriousness if the point is missed.

DIRECTED ACTIVITIES

The kind of activity that keeps the most control, is the easiest to organize, and is the simplest for the children to play is one in which a leader tells or shows the children what to do. Another value of such activities is that the children can play

Outgoing children usually want immediate and continuous involvement.

many of them seated or standing in one location and yet be actively involved in some type of movement experience. Following is a discussion of several kinds of leader-directed activities.

Finger Plays

Finger plays, or little rhymes, songs, or chants that the children act out as they recite them, are very popular with young children. Some classic examples are "The Itsy Bitsy Spider" and "I'm a Little Teapot."

"A finger play gets us warmed up for more challenging activities."

Traditional finger plays are readily available in numerous sources. Many may be made up by the teacher from favorite nursery rhymes.

Single-Action Poetry

Some poetry suggests a single rhythmic movement such as running, hopping, or galloping. While the leader reads the poetry, the children may simply perform the action seated at the desk or standing at the side of it. Actions such as running are done *in place*.

Some examples of single-action poetry are "Hoppity," by A. A. Milne (4); "Jump—Jump—Jump," by Kate Greenaway (4); "Trot Along, Pony," by Marion Edey and Dorothy Grider (4); "Merry-Go-Round," by Dorothy Baruch (4); "Rocking Chair," by John Travers Moore (10); and "Paul Revere's Ride," by Henry Wadsworth Longfellow (4).*

Action Songs

Action songs are also fun to sing and act out. Many are traditional, such as the following: "Did You Ever See a Lassie?" "Here We Go 'Round the Mulberry Bush" (or "This is the Way We Wash Our Clothes"), "If You're Happy and You Know It," "She'll Be Comin' 'Round the Mountain," and "This Old Man, He Played One."

There are also some songs that can easily be made into action songs. For example, the traditional African folk song, "Kum Bay Yah" has a very strong, steady, and slow rhythm. The words are constantly repeated in the different verses with little variation.

Simple gestures of singing, crying, and praying can be added to the song in addition to the clapping and swaying that is usually inevitable when a group sings such a song. *Very simple* dance movements are also easily added when the group is strongly moved by the song.

Another example might be a song such as "Michael, Row the Boat Ashore." One teacher discussed with the children all the activities that sailors must do on a ship. Verses were added that included the children's names and various tasks that everyone acted out: "Sally, help to swab the deck," "Andy, pull up the anchor slow," and so on.

Additional songs that lend themselves to acting out are traditional ones such as "Frog Went A 'Courtin'," "I Know an Old Lady Who Swallowed a Fly," "Old MacDonald Had a Farm," "Sing a Song of Sixpence," "Twelve Days of Christmas," and "Waltzing, Matilda."

---

* Refer to final bibliography for all numbered entries.

Action Games

Action games are also useful. Traditional ones might be "Follow the Leader" and "Simon Says." In each of these games the leader specifies the actions the group is to do. In "Simon Says," however, players are not to perform the action if the leader does *not* say "Simon Says." If they do, they are out of the game, by the traditional rules.

Games that eliminate players, however, should be revised. Ironically, the child who is eliminated is the one who probably could benefit the most from remaining in the game, and practicing the skill. Furthermore, eliminated players may become bored and frustrated with inactivity and with watching classmates excel where they have failed. As a result, they may create diversions to amuse themselves, which are labeled discipline problems. Games need not eliminate players at all, or a player may be eliminated for one turn.

Games like "Follow the Leader" and "Simon Says" can be played with variation. One teacher invented a game using sizes and shapes.

Simon says, "make yourself shaped like a box."
Simon says, "walk in place taking steps like a giant."
Simon says, "make yourself shaped like a piece of pie."
Simon says, "make yourself small as a mouse."

Action Stories

There are some traditional stories that have actions in them for the children to perform. As the leader tells the story and does the actions, the children follow along. Most teachers are already familiar with such traditional stories as "Lion Hunt" or "Bear Hunt" or "Brave Little Indian."

The leader can also make up original action stories. Using traditional stories, one can assign actions to the characters or to any frequently used words. All the children may act out each word, or specific words could be assigned to rows or groups. Sometimes children like to help the teacher think of the actions to use.

For example, the leader might narrate a brief version of "The Three Billy Goats Gruff" with actions for each of the Billy Goats, the Troll, and the bridge.

Older children can enjoy similar kinds of activities with more "sophisticated" subject matter. Topics might include stories with melodramatic themes (complete with villains and swooning lasses), spy stories, or cowboy and rustler adventures. Following is one original example:

Villain: strokes mustache, twirls "cape" and says "Aha!"
Heroine: clasps hands and says, "Oh dear, oh dear"
Hero: flexes muscles and pounds chest
Mother: wipes eyes with corner of apron and shakes head sadly

Sheriff: twirls two six-guns, shoots them in the air, and says, "Bang"

Story: This is the tale of a young girl named *Nell*, her *Mother*, and a *Villain* named Evily Pete. And a show-off *Sheriff* named Sam and a *Hero* named Hal. Our story takes place in the town of Junction City. *Nell* and her widowed *Mother* have fallen on hard times and have no money left to pay the rent. The landlord (none other than our *Villain* Evily Pete) goes to demand payment. *Pete* knocks at the door, but *Nell* and her *Mother* are too frightened to answer. *Pete* goes off to get the *Sheriff* to arrest them. Meanwhile, the *Sheriff* and his friend, *Hero* Hal, are at the saloon having their after-noon drink of sarsaparilla. . . .

SIMPLE PANTOMIME

Simple pantomimes are brief ideas that can be acted out without dialogue.* All the children can play them at their desks at the same time. They are not to be guessed but are intended to give the children a chance to explore pantomime action without being evaluated. Particular learning benefits are that they require the children to concentrate on remembering past experiences, to recall information they have read or heard about, and to form mental pictures. These skills are necessary for most learning tasks and can be sharpened through exercises that simple pantomime activities provide.

Variety of action in pantomimes is important. For example, the leader may create action to involve the entire body.

T: Wonderperson! There isn't a thing you can't do! You can leap tall buildings . . . run faster than a speeding bullet . . . break chains with a snap . . . hang by your teeth . . . twirl a rope on the end of your little finger . . . now with both hands . . . and rotate a hula hoop around your neck at the same time!

Movements can involve levels and directions: up and down, back and forth, left and right, bending over, turning around, going in reverse, and so forth. The following example uses directions in movement while the children pretend to be a power shovel in operation:

T: . . . you drive over to your job. Now swing the cab around to the left and lower the dipper (outstretched arms) to that mound of dirt. Slowly, now . . . scoop up the dirt. Now raise the dipper and swing back to the right. . . . that's it . . . Now very slowly and carefully swing the dipper over the dump truck. . . . Now open the dipper and drop the dirt in. . . .

The leader can also concentrate on changes of tempo. Actions can be done in double time or even triple time, speeded up like an old-fashioned movie. Or they can be done in "slow-motion time" as if one were in space, or performing in a television replay. Note these techniques in the following example:

---

* Extensive discussion of techniques for developing pantomime material can be found in Chapter Four. Pantomimes for audience guessing will be discussed in Chapter Eight.

T: Pretend you are a bow-legged cowboy walking down a frontier town's dusty main road. . . . Now do that same walk a little faster . . . a little faster . . . Now stop! In slow motion take your pistol out of the holster. . . . Now reverse that action. . . . Take out the gun even slower. . . . Now reverse that action just as slowly. . . . Practice taking the gun out in double time . . . triple time. . . .

In addition to focusing on a variety of action, pantomimes can also involve a variety of characters and topics.

A. COMMUNITY HELPERS

T: First let's pretend to be a doctor giving children shots to help their bodies fight disease. . . . Now let's pretend to be a mail person, driving a truck and stopping to deliver some mail. . . . The foresters who trim the city trees are important. Let's pretend to be a forester carefully sawing limbs from a tall tree. . . .

B. STORYBOOK CHARACTERS

T: Let's first pretend to be the Wolf, sneaking through the woods, looking for Little Red Riding Hood. . . . Now let's be the Giant in "Jack and the Beanstalk" coming home for dinner and sitting down to eat a mountain of food. . . . Now we're Pecos Bill lassoing a cyclone to ride. . . .

Senses

Pantomimes can also focus on sensory awareness. The following are some examples:

T: Pretend that you are:

(Tasting)	Taking a dose of bitter medicine. Biting into a piece of your favorite cake. Eating a dill pickle.
(Touching)	Threading a needle. Shuffling cards. Playing a musical instrument.
(Hearing)	A bird listening for a worm. Asleep and the alarm rings and wakens you. Hearing a small voice inside your pocket.
(Seeing)	Observing the actions of a small insect on your desk. Peeking through a knothole in a board fence. Flipping through a magazine looking at food ads.
(Smelling)	Opening a carton of milk and finding it sour. Peeling onions. Smelling smoke coming from inside your desk.

Emotions

Pantomimes may also include emotional feelings. For example,

T: Pretend that
You are watching a scary television show all alone.

You are a cautious rabbit. You never take chances. You are eating a carrot for the very first time.

You are a mean witch mixing a powerful brew in your cauldron.

You are a very shy person at a party drinking a cup of punch.

Conflict

Many of the previous pantomimes have had conflict in them to heighten their dramatic impact. Notice how conflict is added to the following pantomimes, making them more intriguing and involving:

Pantomime Activity	*Pantomime with Conflict*
Eat an ice cream cone.	Eat an ice cream cone; the temperature is 100°.
Pretend to read a book.	Pretend to read a book; a pesky fly keeps bothering you.
Pretend to be listening to a very boring speech.	Pretend to be listening to a very boring speech; your boss is giving the speech and will be upset if you don't act interested.

As the student teacher gains practice in developing pantomime activities, it will become easier to create original ideas or to modify an activity to make it fit particular needs. In the following example, a student teacher used an idea he called a "Time Circle Machine." He wanted to give his class a lot of controlled action and to cover some historical events in chronological order. The children played the activity, standing at the sides of their desks.

> **T:** We're going to take a quick historical tour through time in a Time Circle Machine. For each period of time we change to, we'll have to go through certain actions in order to make the machine work for us.
>
> To go all the way back in time, turn in a circle once. Now you are back in prehistoric time. . . . You are a caveman or cavewoman looking about, hunting for food. . . . Look all around . . . up and down . . . search. . . .
>
> Now stop. Turn around in the smallest circle you can. Now crouch down. Now stand up. Now we are in another time period. You are on the *Mayflower*, traveling to the New World. The boat is rocking back and forth . . . back and forth. . . . You've been on the ship for many days. . . . Oh, boy, we'd better go to another time period before we get seasick. . . .
>
> Now stop. Stand perfectly still. Close your eyes. Turn around once to the right, now once to the left. Wiggle your nose. Snap your fingers once—only once. Now open your eyes. You are Paul Revere riding your horse. You are galloping, faster and faster, because the message must be carried through that the British are coming. Hurry, make your horse go faster. Halt! Whoa! The Time Machine moves on.

The activity continued through being the Wright Brothers flying their plane at Kitty Hawk and Neil Armstrong landing on the moon. Almost any type of information, however, could be included in such a format.

Statues can't move a muscle.

GAMES

Games are also useful for beginning creative drama work. In fact, games have been used predominantly in the work of Viola Spolin in her book *Improvisation for the Theatre**. Many of the games she has devised are specifically intended for instructional purposes with actors in training. There is also a section devoted to work with children. The leader will find many of Spolin's games helpful. In addition, many traditional games are also usable.

The games selected for drama work should involve action or the development of some skill needed for further dramatization. Many games can also serve double duty if the leader incorporates additional curricular concepts into them.

There are some cautions about games, however. Many traditional games encourage competition, and when competition is overemphasized, the learning of the skill of the game can be lost. Children are more interested in gaining points, or jeering those who lose. In some games the winner gets to become the next leader or gets to choose the next player. Many children will never be the winner or will never be chosen by their classmates. Such games should be avoided or redesigned.

---

* Evanston, Ill.: Northwestern University Press, 1963.

Sensory Games

Some games can teach a variety of skills helpful for further creative drama work as well as for other benefits. For example, games that emphasize developing skills in sensory awareness are useful in many areas of the curriculum, such as science and language arts.

SEEING

Scavenger Hunt. The children are given a list of articles to collect within a given time limit. The articles may be a green pencil, a paper clip, a book with a picture of a Toltec temple, a paragraph with the word "magnet" in it, or a picture of a scientist conducting an experiment. The children may work on their own, in pairs, or in groups.

Concentration. (a) Arrange a variety of items on a table and allow the children to study them for a minute. Then have them write the names of the items on a piece of paper from memory. (b) A variation could be to rearrange some of the items and remove one or two while the children close their eyes. See if they can guess which item has been removed. (c) A third variation is to arrange items in a sequence, rearrange them while the children's eyes are closed, then see if the children can replace them in the original order. (d) This observation game can also be played by adding or changing an item in the classroom every day for a week and see if the children can detect the changes.

HEARING

Guess the Sound. The leader (and the children) can tape record a number of familiar sounds. Or the sounds could be made behind a screen. Examples of sounds might be tearing a piece of paper, snapping fingers, the sound of a vacuum cleaner, or a running faucet. As the children listen to the sounds, they are to guess the source. The fun of the game is in the variety of identifications that can be made of one sound.

Who's My Partner? The leader distributes to each child a slip of paper with directions for a specific sound such as "mew like a cat," "whistle a bob-white call," and so forth. Each sound has two (or more) children performing it. On a signal everyone begins making the sound softly, repeating it until the partner is found. When the partner is located, the sounds stop, and the pairs wait where they are until all partners are discovered. Papers may be redistributed for repeated playing.

TOUCHING

Guess the Object. Have the children try to identify numerous items by their shape and texture. The objects might be in paper bags; the children might be blindfolded; or they may sit in a circle and have the objects passed behind their backs. Objects might be a fingernail file, a toy truck, a key chain, and so forth.

Leading the Blind. Have children work in pairs, one with eyes closed and the other as leader. They explore the classroom, discovering that what is usually taken for granted is different when "viewed" in this way. Usually it is best not to allow any talking during this activity in order to aid concentration. (For organizing the classroom, see "Space Considerations" in this chapter.)

TASTING

Discuss the differences in tasting and smelling with such items as onion, chocolate, peppermint, and potato. We taste only sweet, sour, salt, and bitter. We smell rather than taste foods we eat. By holding the nose when tasting, it is difficult to guess a number of foods and flavors.

SMELLING

Put a variety of items with distinctive odors in small containers. Have the children guess the items by sniffing *gently*. Items might be vinegar, ammonia, turpentine, coke, banana oil, vanilla, cedar wood, and onion. Items can be diluted with water to subdue the smells for safety as well as for greater challenge.

Imagination Games

Many drama leaders speak of imagination as a muscle that needs frequent exercising. A number of games which focus on stimulating children's imagination may be played.

Pass the object I. Children sit in a circle. The teacher passes a simple object such as a ball or a pencil and suggests that the object is "a bird with a broken wing," "a very sharp knife," or another significant item. Silence is required so that the children may concentrate on the object, handle it, and respond to it before passing it on.

Pass the object II. The children pass an object of their own choosing. After the first child responds to the teacher's suggestion, he or she gives a new suggestion to which the next child must respond, and so on. The suggestions should remain an appropriate size for passing hand to hand.

Mystery box. The leader brings an imaginary box of any size into the center of the circle. For a very large box, several children may help carry it in. Volunteers, singly or in pairs, may come and open the box which may become a packing carton, an elaborately wrapped gift, a cage, and so forth. Children take the item out of the box, handle or use it in some way, and then return it. The item should be appropriate to the size of the box.

What could it be? The leader shows children objects which they are to imagine might be something else. For example, a pair of scissors might become a dancing puppet, a spear for catching a fish, or a lorgnette. An interesting piece of driftwood might take on a variety of shapes as it is turned in different ways and examined. A conch shell might become a large rosebud, a horn, or a fairy's palace.

Communication Games

Some games also help children to increase their communication skills, both in speaking and in listening. Such games are designed to help children realize the importance of sending and receiving messages as accurately as possible.

What's This? One person describes an object such as a safety pin, a paper clip, a light bulb, or an article of clothing, without naming what the item is. The listeners must draw each part of the object as they listen to the description. They cannot ask questions. Whenever listeners think they know what the drawing is, they may guess.

Giving Directions.   This is similar to the above game. Two children stand back to back with a desk or table in front of each of them. On each desk two or three identical objects are placed. For example, each child may have a pencil, an eraser, and a book. A third child arranges the objects on one child's desk. That child must then tell the partner how to place the objects so that the arrangements are identical. Again, the listener cannot ask questions. Note: To help children see how questioning for clarity is of value, one partner may be allowed to question when the game is repeated. In a third playing, both partners may be allowed to question.

Character Voices.   Different types of people speak with different voices. Even an inanimate object might have a voice that is affected by the material it is made of. For example, tin produces a metallic sound while cotton has a muffled quality.

Place a number of simple sentences on cards and distribute them. On another set of cards, a variety of characters could be listed. Children try to say the sentence as the character might sound. Simple sentences might be, "Good morning." "Hello." "How are you?" Characters might be Papa Bear, Paul Bunyan, a grandfather clock, a tin soldier, a weeping willow, or a wooden spoon.

The Olde Junke Shop.   Children pretend to be items in an old junk shop. They create sounds for each item to make as it moves. For example, one child may choose to be a squeaking old rocking chair, another, a scratchy gramaphone; another, an out-of-tune music box.

SPACE CONSIDERATIONS

Frequently teachers are told that they should use gymnasiums or activity rooms if they are going to do creative drama. In fact, if large rooms are not available, some teachers assume they cannot do creative drama at all.

It has been our experience that one of the prime reasons for many leaders' difficulties with creative drama is inattention to the use of space. It is our belief that the classroom provides sufficient space for the beginning teacher, and even

Playing at the desk area provides control as well as
psychological security.

the use of that fairly well-defined space requires a number of considerations. It seems to us that expanding space *by degrees* is important. For this reason we begin by using the desk area before moving to larger areas of space. This procedure seems more practical, safer, and is definitely easier on everyone's nerves.

There are advantages to using the children's desks which the inexperienced leader should not overlook. The desk area is a convenient and concrete tactile boundary. It separates the children from each other and minimizes distractions. There are also psychological reasons for using desks. The desk is a familiar territory and a home base to the child. It may give the sense of security needed to risk participation.

Almost all of the games mentioned thus far can take place in a limited space. Even the following games, which emphasize movement, can be played at the desk.

Move to the beat. The children sit at their desks. The leader beats the drum while the children move in as many different ways as possible. They may move *only* when the drum beats, so the leader should vary the beats, halt suddenly, and the like, so the children are encouraged to listen closely.

Balance movement game. While standing by the sides of their desks, the children can perform a variety of movements the leader calls out. For example, they can stand on tiptoes, crouch and touch both knees, take one step forward, one step back. The challenge: all of the actions are to be done while they balance a book on their heads!

Painting. Children pretend to paint with a small brush that grows into a

"We pretend to paint a very big picture."

larger and larger brush until it is the size of a broom. Then it shrinks again. Children move from painting on their desk top, to doing it in the air, and then at the side of the desk. Children return to a seated position as the brush shrinks back to its original size. Encourage children to think of themselves as famous artists painting with great skill. Leroy Anderson's "Waltzing Cat" record is a useful accompaniment.

   Activities with a ball. Children pretend to be bouncing different-sized balls: a basketball, volleyball, tennis ball, and so forth. Change the weights of the balls—the ball is heavy, and then it is light. The Harlem Globetrotters' theme "Sweet Georgia Brown," is wonderful background music for this one.

Rearranging the Room

When a game requires the use of more space, it takes preparation and foresight. In the traditional classroom, the usual procedure in expanding space is to move the furniture against the walls. This sounds simple, and the experienced teacher can make it look ridiculously easy; but for the new teacher it may be an awesome experience.

   Frequently a novice will tell an entire class, "Quietly push your desks against the wall," and then expect that this can be done in absolute silence. The sound of thirty desks scraping and thirty pairs of feet scuffling, added to spontaneous whispering and quiet chattering, may be enough to convice the new teacher that the seasoned teacher possesses supernatural powers.

   The new teacher, whose voice often lacks assurance, can make a direction sound more like a question. This in itself can cause perfectly normal children to take advantage and "cut loose." They can create pandemonium with zestful abandon and never hear it at all. But the rest of the school probably will!

   What the new teacher often does not realize is that the seasoned teacher usually sets up an efficient procedure for moving desks and the children have rehearsed it many times. It *seems* spontaneously organized, but often much work has gone into it. Until the new teacher sets up a similar procedure, there is no substitute for caution. It is much wiser to take a little more time and proceed step by step.

   T: Row one, pick up your desks and place them here. (When they have finished and are seated, continue.) Row two, over here, etc.

   Sometimes teachers try to make a game out of moving desks. They may suggest that the children pretend that the desks are "explosives," which have to be moved carefully so that they don't blow up. However, such a direction may be too tempting for some children. "Exploding" may be more interesting than the planned activity! It is usually best to be honest and straightforward about getting the furniture rearranged.

Controls in Space

Once the space is expanded, the leader should incorporate control features in each activity. For example, games played in a circle keep the children in a specified area. This formation is a built-in control that aids organization and orderly playing. Numerous circle games lend themselves to playing in the classroom, such as *Hokey Pokey* (or *Looby Lou*).

Another circle game that is excellent because it combines both actions and development of observation skills is *Who Started the Motion?* For this game, players form a circle. One child leaves the room. A leader in the circle is chosen to perform actions that the other players must imitate. "It" returns to the room and must guess who is the initiator of the actions.

The circle formation can also be used as a basis for creating other kinds of games. One teacher developed the following:

> **Circle Game.** Two concentric circles are formed. They rotate in opposite directions. Players are to remain equally spaced as they march around the circle to lively music. When the leader calls out "Change," the players must reverse directions. After this much of the game is learned, the next stipulation can be added.
>
> The added challenge is for the leader to move around the circles and tap players on the shoulder. The tapped person must move to the opposite circle and change directions while still marching. Other players must adjust the spacing so that the space is still equidistant between players. The leader may continue to call out "Change" at any time.

Another way to control is to direct the children to stop and "freeze" at various moments on signal. For example, a game called *Freeze* might be de-

"Freeze" can be a game and a control device.

signed. The children might be allowed to move about the room in any way they wish (without bumping into each other), but on signal they must freeze into a position or an expression. The leader might ask them to look funny, to be historical statues, or to be animals.

The signal for freezing should be definite and clear, and in order to teach the signal and test it out, it would be wise to use only a few children for the first brief playing. Additional children can be added gradually.

A variation of freezing might be for the leader to beat a drum and allow the children to move only when the drum is beating. In this way the leader can stop the children by stopping the drumbeat.

Another way to control is to have the children root their feet in one spot. A game called *Caught in the Act* incorporates this control. The children move in any way they wish while their feet remain stationary. A signal is given to stop. On a second signal they must move about the room as fast as they can in their frozen position. On the next signal they are again rooted to the spot and are free to move the rest of their body.

Slow Motion

Slow motion is another good way to control movement. It is also an excellent exercise in disciplined, thoughtful movement, focusing concentration and involvement on an idea as well as on body awareness. And when slow motion is mastered, it can be as fascinating to watch as it is to perform.

Moving in slow motion is not always easy, and requires the guidance of the leader. Children have to be reminded to keep the movement slow; in the excitement of moving, the tendency is to speed up.

> **T:** That's it. Keep it slow. Freeze. Now this time go even slower—three times as slow as you just did. (The leader might give these directions in a slow-motion voice, like a record playing on slow speed.)

It is also helpful to compare slow motion to the replays of televised sports events, to time-lapse photography, or to moving through heavy syrup. Music can aid many slow-motion activities. With a variable-speed record player, a slow-motion effect can be gained by playing a record at a slower speed. Or selections such as Debussy's "Clair de Lune" or "Afternoon of a Faun" can be useful.

Many games can be played in slow motion. A simple game of tag is suggested by Viola Spolin in her book. However, the leader will find slow motion a useful technique in almost any activity.

Encouraging Children
to Organize Space for Themselves

Some children have very little trouble using space. Their motor control is excellent, and they sensitively adjust their movements to accommodate a variety of spaces—the gym, activity room, and classroom. They can move freely and with control. They can run in random patterns and never collide or even touch each other. They can work closely together, sensitively respecting the needs of their peers.

It would be ideal if all children could operate in this fashion. Realistically, however, many children will not. Such factors as age, motor control, and social and emotional maturity will play a significant role in determining their ability to use space. The teacher has the responsibility for guiding children who have greater needs.

Eventually the leader will want to encourage and guide children to allow their physical needs and their ideas to determine the use of space. They may move wherever they feel they need to and where their ideas take them, provided they can remain absorbed in their work and can be aware of the others in the group. Such an experience in democratic responsibility is extremely valuable but may need to be approached systematically.

The teacher and the children may discuss what people do in order to share space. For example,

T: When people move about in crowds, how do they manage to share their space with each other?
C: They watch each other.
C: Sometimes they have to speed up or slow down; sometimes you have to stop so you won't bump into someone.
C: Sometimes you pass around them and sometimes you let them pass you.

Exercises are also helpful. At first it may be easier if the movement is simple, such as walking. The teacher might also play "walking" music, or music with an easy, specific rhythm the children can follow, such as Henry Mancini's "March of the Cue Balls." After the simple activity of walking, it is a

"We pretend to go supermarket shopping as fast as we can
without bumping into anyone."

good practice (and fun!) to increase and vary the speed. It may be necessary to begin with only a few children at a time and then add more.

ORDERLY, ORGANIZED PLAYING

It is very important that the leader communicate the directions for playing as clearly as possible. Children need to know what is wanted and expected of them. From their point of view there is nothing so frustrating as having to second-guess what the teacher has in mind. From the teacher's point of view, clearly stated directions can avoid many problems.

Wording Directions

Often, inexperienced teachers want to appeal to the children's imagination by sugarcoating directions in fantasy. For example, they may want the children to remain in a designated area; yet they warn:

> **T:**   You're like a sticky gum, so don't touch anyone or you may stick together.

For most children this kind of statement is like a "Wet Paint" sign. It becomes an interesting possibility and announces itself as a challenge to be tested. Then they are ironically beguiled into doing exactly what the teacher was trying to avoid. Not only do they touch each other; they may clump in a huge mass before the teacher ever figures out what happened! Being straightforward about directions is usually safer.

> **T:**   During this activity you are to remain in your own space. Give yourself enough room so that you will not touch anyone.

Often the leader needs to be explicit about no talking. This is hard for some teachers to do, and they will try to down-play these directions. For example, the material may be a poem about snowflakes, so the teacher says:

> **T:**   Remember, now, snowflakes don't talk.

But if children can imagine being a snowflake, they can also imagine that the snowflake is capable of speech. And in fact, the teacher just might ask for this kind of imagination on another occasion. Being straightforward, the teacher should say simply and directly:

> **T:**   For this activity I want you to move as silently as possible. There should be no talking at all. When everyone is quiet, we shall begin.

Getting Attention

To help in giving directions, the leader may need some attention-getting device, such as the ring of a small bell or the beat of the drum; it may be a visual signal, such as the flicking of lights or the raising of a hand.

A cue other than the teacher's voice is often more effective in gaining attention. When the teacher shouts above the group's noise, it only adds to the din and confusion. The children often have no idea that the teacher is talking to them. Furthermore, when teachers raise the volume of their voice, they usually raise the pitch as well, which contributes to cacophony.

In time, however, with patience and guidance, the group can become sensitive enough that the leader need only say:

> **T:** Groups, go to your areas, and when you're settled I'll give you some further directions.

Directions can be fun and still challenging and effective. For example, children usually like the word "freeze" to call them to attention. It becomes more of a game rule than a command. However, "freeze" can easily become overworked. If the teacher uses it more than two or three times in one period, the situation should be reexamined.

Nonverbal Directions

The teacher should also look for ways to remain in control and yet not be scolding or constantly reminding children of how they are to behave. Much of this control can be done nonverbally.

Student teachers have noted that the experienced teacher can do much with a glance, a definite shake of the head, or other simple tactics that convey as strong a message as a verbally stated one. Many of these tactics will take time to learn and to perfect. But student teachers will do well to think of some possibilities for themselves. One student teacher who was having a hard time getting the children's attention because of her soft voice drew a large colorful sign saying in bold letters, "Cool It!" Whenever she wanted the group to be quiet and listen for further directions, she simply held up the sign and waited for a few seconds until everyone saw it. Then she proceeded with the activity. For her it worked.

The new teacher should also get into the habit of taking direct action when it is needed. Frequently student teachers prefer to look in the other direction rather than face a problem. There are many situations that can be overlooked, but when an activity is getting raggedy around the edges because of the behavior of some children, the whole session can deteriorate quickly unless action is taken immediately.

For example, some children have a tendency to chatter to one another or to engage in horseplay. Often they will stop when the teacher moves over in their direction. The close proximity of the authority figure speaks for itself. A hand on the shoulder might also be helpful.

Repeating Directions

The teacher should not assume that directions which are given once are internalized by the children immediately. For example, it may be difficult for the children to stay in their area once the playing begins. They mean well, but it is very natural to gravitate (sometimes friends are tempting), and soon social and sometimes physical interaction completely overshadows the activity. Of course, concentration is usually lost.

When this happens it is best to stop the activity. Inexperienced teachers are often hesitant to do this; they try to muddle through rather than trying to solve the problem. But insistence upon remaining in separated areas is not an arbitrary decision; it is an aid for concentration. It may take practice to stay in a separate area, particularly for young children whose bodies are often constantly in motion. Directions and the reasons for them may need to be repeated before children can follow through. When children see that keeping their concentration makes the playing more interesting, it will be easier to accomplish.

Understanding Problems

When children are involved in creative drama, they often get excited and find it difficult to listen to and follow directions. At times the leader contributes to children's hyperactivity. Sometimes one takes too long to get to the playing, causing the children to be restless and fidgety. Sometimes one proceeds too quickly with an idea before the children are ready to handle it. Recognizing and admitting one's own mistakes is important so that the children know that the difficulty may not have been their fault.

> **T:** I think I've kept you sitting a long time while we've discussed this. . . .
>
> **T:** Sometimes I get so excited about what we're doing that I try to rush you too fast. I think that may be what happened just now. We were really getting ahead of ourselves.

When things do go wrong, the best thing to do is to stop before they get worse and try to sort out what has happened and how to remedy it. There are ways to keep the excitement down without scolding the children for something that is a quite natural response. This can be done good naturedly.

> **T:** Whoops, I can see we've got a problem. Let's work on it.

But the problem usually cannot be worked on until everyone is quiet and the children have stopped moving. The teacher should be sure to get these things accomplished before going on with discussion. If the movement is stopped first, the children's talking usually stops automatically. If not, a finger to the lips for a moment or two should be all that is necessary. Then the teacher is ready to find out what went wrong.

Even the children are aware that this procedure can be helpful. One of the authors vividly remembers a helpful suggestion from a five-year-old during a chaotic moment with kindergarten children. As the children were pretending to be baby animals, they suddenly turned into ferocious tigers and lions, fighting one another. The leader recalls standing in a kind of daze until "out of the mouths of babes," a child suggested: "Teacher, I think we need to sit down in a circle."

Sometimes things go wrong in spite of all one's precautions. Directions may sound logical and clear to the leader; one could assume that they are clear to everyone else. However, this is not always true. Once one of the authors, in trying to organize a group, became exasperated with one child who was talking with a friend. Accusingly she asked, "Can you do this?" and pointed a finger at him. He, puzzled but cooperative, nodded his head and pointed his finger also! At a time like this a sense of humor is very helpful.

In summary, we remind the teacher that by beginning with the most restricted area and expanding space by degrees, and by using organization, planning, and the clearest directions, children can learn to function with less teacher control and greater self-control.

GAMES FOR SELF-CONTROL

While games in themselves have a built-in control, there are several games which particularly focus on building self-control and self-discipline. The student teacher will find them helpful in enticing children to work at developing these important skills. Some can be played in limited space; others will need more room.

Be careful! Pantomime walking over stepping stones, on a tightrope, or fence top, retaining balance. Do this at the side of the desks or have small groups go from one end of the room to the other.

Conduct an orchestra. All the children are orchestra leaders and must keep with the beat of a particular record. "Sabre Dance" by Khachaturian or the *Star Wars* theme is useful.

Burglars. In groups (one group at a time), be burglars sneaking through a museum guarded by electronic eyes. Children must move as rapidly as possible from one side of the room to another, but must go down to the floor whenever they hear the sound cue which indicates activation of the electronic eye. (An alarm-clock bell or buzzer works well for this.) The objective is to move quickly *and* quietly. Groups could work to improve their speed.

College student works to get a smile in the game "I Won't Laugh."

I won't laugh. Several students at a time sit facing the class. They cannot close their eyes or plug their ears. The rest of the class volunteers to tell jokes, make faces, or whatever else they can think of (without touching the contestants) to make them laugh. Again, groups and/or individuals could work to increase the length of time they can hold out.

Interrogation. In each group, one child is the questioner. The questioner focuses on one person, but it is the person on the right of the questioned person who must answer, and with a straight face. The questioned person must maintain eye contact with the questioner and not laugh. Whoever in the group cannot remain solemn throughout the proceedings becomes the next interrogator. For an added challenge, if the questioner points a finger at a subject, the person on the *left* must answer. Try going fast.

Falling. Children love to fall. Suggest that anyone can fall, but that it takes real skill to do it with control. Caution them not to fall on unprotected parts of their bodies like elbows, knees, and heads. Think of different kinds of objects that fall: a leaf, a balloon losing air. Fall in slow motion. No one can reach the ground before the leader counts to a slow 10. Have them close their eyes so they concentrate only on their own work.

To tire out an overactive group, make them fall in a variety of ways very quickly. "Up again—this time fall quickly like a falling star. Now! (They fall.) Up. This time you're a feather. Fall on the count of five. (They fall.) Up again . . ."

Making noiseless sounds. Children pantomime making a vocal sound by using their face and body but not their voice. Try it in slow motion. Cough, sneeze, gulp, gasp, sigh, and shout.

In-service teachers practice falling in slow motion.

Pair and Group Work in Self-Control

Many groups of children need assistance and motivation in order to work together. The games in the next section are useful in achieving this goal.

For pair and group playing the children can be grouped by the leader or they may group themselves, depending on their maturity. Often children work best when they are allowed to choose their coworkers. Some classes can pair and group themselves with few arguments and no hard feelings. Eventually, however, the leader will want to encourage various groupings so that cliques do not form.

When children do have problems with grouping decisions, the leader will need to step in. During these moments it is best to make the decisions quickly and get on with the playing. If the leader acts as if the groups can get along with each other, they frequently live up to that expectation. Often the excitement of playing the game is strong enough to help them forget about arguing over coworkers.

Sound pantomime.   One child pantomimes while another creates the sound effects. First the sound effects should fit the timing of the pantomime. Then let the pantomimer fit movements to the lead of the person doing sound effects. Use simple ideas at first. For example, someone is sneaking across a creaky floor trying not to be heard; sawing a piece of lumber; cutting down a tree with an ax; trying to start an old, junky car; a robot moving with creaking joints.

Two-person jobs.   Select a task which requires two people to perform. Pretend to fold a flag or tablecloth; saw wood with a cross-saw; play see-saw. Pairs must concentrate on the pantomimed object and cooperate to make the pantomime appear real.

Mirroring.   Two people face each other. One is the mirror and the other, the person using the mirror. The mirror must follow the leader in putting on makeup, washing face, shaving, and so on. Consider possibilities with a full-

Kindergarteners play the "Mirror Game."

length mirror also, as in practicing a dance step. Switch parts so the follower can become the leader. It is helpful to do this in slow motion to keep the actions carefully "mirrored."

Sculpturing. One person is the sculptor and the other, a piece of clay. The sculptor molds clay into a statue, giving it a particular stance and/or emotional attitude. The statue must allow itself to be moved about. Nontouchers and the ticklish will find this a real challenge.

Group jobs. Five people are carrying a large piece of glass from one side of the room to the other. The five people must coordinate their movements so the imaginary piece of glass really seems to exist. As the group walks, the pane of glass must stay in one piece! As an added challenge, have the group walk as fast as possible, "upstairs," "downstairs," and the like. Other group jobs might be firemen carrying an extension ladder, pirates carrying a large treasure chest, or police moving a very tall murder victim.

Tug-of-war. Two teams of three or more pretend to pull on an imaginary rope. The rope must seem to exist. The leader needs to sidecoach the game. "Team I is ahead—now it's Team II . . ." On the leader's signal, the rope breaks and the players fall in *slow motion.* Players cannot reach the floor until the leader, who is counting slowly, reaches the count of 10.

Conducting an orchestra. This time the children are in groups pantomiming to a record. One is the conductor while the others are playing specific instruments. Drums, cymbals, violins, and trombones are particularly good because they require large movements. March music (Sousa) is easiest to begin on. For further self-discipline, stop the record periodically so players have to freeze.

Mirroring in groups. After experiencing pair mirroring, the children can try pairs mirroring pairs. For example, a person at beauty or barber shop is

"Tug of War" encourages concentration and focus.
(Photo courtesy of Jon Vander Meer.)

mirrored; then the hairdresser or barber is mirrored. A manicurist and shoe shiner, both mirrored, may even be added.

One at a time. Several players (five) pretend to be in a given setting, perhaps a living room. They are seated randomly. They may move about the room as they like, but they do not interact. However, only one person may move at a time. The action of the next person moving freezes the first mover in place until that player decides to initiate movement again. For example, Person #1 gets out of a chair and turns on an imaginary TV set. Person #2 picks up a newspaper from a table, which freezes Person #1 at the TV. Perhaps Person #3 crosses her legs and freezes Person #2. Then Person #1 might decide to return to his seat, and so forth. Children must become very sensitive to each other's movements or the game fails. They must also be assertive if they want to move. The leader monitors and coaches, "Only one person can move at a time . . ."

To help children learn the game, it is helpful for the leader to give players a number and call the numbers at random to indicate when the children may move. Once the children understand how the game is played, they initiate their own actions.

A variation of the game is to have children sit in a circle and not move from their seats. All initiated action must be in a seated position. Work toward using smaller and smaller actions. Groups of five-ten work best. More than one group may play at a time.

(Note: The spontaneity of this game makes it fun for the rest of the children to watch.)

QUIETING ACTIVITIES

A creative drama period should come to a quieting end. There will probably have been a lot of action, concentration, and hard work. It is usually essential to calm the children down rather than to let them go on to their next work at a high pitch.

One technique is to narrate a very quieting selection. There are several poems suitable for this purpose. The characters in the poems are relaxed or tired; thus, the actions are subdued. Some examples are "Fatigue," by Peggy Bacon (30); "Lullaby," by Robert Hillyer (31); "Slowly," by James Reeves (47); and "Sunning," by James S. Tippett (4) (31).

Usually it is helpful to have the children close their eyes as they enact the poem. The leader should try to capture the quieting mood in the voice or perhaps use a quiet record for accompaniment.

The leader may also create simple quieting activities. One may narrate a few sentences about a candle burning and slowly melting away, or ask the children to pretend to be floating on a sea of tranquility.

A quieting activity brings the period to a restful close.
(Photo courtesy of Jon Vander Meer.)

The importance of the quieting experience is to relax the group and to calm down any hyperactivity. Perhaps more than that, however, it helps the children to absorb the concepts, experiences, and feelings covered during the drama period.

FOR THE COLLEGE STUDENT

1. Collect or design five of each of the following:
   a. finger plays
   b. single-action poetry
   c. action songs
   d. action games
   e. action stories
   f. quieting activities

2. Find a game or design one of your own that has action in it but can be played at the desk.

3. Select a game to lead your classmates in. Give the directions for playing the activity. Organize the group for playing the game. Bring the playing to a close. Afterward discuss with your classmates what your strengths and weaknesses were. Brainstorm for ways to improve the activity.

4. Select or design three games that illustrate the use of controls.

5. Find or create a game to develop children's imagination.

6. Select or design five sensory games, one for each of the senses.

7. Select or design a communication game, emphasizing either speaking or listening skills.

8. Write a pantomime, of at least fifty words, which emphasizes a variety of actions.

9. Write ten sensory pantomimes, two for each of the five major senses.

10. Write five pantomimes emphasizing emotions.

11. Make a list of ten brief pantomimes; then in a second list add conflict to each.

12. As a class, play some of the games for self-control. Afterward, discuss your reactions. Were you able to improve your skills as a result of the playing? How do you think this was accomplished?

13. Discuss various classroom physical environments. Consider such factors as fixed desks, rows of desks on runners, large rooms with movable furniture, small rooms with tables and chairs, carpeting, thin classroom partitions and walls, skylights, and shades. Consider ways to accommodate any of these physical features. Include selection of material, planning and organizing space, and giving directions.

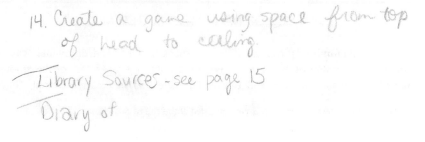

Chapter Three

Stories and Poems for Narrative Pantomime

The pantomime materials we will focus on in this chapter are those that the leader narrates for the children to interpret in their own way. There are a number of stories and poems describing interesting and dramatic action that the children can easily play as the teacher reads them.

> **T:** As I read *Harold and the Purple Crayon,** you pretend to be Harold, drawing what he draws and doing what he does . . .

At the end of this chapter we have listed a number of selections suitable for playing in narrated fashion. Some of the better-known pieces include Paul Galdone's *The Three Bears,* Beatrix Potter's *Peter Rabbit,* and Dr. Seuss's *How the Grinch Stole Christmas!* Many selections can be found in basal readers. Some of the selections are realistic adventure stories of people and animals and could correlate with science and social studies lessons.

VALUES OF NARRATIVE MATERIALS

Narrative pantomime provides an expedient, efficient, and enjoyable way to dramatize a number of materials. It is a useful activity regardless of the amount of experience the children and the leader have had in creative drama. Since

---

* All materials referred to in this chapter are listed at the end of this chapter.

46

pantomime materials are often easier to enact than dialogue materials, they are useful for beginning groups as well as for warm-ups with experienced groups.

Narrative materials are also a foundation for further creative work. Later, dialogue can be added to some of these materials, or they can be elaborated in a variety of ways.

Also, in using these materials, the children will be able to enact completed little dramas from the very beginning. This can be very satisfying for both the children and the teacher.

Values to Children

Through narrative pantomimes the children will be able to "try on" a number of characters and situations in literature, moving with them through the action of the story or poem. Through this process they should be able to interpret and understand the literature more completely.

Because the materials are narrated, the children must listen carefully in order to know *what* to do and *when* to do it. For this reason, narrative pantomimes are excellent for encouraging children to focus on an activity, to concentrate their thinking, and to develop their listening skills.

Narrative materials are relatively easy to do. Many children feel pressured if they are required to create on their own before they are psychologically ready. In narrative activities everyone can be successful since they need only follow the actions the material prescribes. Thus, the materials help build confidence and develop positive self-concepts in the children for more challenging material later.

Values to the Leader

Narrative materials are orderly, consistent, and provide a built-in organization. This is an important aid for the beginning leader. By narrating the action, the leader gives the cues for playing and has control of the dramatization.

Narrative materials also provide a basis for developing the leader's skills in guiding other creative drama activities. After becoming proficient in narrative materials, the leader will be more confident in editing passages from longer selections and in writing original materials. This will be discussed further in the next chapter.

One of the most important skills for the leader of creative drama is side-coaching. Side-coaching is the encouraging and descriptive commentary the leader gives as the children play their own ideas. We will speak of side-coaching often, but for now the leader is simply alerted to the fact that side-coaching is in many ways very similar to narrative pantomime. The leader will thus be preparing for that skill while guiding narrative pantomimes.

TYPES OF MATERIAL

The type of material suitable for narrative pantomime must have an emphasis on action. The action must be continuous enough for the children to have something to enact without having to pause and wait for long periods of time.

Material for Individual Playing

Most frequently the material for narrative pantomime contains only one character. When authors write about single characters, they usually have to give them action to perform since there isn't anyone to talk with. All the children play this character together.

Sometimes the character lives alone, as does *The Man Who Didn't Wash His Dishes*. Or the character may be alone on an adventure, as is Harold in *Harold and the Purple Crayon*. Some material has two or more characters who act independently of each other. For example, *The Pond* describes the movements of several characters, one at a time: the water, a dragonfly, shadows, and so forth. In these materials the child can play all of the parts, changing from one to the other with relative ease.

Material for Paired Playing

For paired playing, stories or poems with two fairly equal characters are required. Such a story might be Beatrix Potter's *The Tale of Two Bad Mice*. There can also be paired playing with material which has more than two characters. For example, in some stories a main character goes on an adventure and meets a series of different people along the way. One child in each pair can play the adventurer and the partner can play all of the people who are met.

Even in a story like *The Three Bears,* one child can play the part of all three bears simply by switching back and forth. Or in a story like "Gertrude McFuzz," the same child who plays Lolla-Lee-Lou could also play Uncle Dake.

Material for Group Playing

Material which contains several characters (or has the potential for adding characters) can be played in groups. The playing of narrative pantomime group stories is similar to a popular theatre form called *story theatre.*

Some of the characters in group stories have small parts, but if they are interesting characters, the children will want to include them. For example, in *Ittki Pittki* there is, in addition to the title role, the prince, the wife, four sons, the prince's messenger, the doctor, the funeral director, and all the customers and mourners. Some appear only briefly, but they are all important to the plot.

Varying Cast Size

Frequently the number of characters in group stories can be expanded or reduced. By adding characters or by double casting, the entire class can be involved in a single playing. For example, there can be two or even three wives and husbands in *Brownies—Hush!* and any number of elves.

If it is preferable to have a small "cast of characters," several of the minor parts in a story can be played by the same person. Then two or more groups can enact the story simultaneously. For older or more experienced classes there can be several groups, each with a different story to prepare. In the latter case, children will probably serve as their own narrators; therefore, it will be important to have a skilled reader in each group.

CREATIVE INTERPRETATION

Although narrative materials contain numerous ideas of *what* to do, the children are not told *how* to do them. Thus they may interpret their ideas through pantomime in whatever way they choose.

Many of the lines of the material can be played easily and simply. Yet creative interpretation is possible even with a fairly explicit line such as "frogs hop." Some children may choose to enact their frog in an upright position, hopping on hind legs. Others may want to be on all fours, perhaps even crooking their arms to represent the frog's bowed front legs.

Some lines may be more challenging. For example, in Carl Sandburg's "Lines Written for Gene Kelly to Dance To," the children are asked if they can dance a question mark. This could be interpreted in a variety of ways: the feet might draw a question mark on the floor; the hands might inscribe one in the air; or the whole body might form one, dissolving and reforming in a rhythmic dance.

Sometimes the material calls for action that has to be interpreted symbolically. The children have the opportunity to exercise their creativity to interpret "disappearing," "being swallowed," "dissolving," "swinging from a rope," and so forth. Often the players will have to "read between the lines" in order to create action for themselves. Even with illustrations, Ungerer's line in *The Beast of Monsieur Racine,* "Unspeakable acts were performed," leaves room for inventiveness (within reason, of course!).

PREPARATION

There is no set way for the leader to prepare the children for enacting narrative pantomime. The nature of the material and personal preferences will play an important part in the final decision. Following are some suggestions the leader may want to consider.

Editing Action

Stories and poetry are not generally written with narrative pantomime in mind; therefore, almost any selection can benefit from minor editing. Some material benefits from shortening or tightening the physical action. As a check for the amount and placement of pantomime in a story, the leader should locate and underline the verbs or action words. Frequently sentences with no action in them can simply be omitted without destroying the plot.

Endings of stories should come to a quieting close, with the children in a settled position. Many stories do this naturally. For those that do not, the leader may reword them. For example, in Ezra Jack Keats's *The Snowy Day,* the story could end when Peter goes to bed, rather than continuing with Peter waking up the next day and going outside to play again. The ending line might be:

> And Peter went to sleep, dreaming of tomorrow and another day of play in the deep, deep snow.

Additional Action

The leader may want to narrate a few words of additional action to give the children increased involvement. For example,

> "While Fritzl stayed at home to do the housework, Liesi did the work in the field, *cutting and stacking the hay.*

Or if the leader wants to give the children something specific to do but doesn't want them to be physically active, the narration might read,

> "The bears walked so long in the woods, waiting for their porridge to cool, that they became tired and *sat down under a tree to sleep.*

With picture books, important parts of the plot and action are often told in the pictures rather than the text. In such cases the leader should add important pictured action to the narration.

Editing Dialogue

In most cases, unimportant dialogue can easily be omitted or reworded without destroying the plot. If, however, the bits of dialogue are very short and compelling, the children may want to repeat them after the leader reads them. For example, it is almost crucial to let the children say, "Gwot, I ate it!" the final line of George Mendoza's "The Hairy Toe." Or in Russell Hoban's *The Little Brute Family,* the lines "How nice," or "May we keep it?" are fun to repeat.

Some dialogue can easily be pantomimed, such as shaking one's head for "No," or gesturing with a shrug of the shoulders for "I really don't know what to do next.'' However, it is best not to have the children mouth any words of dialogue, since that is usually too distracting.

Presenting the Material

First, the leader may want to read the material to the children to see whether they like it well enough to play it. The teacher's reading will affect the children's initial interest as well as their interpretative playing of it. It may be necessary to give one's all to making the material sound exciting, dramatic, or funny— whatever the material calls for.

A prior reading is particularly beneficial when there are certain concepts in the material the teacher wants the children to understand. For example, there is a small science lesson in Jean George's *All Upon a Stone*.

> **T:** As I read the story, you listen to the description of the mole cricket and the things he does. A lot of what he does will be different from the way you do them. That's because his sense organs are different from yours. He hears with his knees, and breathes through his belly, and smells through his antennae. You'll have to keep all that in mind when I read it the second time for you to play it.

Or, if the material is lengthy or time is limited, the leader may prefer to give a brief synopsis of it.

Discussions and Preview Playing

Before the material is played, the leader will want some assurance that the children will be successful. This means that

a. they have some idea of what they will do for the challenging and/or symbolic lines;
b. they understand how to use limited space;
c. they can handle the physical action safely.

Discussions and preview playing generate ideas and help the teacher assess the children's readiness. The following examples illustrate how the teacher can guide children to discuss and preview play:

> **A.**
>
> **T:** In the poem, "Boa Constrictor," you will be pretending to be swallowed up, starting with your toe, until you are completely swallowed. How could we pretend that is happening to us? You may all have different ideas.
> **C:** I could stand behind my desk, see, and then go down behind it a little bit at a time.
> **C:** You could sink down on the floor.
> **C:** You could just crumple until you were a ball of nothing.

B.

T: In Ray Bradbury's story, "There Will Come Soft Rains," how might you play the part of the machines that are like little mice cleaning the house while you remain at your desk area?

C: I have suction cleaners on my feet that neatly and quickly eliminate all dirt. When I scoot to the front of my desk, I clean the living room; at this side, I clean the bedroom; this is the kitchen; and this side is the study; and up here, you find the bathroom. I clean that last.

C: I'll be a giant machine here in the middle of my desk. I'm all folded up, but when I begin to work, I slowly unfold. My long arms extend throughout the house. One arm is equipped with a vacuum cleaner hose and the other has furniture polish and cleaning spray.

C.

T: There is one line in *Hildilid's Night* that tells us she hated the night so much she "spat" at it. Those in Row 1 who think they can pretend but not really spit, let's see how you'd do that. On the count of three—one, two, three!

D.

T: In the story *Oté*, the devil gives you a command and you fall in a faint. How can you pretend to fall so that you don't get hurt?

C: The gym teacher has taught us to fall part by part so you land on your muscles.

T: That sounds very safe. Would some of you like to demonstrate how you would do that?

E.

T: Also in the story *Oté*, the devil hops on Oté's back and makes him take him home. How can that be done?

C: The devil could just walk real close behind Oté and maybe put his arms around his neck like he does in the picture.

T: Les, could you and Mack show us how that could be done?

Usually children prefer to keep all the exciting action in the story and rehearse it carefully. Knowing they will have to forfeit the privilege of playing exciting drama if they cannot follow the rules usually motivates them to comply.

If the leader feels the children are not ready to handle particular lines or actions, they may be omitted or reworded. For example, the leader may substitute "made a face at the night" for spitting. Instead of "falling in a faint," the characters could "freeze."

Casting for Preview

The demonstrators for preview playing should be volunteers since they will probably be the most confident children. It is also a good idea to have more than one demonstrator. In this way there is no pressure on any one child.

Since preview playing usually becomes the model for the entire class to follow, it is important that it be successful. If several children volunteer to be demonstrators, it is valid and desirable to use some selection procedures. The leader may explain that those who are selected must be able to remain involved and not be distracted by the fact that others are observing them. Confident and even "hammy" children might feel at ease in front of their classmates if the material is humorous. If the material is serious, however, the "comedian" may not be a wise choice. Serious material may turn into farce in this child's hands. Then the entire class may decide that they want to play the material in the same way! Sometimes it is the quiet children who, if they volunteer, make the serious scenes convey the poignancy called for.

Audience for Preview

Even at this early beginning it is good to establish the audience rules. Any time that children are observing their peers, they are doing so to learn something and to share ideas. They should remain quiet and not be allowed to boo and hiss even in a playful way, because such action will interrupt the demonstrators' concentration.

Perhaps it is important to point out that "work" is a good word for the leader to use. The play and fun part of creative drama is obvious enough to them. Usually children are surprised, yet pleased, to think that something they enjoy can also legitimately be called "work." And it *does* take concentration and involvement to produce the most satisfying results.

PLAYING

Unison Playing

It is important, particularly in the beginning stages of creative drama, for children to play in unison. *Unison playing* means that all the players perform simultaneously, whether in pairs, groups, or by themselves.

Unison playing allows children a chance to experience their ideas for their own enjoyment without worrying about audience evaluation. It allows them an opportunity to rehearse and polish their ideas in case they later decide to share them with classmates.

Another benefit of unison playing is that it reduces the time spent waiting to take turns. For active groups who cannot bear to sit and wait, convinced that their turn will *never* come, unison playing is most satisfying.

Individual Playing

Individual playing means that each child is the solo performer in a private drama. All the children can play the main part in a story without having to share the role with someone else. For many children, particularly the younger ones, it is important to have this immediate gratification. Once they have had a chance to be the

"Individual playing means I work by myself and enjoy my own ideas."
(Photo courtesy of Jon Vander Meer.)

main character, they are usually more interested in sharing parts and playing in pairs and groups.

Also, when children play individually they need only a small amount of space. This can be the desk area, which minimizes the need to reorganize the classroom.

Pair and Group Playing

While older children can benefit from the privacy and concentration afforded by individual playing, they are usually more comfortable at first with *pair and group playing*. However, pair and group playing involve both social and physical interaction. These two factors will necessitate additional considerations in organizing the playing.

First of all, with pair and group playing, the children will be dividing their attention between the teacher and other players. Once they are grouped, getting their attention and giving additional directions will be difficult.

Secondly, the physical contact in pair and group materials usually has to be faked as it is done in the movies and on T.V. For example, "The Crack in the Wall," by George Mendoza, is fun to play with one child being the hermit and one being the expanding crack. But the hermit pounds and kicks the wall. This action can be done *close* to the "wall" without actually touching it. This means the players will have to be careful in judging their distance from each other, and the hermit will have to control his or her actions.

If the inexperienced teacher is not already aware of this, it should be noted that children frequently introduce aggression and physical contact if there is the slightest suggestion of it in the material. A seemingly innocuous line such as, "When John headed for the door, Sam stopped him," might seem to be a good line for practicing a flying tackle! The children often see such action in dramatic shows. For them it is logical and impressive.

As another alternative, it may be useful to begin with individual playing and work up to pair and group playing gradually. For example, in a first playing of "The Sorcerer's Apprentice," all the children might be Fritzl. A second playing might be in pairs, adding the broom since it creates the conflict and causes all the excitement in the story. Then, for trio playing, the Sorcerer can be added.

Another problem is sustained physical contact, as when a character rides an animal. Often it is best to imagine that the animal is being ridden.

However, in a story such as *Gregory,* the bear and the mule that he rides have some human qualities and are necessary to the story. These parts should be cast, and the riding should be done so that the rider does not actually sit on the "mule's" back. This leaves the "mule" room to move freely without bearing the weight of the rider.

Children like to include physical contact, but it can get out of hand.

Limited Space

As a general rule, for first playings of individual narrative pantomime, the children should remain at the desk area. The desks can become part of the drama itself. They can be the various kinds of transportation for Lois Lenski's stories about Mr. Small. The desk can be a table, sink, and easy chair, as well as the truck for *The Man Who Didn't Wash His Dishes.*

Pair and group work can also be done in limited space. For some classrooms the space between aisles or at the corners may be sufficient.

If necessary, pair and group stories can be handled in limited space in another way. For example, in a story with two characters, one-half the class can play one character while the other half plays the second character. But instead of interacting as pairs, they play at their desks, imagining their partner. They can see the other part being enacted, but they remain separated from each other.

This same method may also be used for material with several characters. For example, the children might play Goldilocks and the Three Bears, with Row 1 (or one group) being Goldilocks, and Rows 2, 3, and 4 being each of the Three Bears. The desks could be the table, the chairs, and the beds in the story.

Organizing and Casting for Pair and Group Stories

For pair and group playing the children can be grouped by the leader or they may group themselves. Usually it is best at first not to work with groups larger than five; otherwise the interaction process can get too complicated.

Another decision to be made involves the casting of parts. In paired playing, the children can usually decide between themselves who will play which part, particularly if they know there will be a replaying and parts will be switched. If there is not enough time for everyone to play every part in a group story, the leader may need to help with the decision making.

Narrating the Material

The leader should be familiar enough with the material so that it can be read by glancing down only *occasionally*. This gives the leader more opportunity to watch the children and to time the pauses for playing.

One student teacher learned the value of good reading most graphically. She began by selecting a poem too difficult for her kindergarteners to understand. Then she read the poem, haltingly and without once glancing up. The children stood patiently, listening, but had no idea of what to do. At the end of the poem and after a moment's silence, one little voice piped up, "Is that it?" Although the student had made an error in selecting the material, it would have helped to know that the children were doing nothing. A couple of glances up from the page would have made this clear.

Leaders should also take their voice into consideration when deciding how many children will be playing the material. Many teachers, particularly the inexperienced, may not have voices strong enough to be heard when more than ten are playing. Some experimenting and practicing may be necessary to determine one's vocal capabilities.

Generally it is best to make pauses too short rather than too long. Pauses can always be lengthened on repeated playings, when the children have more ideas and feel more comfortable with the material. Since the narration contains the cues to the action, the leader's timing and intensity in reading can help control the noise level. If the children become a little boisterous, the leader can pause for a moment. When the children become quieter in order to hear the next cue, the leader can speak in a softer voice, and the children's playing will become quieter.

Because of the many considerations involved in narrating the material, it is perhaps best that the leader rather than the children be the narrator, at least in initial work. It is possible, however, to find some children who can narrate as well as the leader. One of our best narrators was a second grader who read *Seven Skinny Goats* for his class to play. His only problem was trying not to laugh at the antics of the players!

With time and experience there may even be several children who can alternate in the role of narrator. Sometimes two or three narrators can be used in a single playing by dividing the story into logical units.

It might be added that when children see the importance of the narrator role and have a desire to try it, they are often motivated to perfect their reading skills. Sometimes the narrator role becomes as significant to the children as the "lead" part in the story.

Music

The use of recorded music during the playing, while not required, has advantages for some materials. It can lend atmosphere and sustain involvement as well as encourage ideas. Some suggestions of music titles are indicated in the bibliography. The leader will, of course, need to rehearse narrating with the music before trying it in class.

EVALUATION

Throughout the discussions, preview playing, and the eventual playing, the leader should convey to the children general enthusiasm and enjoyment.

Comments can be made that acknowledge children's inventiveness, but no one idea need be praised over another. Statements should be made in a general way.

"Look at the world upside down . . . "
(Photo courtesy of the *Kalamazoo Gazette.)*

That's interesting.
That's another way it could be done.
I saw many different and good ideas.

The leader can express appreciation whenever children handle space or difficult lines creatively or when they follow the audience rules.

I like the way you listen to each other.
You did very well putting all of the actions into one small area.

Perhaps the most important evaluation, however, is the children's own. Self-evaluation can be encouraged by asking,

What's the one thing you did that you liked the best?
What changes do you think should be made next time?
What was the hardest part for you?
What can we do about the difficult parts? In what ways can we help one another with them?

When a spirit of working together to create an enjoyable experience can be established in any learning situation, the highest achievements are gained.

REPLAYING THE MATERIAL

It is often important to play the material more than once. The first playing can serve as a run-through. In repeated playings the children perfect their ideas on their own and with the leader's encouragement of new goals.

T: This time I'm going to read the story a little slower so you can add more ideas.

T: Now that you know what the poem is about, I think you'll be able to work harder at being these different animals. Last time I saw more second graders than rabbits.

In replaying pair and group material the children exchange parts. In this way they can see the ideas of other children as well as the perspective of the other characters.

Additional Characters

In replaying there is an opportunity to invent additional characters or interesting inanimate objects. For example, Richard Rostron's "The Sorcerer's Apprentice" would seem to have only three playable characters: the Sorcerer, Fritzl, and the Broom. But children delight in being various articles such as magic books, bottles, baskets, or flasks found in the Sorcerer's cellar which bob around, sink, or float in the rising water.

In adding characters, the leader should be sure the children have ideas for action. For example,

T: Several of you have mentioned that you would like to be the Sorcerer's magic book. Let's think about that for a moment. What will happen to you as a magic book in a flood?

C: I'll be open, lying on the table. Then, because I'm magic, I can see the water getting higher and higher. So I will close slowly so my insides won't get wet. Then I float until the end of the story.

C: I'm on a shelf like a library book. The water never gets up as high as I am. But I fall off the shelf because there's so much commotion. And because I'm magic, I grow legs and arms and swim out the door.

As another example, in the story *The Little Auto,* some groups might like to create the auto itself. In addition to Mr. Small, four children on their hands and knees can be the tires of the car. To give them a little more to do, they can also be the engine humming and the horn beeping. The action can be controlled if the auto bounces along "in place" rather than moving about. A sixth person could act all the parts of the other characters: the policeman, the gas station attendant, and even the person who sells the newspaper to Mr. Small.

GROUP STORIES INTO PLAYS

Many of the group stories can be turned into simple, informal plays, if desired. When the class likes a story particularly well and enjoys replaying it, the children begin to perfect it much as they might in rehearsing a play. The leader may then wish to encourage this idea further.

Adding Dialogue

Dialogue flows more easily when children are interested in the material and are so involved in it that it seems perfectly natural to include verbalizing. Working with the group stories, the children will probably see opportunities for dialogue. To encourage verbalizing, the leader pauses in the narration for the moments when dialogue would be appropriate and lets the children improvise. Sometimes the children can carry the story along so completely that narrating isn't even required.

There is an advantage to using the pantomime materials since verbalizing is not essential to the story. Those children who are hesitant about verbalizing can still participate in the playing, while those who are ready for dialogue have the opportunity to add it. And as long as the pantomime action of the story progresses, the "play" goes on. The children are not pressured by the worry of "forgetting lines," usually the biggest fear with a scripted play.

A few simple costumes can add to the dramatization.

In-service teachers prepare for dramatizing *Strega Nona*.

Adding Costumes and Props

Often children like to add embellishments to the group stories. The simpler these additions are, however, the better. While some suggestion of costuming and props can help tell the story and aid involvement, they should never clutter the playing and become more important than the story itself.

If costumes are desired, they can be made of simple squares of material. In this way they can be draped on any child of any size. Old drapes, blankets, tablecloths, and remnants of fabric are usually all that are needed for most stories.

Props can be found around the house or schoolroom or made of simple materials. It is not necessary to have props for all items mentioned in the story; many can still be pantomimed effectively.

Sharing

As the children gain more confidence in themselves and become pleased with their work, they may want to share it with another class. It is most important, however, that any sharing be the collective desire of the group. It should not be imposed by the leader but should grow out of a pleasurable and confident experience the group has first enjoyed together.

Example from "Urashima Taro and the Princess of the Sea"

The following is a description of the development of a group story into a classroom play with a fourth-grade class. The story was a condensed version of the Japanese folktale, "Urashima Taro and the Princess of the Sea," which the students had read in their basal reading series. In this story, a young man who saves a turtle is rewarded with a trip under the sea. While enjoying himself there for what he thinks are three days, many years pass on earth. One day he asks to return to visit his parents. He is given a box which he is told not to open so that he may use it to return to the sea again. When he finds that he is in another time period on earth, he opens the box and is transformed into an old man.

A narrative pantomime was developed from this story for the entire class to play. The story was shortened, the action tightened, and all but the simplest of dialogue was edited out. The major characters in the story were Urashima Taro, the Princess of the Sea, and the Turtle. Other characters were added by focusing on the underwater sea life (crabs, fish, octopus, and so on) which Urashima would pass on his ride to and from the sea on the turtle's back. Then, when the Princess showed Urashima the seasons, several children pantomimed actions appropriate to each—swimming in summer, skiing in winter, and so forth. Other characters were a group of children who taunted the turtle in the opening scene, courtiers under the sea, and a couple who greeted Urashima at the end of the story.

The action of the play began at the front of the room, moved around the side, and then to the back of the room for the Princess's palace. The return trip was made on the other side of the room, and the story ended in the front of the classroom again.

For the costumes, pieces of sheer pastel fabric were used, mainly of green and blue shades, to represent the underwater world. The only scenery was crepe-paper streamers of various colors which were twisted slightly. With two children at each end of a streamer, several streamers were alternately raised up and down. The effect was of sea waves, so that as Urashima and the Turtle moved in between the two streamers, they appeared to be swimming in the sea. At the back of the room, the same technique was used with various-colored streamers depicting the seasons: red and orange for fall, blue and white for winter. The pantomimes of the seasons were enacted between the streamers. A small jewelry box served as the Princess's gift to Urashima and was the only prop used.

The actions under the sea, as well as Urashima's turning into an old man at the end of the story, were done in slow motion to add to the mood. For background music, a recording of Orff instruments was used because of its somewhat oriental sound.* With more time, the children could have played the instrumental music themselves.

The entire process took only about forty minutes to complete. At the end of the lesson, the children expressed pleasure with their work and thought that the story was a beautiful one.

The major objective was to enhance a reading lesson, not to prepare a play for performance. However, if the children had wished to share it, this could easily have been done.

---

* Carl Orff and Gunhild Keetman, English version by Margaret Murray, *Music for Children,* Angel Records, 1959.

FOR THE COLLEGE STUDENT

1. Select a story and a poem suitable for a narrated activity. Prepare it to read aloud to your classmates. Practice and experiment with pauses, timing, vocal pitch, and quality to make the selection as interesting as possible. Find some background music suitable to the mood of the selection and play it as you read.

2. Select a narrative poem or story suitable for individual playing. Lead your classmates through a playing of the material you have selected. Consider whether or not a discussion will be necessary; whether preview playing is required. Give all the necessary instructions for organizing the playing. Consider the possibility of special lighting effects, sound effects, and so forth. Evaluate the playing.

3. Select a narrative poem or story to be played in pairs or groups, following the format in Exercise 2.

4. Divide into groups. Select several group stories for each of the groups to prepare. Rehearse and arrange the story as a play, perhaps adding simple costumes and props. Share your stories with the class.

5. Find as many other suitable materials for narration as you can. Keep a file of these materials. Select from reading books, social studies, health, science, and other trade books used in the classroom.

SELECTED BIBLIOGRAPHY FOR NARRATIVE PANTOMIME

The following stories and poems are suggested for narrative pantomime. They are arranged in alphabetical order according to title. Numbers in parentheses refer to sources listed in the final bibliography. All the books listed are picture books. The following symbols are used to indicate the age level the material might be best suited for:

Y   young children in kindergarten, first, and second grades
M   middle-grade children in third and fourth grades
O   older children in fifth and sixth grades

Y   *Alligators All Around,* Maurice Sendak. New York: Harper & Row, Pub., 1962. Something to do for each letter of the alphabet.

M   *All Upon a Stone,* Jean Craighead George. New York: Thomas Y. Crowell, 1971. A mole cricket searches for and finds his fellow crickets. After a brief meeting he returns to his solitary life once again. Solo.

Y—M   *Andy and the Lion,* James Daugherty. New York: Viking, 1966. Young boy reads about lions and imagines himself in an adventure similar to that of the fabled Androcles. Pairs. Begin with Part II.

M   *The Barn,* John Schoenherr. Boston: Little, Brown, 1968. In an old barn, a skunk searches for food; yet to the mother owl, the skunk is food for her babies. Solo.

O   "Base Stealer," Robert Francis. (31)
Baseball player's actions described as he hesitates—then decides to run. Poem.

Y   *Beady Bear,* Don Freeman. New York: Viking, 1954. A stuffed toy bear thinks he should live in a cave. Edit for solo or pairs.

M—O   "The Bear in the Pear Tree," Alice Geer Kelsey.   (29)
The Hodja meets a bear and hides from him in a pear tree. Pairs.

M   *Bear Mouse,* Berniece Freschet. New York: Scribner's, 1973. A meadow mouse hunts food for her young, escaping a hawk and a bobcat. Solo. Edit to condense.

M   *The Bears Who Stayed Indoors,* Susanna Gretz. Chicago: Follett Publishing Company, 1970. Five bears on a rainy-day play spaceship. Solo playing of all bears or group.

O   *The Beast of Monsieur Racine,* Tomi Ungerer. New York: Farrar, Straus & Giroux, 1971. A retired tax collector discovers a rare beast, befriends it and takes it to the Academy of Sciences. May be played in threes (two are the beast) or with added crowd scenes. Try a series of frozen pictures (see Chapter 8) for the line, "Unspeakable acts were performed."

M   *The Big Yellow Balloon,* Edward Fenton. New York: Doubleday, 1967. With his yellow balloon, Roger manages to lure an unlikely parade of a cat, dog, dog catcher, lady, thief, and policeman. Organize this one carefully.

M   "Boa Constrictor," Shel Silverstein.   (3) (28) (48)
Very brief poem. The complaint of one being slowly eaten by a boa.

Y—M   *Brownies—Hush!* Gladys L. Adshead. New York: Henry Z. Walck, 1938. A version of "The Elves and the Shoemaker" story. There are fourteen separate elves, but can be reworded so all elves perform all tasks.

Y   "Busy," A. A. Milne.   (27)
A little boy pretends to be different people. In between, he turns roundabout.

Y—M   *Caps for Sale,* Esphyr Slobodkina. New York: Scholastic Book Services, 1947. Thieving monkeys take a peddler's caps. This version is easiest to use for narrative. Flexible casting.

M   "The Cares of a Caretaker," Wallace Irwin.   (28)
An old woman has her work cut out for her trying to take care of life on the seashore. Poem.

Y—M   "Cat," Mary Britton Miller.   (4)
Cat's movements described in this poem.

Y—M   *Cowboy Small,* Lois Lenski. New York: Henry Z. Walck, 1949. A little cowboy ropes cattle, takes care of his horse, and plays a guitar, among other activities in his busy day.

M—O   "The Crack in the Wall," George Mendoza.   (11)
A hermit loses his house to a crack in the wall that won't stop spreading.

Y—M   *Curious George,* H. A. Rey. Boston: Houghton Mifflin, 1941. The antics of a curious little monkey who cannot stay out of trouble. Everyone will want to be George. Edit for solo playing.

M   *"Could Be Worse!"* James Stevenson. New York: Morrow, 1977. Grandpa tells a tall tale about what happened to him during the night. Edit for solo.

M   *A Day of Winter,* Betty Miles. New York: Knopf, 1961. Numerous sensory experiences with snow.

O   *Drummer Hoff,* Barbara Emberley. Englewood Cliffs, N.J.: Prentice-Hall, 1967. Simple cumulative story of cannon being loaded and fired off. Older students will like the challenge of mechanical movement in this one. Be sure to add flowers growing at the end.

M—O   *The Duchess Bakes a Cake,* Virginia Kahl. New York: Scribner's, 1955. A bored Duchess tries her hand at baking and winds up on top of a huge cake. Told in rhyme; dialogue can be pantomimed. Numerous characters.

M—Y   "The Elf Singing," William Allingham.   (35)
A story poem about a wizard who almost catches an elf. Pairs.

M   *Fortunately,* Remy Charlip. New York: Parents', 1964. Good fortune and bad fortune go hand in hand in this adventure.

M—O   "Foul Shot," Edwin A. Hoey.   (31)
Careful, poetic description of all the minute details of a basketball shot. In solo playing, children can be the player and then the ball. For a final touch, be the crowd giving a *silent* "roarup," and then freeze. Poem reprinted on p. 122 of this text.

Y   *Frances Face-Maker,* William Cole and Tomi Ungerer. New York: Collins Publishers, 1964. Frances doesn't like to go to bed at night. Daddy plays a game of face-making. Can play seated.

M   "Gertrude McFuzz," Dr. Seuss.   (52)
Gertrude finds that growing a big, beautiful tail may not be what she really wants after all.

M—O   *The Goblin Under the Stairs,* Mary Calhoun. New York: Morrow, 1967. A boy and his parents each have a special way of viewing the goblin who lives in their house. And the goblin lives up to each one's expectations. Fun in groups. Narrator can be the neighbor.

Y   *The Golden Egg Book,* Margaret Wise Brown. New York: Simon & Schuster, 1947. A bunny and a newly-hatched duck discover each other. Pairs. Edit interaction carefully.

M—O   *Gone Is Gone,* Wanda Gag. New York: Coward McCann, & Geoghegan, 1935. The old tale of the man who swaps chores with his wife, only to discover her work isn't as simple as he had thought. Another version is "The Husband Who Was to Mind the House."   (4)
Can combine the best features of both. Pairs.

Y—M   *Good Hunting, Little Indian,* Peggy Parish. Reading, Mass.: Addison-Wesley, 1962. A little Indian gets more than he bargained for in his hunting adventure.

Y—M   *The Great Big Enormous Turnip,* Alexei Tolstoy. New York: Franklin Watts, 1968. Grandfather, grandmother, granddaughter, dog, cat, and mouse finally succeed in pulling up a turnip. One child could be the turnip. Simple story. Encourage character differences.

M—O   *Great-Grandfather in the Honey Tree,* Sam and Zoa Swayne. New York: Viking, 1949. A very tall tale about a hunting adventure.

Y—M   *Gregory,* Robert Bright. New York: Doubleday, 1969. Proud Gregory is fast, can jump high, and holler loud, but he has a problem listening. Group playing. Use caution with the mule and bear riding.

M—O   "The Hairy Toe," George Mendoza.   (19)
Deliciously weird tale similar to the tale of "Teeny Tiny."   (35)

Y—M   *Harold and the Purple Crayon,* Crockett Johnson. New York: Harper & Row, Pub., 1955. A little boy has many adventures with the help of a purple crayon to draw them. Solo, or try in pairs with one person becoming the things being drawn.

M   *Harold's Circus.* Crockett Johnson. New York: Harper & Row, Pub., 1959. Harold creates a circus in this story.

M   *Harold's Trip to the Sky,* Crockett Johnson. New York: Harper & Row, Pub., 1957. Harold goes off on a rocket in this adventure.

Y   *Harry the Dirty Dog,* Gene Zion. New York: Harper & Row, Pub., 1956. Harry won't take a bath and his family doesn't recognize him.

Y—M   *Hildilid's Night,* Cheli Duran Ryan. New York: Macmillan, 1971. Woman tries everything she can think of to get rid of the night.

Y—M   *How the Grinch Stole Christmas!* Dr. Seuss. New York: Random House, 1957. The modern classic of a spiteful character who learns the true meaning of Christmas. Can be done solo or in pairs for Max, the dog, and a Who child.

M—O   *How the Rhinoceros Got His Skin,* Rudyard Kipling. New York: Walker, 1974. A Parsee gets even with a rhinoceros who keeps stealing cakes.

M—O   "Hungry Mungry," Shel Silverstein.   (48)
A nonsense poem about a boy who eats everything, including himself.

Y—M   "The Journey," Arnold Lobel.   (25)
A mouse goes off to visit his mother, using various forms of transportation.

Y—M   *If You Were An Eel, How Would You Feel?* Mina and Howard Simon. Chicago: Follett Publishing Company, 1963. Various animals described according to their characteristic actions. Solo.

Y   *Indian Two Feet and His Horse,* Margaret Friskey. New York: Scholastic Book Services, 1964. A little Indian wishes for a horse and gets one.

O   *Ittki Pittki,* Miriam Chaikin. New York: Parents', 1971. Ittki Pittki, a merchant, fears he has been poisoned at the palace. Flexible casting.

Y   "Jump or Jiggle," Evelyn Beyer.   (4)
Brief poem naming animals and their style of walking.

Y—M   *Just Suppose,* May Garelick. New York: Scholastic Book Services, 1969. Suppose you were a number of different animals, doing what they do.

Y—M   *The King, The Mice, and the Cheese,* Nancy & Eric Gurney. New York: Random House, 1965. To get rid of mice, cats are brought in. Dogs replace cats, followed by lions, elephants, and then a return to mice. Flexible casting.

M—O   "Lines Written for Gene Kelly To Dance To," Carl Sandburg.   (50)
Poem asks famous dancer to dance different ideas. First section is most fun to do. Try with Leroy Andersen's "Sandpaper Ballet" as background music.

Y   *The Little Airplane,* Lois Lenski. New York: Henry Z. Walck, 1938. Pilot Small takes his airplane up for a ride.

Y   *The Little Auto,* Lois Lenski. New York: Henry Z. Walck, 1934. Mr. Small has a little auto which he cares for and drives all around.

Y—M   *Little Bear's Sunday Breakfast,* Janice. New York: Lothrop, 1958. The Three Bears story in reverse. Little Bear visits *her* house this time. May want to edit dialogue. Groups of four.

Y—M   *The Little Brute Family,* Russell Hoban. New York: Macmillan, 1966. Papa, Mama, Brother, Sister, and Baby Brute consistently have grumpy and unpleasant days until a little lost feeling enters their lives. Group playing.

Y   *The Little Sailboat,* Lois Lenski. New York: Henry Z. Walck, 1937. Captain Small has an adventure with his sailboat.

Y—M   *Lizard Lying in the Sun,* Berniece Freschet. New York: Scribner's, 1975. A lizard has a peaceful day in the sun until an eagle flies by. Play in pairs.

M   *The Man Who Didn't Wash His Dishes,* Phyllis Krasilovsky. New York: Doubleday, 1950. A lazy man's neglect poses problems in housekeeping.

M—O *Mrs. Beggs and the Wizard,* Mercer Mayer. New York: Parents', 1973. Mrs. Beggs owns a boarding house. A strange renter creates havoc and she is forced to use her witchery kit. Flexible casting.

M "The Mouse and the Flea," Charles E. Gillham. (5)
Two friends get tired of each other and begin to play tricks. Alaskan Eskimo tale. Pairs.

Y—M "On Our Way," Eve Merriam. (7)
In this poem children experiment with the walks of various animals.

M—O *Oté,* Pura Belpré. New York: Pantheon, 1969. A Puerto Rican folktale about a man and his family who are plagued by an unwanted, nearsighted little devil. Group.

Y *Papa Small,* Lois Lenski. New York: Henry Z. Walck, 1951. The story of the Small family, who all work together. Group.

O "The Passer," George Abbe. (33)
Brief description of a football pass. Try this one in slow motion.

Y *(The Tale of) Peter Rabbit,* Beatrix Potter. (3) (35)
The timeless story of a misbehaving bunny who finds adventure in Mr. McGregor's garden. Solo or in pairs with Mr. McGregor. May want to simplify wording.

M—O *The Pond,* Carol and Donald Carrick. New York: Macmillan, 1970. Sensitive, poetic description of movements of water, insects, and all life near and in a pond. Try Debussy's "La Mer" as background music.

O "Rodeo," Edward Lueders. (31)
Description of a cowboy readying to mount and ride a Brahma bull.

M *Salt Boy,* Mary Perrine. Boston: Houghton Mifflin, 1968. Young boy rescues a lamb in a storm and gets his wish: to learn to rope the horse. Edit for solo playing.

Y—O *Seven Skinny Goats,* Victor G. Ambrus. New York: Harcourt, Brace Jovanovich, 1969. Jano doesn't realize his flute playing, which causes everyone to dance, isn't appreciated. Flexible casting.

O "The Skunk in the Pond," George Mendoza. (11)
A browbeaten man finally takes care of skunk in the pond by cooking it for his nagging family to eat! Group playing.

M—O *The Sneetches,* Dr. Seuss. New York: Random House, 1961. Sneetches with stars on their bellies feel superior to those without. An enterprising salesman takes advantage of the situation. Fun for children to become the machines, too. Flexible casting.

Y *The Snowy Day,* Ezra Jack Keats. New York: Viking, 1962. Young Peter plays in the snow.

M *Sometimes I Dance Mountains,* Byrd Baylor. New York: Scribner's, 1973. Ideas for dance pantomime. Photographs of a girl dancing illustrate movement ideas. Solo. Simple instruments (wooden xylophone, tambourine, drum, and so forth) can provide background effects.

M—O "The Sorcerer's Apprentice," Richard Rostron. (3) (35)
The young apprentice to a magician remembers only part of a magic spell and finds himself in much trouble. Begin action where Sorcerer leaves.

Y—M *The Story About Ping,* Marjorie Flack. New York: Viking, 1961. The adventure of a little duck on the Yangtze River.

M *The Story of Ferdinand,* Munro Leaf. New York: Viking, 1936. Ferdinand, the Bull, would rather smell flowers than fight in the bull ring. Flexible casting.

M—O   *Strega Nona,* Tomie de Paola. Englewood Cliffs, N.J.: Prentice-Hall, 1975.
Strega Nona, or "Grandma Witch," has a magic pasta pot which Big Anthony
misuses, and the town is flooded with pasta. Flexible casting.

Y—M   *The Tale of Two Bad Mice,* Beatrix Potter. New York: Frederick Warne, 1932.
Two mice find a doll house and create havoc when they discover the play food is
not real. Edit for pair playing.

Y   *Ten Bears in My Bed,* Stan Mack. New York: Pantheon, 1974. A counting story
with each bear going out the window a different way. Line up ten "bears" and
let all the children sing out the "Roll over" lines.

Y—M   *Theodore Turtle,* Ellen MacGregor. New York: McGraw-Hill, 1955. Forgetful
Theodore first loses one of his rubbers and then misplaces almost everything
else he lays his hands on.

O   "There Will Come Soft Rains," Ray Bradbury.   (24)
A chilling science-fiction story about an ultra-modern house that falls apart,
piece by piece, after humanity is destroyed with the final bomb. Challenging
but worth the effort.

Y   *The Three Bears,* Paul Galdone. New York: Seabury Press, 1972. Classic tale
of a little girl who visits a bear's house. This version works nicely for narrative.
Solo or group.

M—O   *The Three Poor Tailors,* Victor G. Ambrus. New York: Harcourt Brace
Jovanovich, 1965. Three tailors go off on the back of a goat to see the city and
find fun, adventure, and trouble. Groups of four: three tailors, with a fourth to
play soldier, innkeeper, and guards. It's more fun just to imagine the goat.

M—O   "Trinity Place," Phyllis McGinley.   (30)
Description of actions of pigeons in a city park, comparing them with men.

M—O   "Urashima Taro and the Princess of the Sea," Yoshiko Uchida.   (4) (12)
Urashima is enticed to live in the sea and spends much more time there than he
imagines. On returning home, he finds out just how much time has lapsed.
Dialogue can easily be edited.

Y   *The Very Hungry Caterpillar,* Eric Carle. New York: Collins Publishers, 1969.
Voracious caterpillar prepares for eventual change into a butterfly.

M—O   "Wait Till Martin Comes," Maria Leach.   (41)
A man has a scary adventure in a haunted house with four cats. Fun to have
man sit in a rocking chair.

M—O   *The Way the Tiger Walked,* Doris J. Chaconas. New York: Simon & Schuster,
1970. Porcupine, zebra, elephant try unsuccessfully to imitate the tiger's regal
walk while monkeys watch the show. When the tiger imitates *their* walks, they
return to their natural movements. Subtle humor. Can be done simply or per-
fected into a finely tuned precision piece, perhaps with rhythm instruments for
sound effects.

M   *We Were Tired of Living in a House,* Liesel Moak Skorpen. New York: Coward, McCann & Geoghegan, 1969. Fill in detail from the pictures. Some children decide to investigate other places to live and find that their house isn't so
bad after all.

Y—M   "What Was I Scared Of?" Dr. Seuss.   (32)
A Seuss character is frightened of a pair of pants with nobody in them, until
it finds the pants are afraid of it! Pairs.

Y   *What Will You Do Today, Little Russell?* Robert Wahl. New York: Putnam's,
1972. A little boy explores a farm.

Y *Whistle for Willie,* Ezra Jack Keats. New York: Viking, 1964. Peter wishes he could learn to whistle for his dog. Edit for solo playing.

Y *Willie's Walk,* Margaret Wise Brown. Reading, Mass.: Addison-Wesley, 1944. Willie goes to Grandmama's house by way of other animal houses. Edit for solo playing.

Chapter Four

Developing Narrative Pantomimes

In this chapter we will examine narrative materials more closely and consider the dramatic principles in them. Understanding and applying these principles should make it easier for leaders to select and adapt as well as write their own materials.

The topics which can be covered through narrative pantomime are almost limitless. Science stories about animals or experiments, biographical data on historical or modern-day figures, information on various occupations, and stories about people in other times and geographical and cultural settings are just some of the many possibilities. The leader may also have information about a topic gained from personal interest and background which can be placed in a dramatic format. By enacting these materials and the facts and concepts presented in them, the children should be able to internalize the information more completely than if they simply read about it.

SELECTING MATERIAL

Action is always the central focus of narrative pantomime. Not all materials the leader finds will have sufficient action in them. Sometimes it is possible simply to select the portions that have the most action.

Sometimes the leader may be able to splice several short passages together. For example, in Michael Bond's *Paddington* (59) stories, the bear's adventures can frequently be handled in this manner by focusing only on those passages in which Paddington appears.

Poetry

While there are some excellent poems one can use for narrative pantomime, such as Edwin A. Hoey's "Foul Shot" (p. 122) or Byrd Baylor's *Sometimes I Dance Mountains*, (p. 67) they are not as readily available as prose selections. The language of poetry can often be abstract, complete sentences may be lacking, wording of phrases convoluted, and the rhythm and rhyme so exact that editing is difficult, if not impossible. Therefore, we urge caution in selecting poetry and recommend that initial attempts focus on prose.

Inanimate Objects

The leader should be sure that materials using personified inanimate objects have enough action to make them interesting for dramatization. For example, Virginia Lee Burton's charming story, *The Little House* (Houghton Mifflin, 1942), tells of the many reactions of a deserted house to its lonely situation, but there is very little if any action the house can perform. Another similar kind of story is Rachel Field's *Hitty* (Macmillan, 1959). This is the fascinating story of a doll to whom many things happen. But since she cannot move by herself, the experiences are all passive ones.

Dialogue

Because the emphasis in narrative pantomime is on action, dialogue should be nonexistent, or almost so. When people talk at great length to each other in literature, they often stop performing actions. This means that the children have to stand for long periods of time looking at one another. They can only feel foolish when this happens and will probably lose interest and involvement in the material.

In searching for narrative material, we have found that a helpful first clue is the absence of quotation marks. This clue makes it possible to flip through the pages of books rather rapidly, eliminating unlikely candidates.

Stories with several characters will probably have some dialogue in them. However, if the plot of the story is action-centered, then it is possible that the dialogue could be edited out. If not, the story will prove to be a poor choice.

Some materials may be made suitable for narrative pantomime if the dialogue is changed from direct to indirect. Note the following example:

"Isn't this a fine piece of cloth?" said the peddler to the old woman.
The peddler proudly held up a piece of cloth for the old woman to see.

EDITING

Continuous Action

The action of the material should be as continuous as possible. In some literature there are interruptions in the flow of the action in order to interject reflective thinking, flashbacks, or additional information. If such interruptions are lengthy, they may require the players to pause and wait before they can continue the action. For example, a passage may read,

> His hand touched the doorknob and in that moment his mind raced back to a thousand memories. *Like the time he opened the door to Old Man Henry's place on that fateful Halloween night. The guys had run off just as he was about to open the door. They had all decided to go in together and then everybody chickened out and left him standing there to hear Old Man Henry's voice bellow out at him.* He shook the thought from his mind, opened the door, and stepped into the darkened interior.

By going back in time, the italicized passage keeps the players poised at the doorknob without moving. Through editing, the leader can tighten the action. In this case, the flashback can easily be omitted.

Word Order

The cues for the action should always be edited to follow chronologically. If they do not, the players may be misled. For example,

> She left the apartment and went down to the first floor. When she got off the elevator and entered the lobby, she . . .

Players who are following this narration might *walk down steps* rather than riding an elevator since this information is not specified until the second sentence.

Immediacy of Action

Action should be condensed into as short a time period as possible. When action is spread out over a period of time, it tends to lose its dramatic impact. For example,

> The men worked, eagerly packing their gear for the adventure. After two weeks they were ready to start off. They left full of energy and with high hopes that they would be successful.
>
> Three months later they were weary and disappointed. Almost everyone in the exploring party was ready to turn back.

Some literature focuses on interesting action but bounces back and forth in time. For example,

You get up in the morning and wash your face . . .

That day he decided to go for a swim. The following day it rained. By the end of summer, he had enjoyed boating, water-skiing, and swimming—but it was the swimming he enjoyed the most.

While there is plenty of action suggested in the above passage, it would be unrealistic to pantomime it as written. Editing or rewording is required.

Present Tense and "You"

A sense of immediacy is sometimes helped by the use of the present tense and the wording "you."

. . .and brush your teeth.

Now you run your hand along the bark of the old tree, lean forward and smell the mossy dampness. . . .

This wording makes the action and the direction compelling and involving. Some children respond more easily to this direct wording since they can feel that the action is happening now and to them. It seems more logical to follow this kind of narration.

Robert McCloskey has incorporated this wording in *Time of Wonder,** but it is not a style of writing frequently used by authors. Although the leader may not want to change literature into this wording style, much original material and side-coaching can easily be worded in this way.

More importantly, whichever person and tense the leader chooses to use should remain consistent throughout the activity. Note the following examples:

Third person, present tense: As the sun rises, the Athenian citizen gets out of bed and folds a piece of wool cloth around himself, pins it at the shoulders, and ties a sash around his waist. Then he sits down to breakfast, drinks a cup of wine mixed with hot water and honey and eats a dry barley cake.

First person plural, present tense: We begin cleaning out the horse's stall, shoveling the old hay into a wheelbarrow and wheeling it carefully to the outside of the barn. We empty it into a large pile. We use the pitchfork to bring fresh hay to the horse's stall and spread it evenly over the floor.

Third person, past tense: To build his wigwam, Running Bear first had to find a level surface. He marked a groove in the ground with a sharp stick. He made an oval shape about twice as long as it was wide . . .

Adding Action

The amount of action the leader includes in narrative pantomime should depend on the needs of the children. Some children will be able to elaborate on ideas more easily than others. For example, a line may read,

They prepared their equipment for the camping trip. . . .

Some children may be observed packing numerous items and making considerable preparations while other children quickly finish only one idea. The leader must make the narration detailed, descriptive, and compelling in order to give an understandable and involving experience. On the other hand, the leader must not make the narration so specific that it interrupts or holds up the children's own ideas. In other words, the leader must be flexible with any narrative material and let the needs of the majority dictate the amount of action given.

---

* Unless otherwise indicated, literature mentioned in this chapter is in the bibliography at the end of the chapter.

The Indian mother shelters her children from the storm.

Descriptive Language

Language that is descriptive is exciting and encourages imagination. When the leader's language helps to paint the mental images of sensory and emotional detail, it can artfully compel the children to be aware of the environment and invites involvement.

In the story of "Goldilocks and the Three Bears," for example, the scene of eating the porridge might be narrated as follows:

> **T:** You see three bowls of porridge and you are so very hungry . . . so you taste the porridge in Papa Bear's bowl. Oh! That's too hot! It burned your tongue!! Oh dear, well, you are still hungry, and maybe the porridge in the middle-sized bowl will be better. You cooop up a big spoonful from Mama Bear's bowl. You take a big bite and . . . oh, no! That one is too cold. And LUMPY! . . . Well, there's one bowl left. This time you take a tiny spoonful of porridge and carefully you taste it. Ahhh, this is perfect. What good porridge; not too hot, not too cold. The cream in the porridge is sweet . . . and you think you detect the flavor of butter and just the tiniest pinch of salt. And you eat and eat and eat . . . until there is just one spoonful left . . . and you eat that one slowly and savor the last bite. . . . Ummmmmm . . . good!

In the following example the leader elaborates on a moment mentioned in a history text:

> **T:** As the door to his Bastille cell slammed shut, the new prisoner surveyed his miserable surroundings. There was one small window in the thick wall crossed with iron gratings. He tried to look out, but the opening was too small to permit a view.

Besides, foul odors rose from the ditch below the walls and choked his breathing. He examined the sparse furnishings. There was a worn, filthy mattress, musty and moldy. He picked it up gingerly at one corner.

STORY FRAMEWORK

The overall outline of a narrative activity, no matter what its length, should have a beginning, middle, and end. One clue is the sense of progression or chronological order. This may be noted in wording such as, "First . . . and then . . . Finally. . . ." By using this wording, the leader can give a feeling of completeness.

> **T:**   All the marionettes' strings are breaking one by one. First to go is the string on the right arm . . . now on the left . . . now the right leg . . . then the left . . . and finally their heads droop and they are as limp as the rag dolls on the shelf above them.

Longer activities are generally built around the performance of a task, the setting of a goal and its accomplishment, or setting out on a journey and the return home. There is one episode in Jane Wagner's *J.T.* (103), for example, when J.T. makes a house out of junk for a stray cat. Another example is Dantes's escape from prison in Dumas's *The Count of Monte Cristo* (72).

A story might involve the process of a day's work as in *Gone is Gone* (p. 65). Or it may be part of a life cycle as it is for the mole cricket in George's *All Upon a Stone* (p. 63).

Suspense and Conflict

Often an activity is based simply on an interesting experience. It may be a pleasant one, as in Keats' *Snowy Day* (p. 67) or a funny one, as in Cole's *Frances Face-Maker* (p. 65). Most dramatic stories, however, have some conflict in them, and the leader should be familiar with the various ways to include it.

Conflict in a story not only makes it more dramatic and suspenseful, it also creates a physical intensity in the players. Sometimes the physical movements also become larger and stronger, and the players must exert themselves in order to solve the conflict. The exertion then more logically leads to the restful conclusion of the story.

Children usually enjoy and want plenty of exciting action and conflict in their activities. Sometimes they will add it even when the teacher has not included it in the narration. The line says to smell a flower; they do and a bee stings them. Or the line says, "He walked carefully so he would not slip"; they walk carefully but slip too! For some children there can never be too much excitement in their stories.

There are many kinds of conflict. Strong conflict is obvious in fights, chases, or meeting of an enemy face to face. Conflict is also present in natural phenomena. A threatening storm begins slowly. Then the winds blow and waves billow while thunder crashes and lightning strikes until a dramatic climax is reached. When the storm subsides, resolution of the conflict of nature occurs. George Maxim Ross's *The Pine Tree* demonstrates the drama in nature.

Conflict can be present in the daily struggle for survival. Even if a task is a rather methodical one, its importance is increased if it is crucial to continued living. Perhaps each step along the way has its own particular importance in reaching the final outcome. For example, Karana in *Island of the Blue Dolphins* must build a house to protect herself from the wild dogs.

Sometimes conflict and suspense can be additionally implied in the words used. If an action is "carefully" done or if a line reads, "He held his breath as he lifted the cargo . . ." an imminent problem is presented.

Often conflict generates more energized and hurried action. For example, we must swim fast to escape a shark. Meeting some sort of deadline also creates hurried action. Cleaning house before company comes, shopping before a store closes, getting the game ended or the picnic dinner eaten before it rains, or getting to work on time are all examples.

T: Here it is Christmas Eve and you haven't done any of your shopping yet. The stores will close in two hours and you have to finish in that time. You've got six things to get in six different departments, so here we go: First over to the cosmetic counter to get cologne for Aunt Mary. But there's a big crowd there so maybe you better go up to the third floor first and pick up the cologne on the way out. Let's hurry, there's an elevator going up . . . . People are blocking your way. . . . Watch out for that lady's packages. . . she's going to lose control of them. . . . There they go . . . better help her pick them up. . . . Going up! You missed the elevator . . . how about the escalator? . . . Hurry . . . hurry. . . .

An animal stalks its prey.

Beginnings and Endings

The beginning of a narrative should be like the warm-up of an airplane for takeoff. The ending should include similar precautions for making a smooth landing. The children begin in a quiet position and are calmed down again for the ending. This procedure is helpful both to them and to the leader.

When an entire poem or story is used, there is often a smooth beginning and ending built in. For example, an animal may be lying in quiet wait for a prey. After he catches it and eats, he often rests. Often there is awakening from sleep, working at a daily task, and then returning to rest again. In adapting or writing original materials, however, leaders may need to create quiet beginnings and endings of their own.

WRITING ORIGINAL MATERIALS

Length of narrative pantomime can vary from a brief paragraph to a story of several hundred words. Whatever the length, the techniques remain the same. Incidentally, it is a good practice for beginning leaders to write out their materials carefully beforehand. As the leader becomes more experienced, an outline for handy reference may be all that is needed.

Creating original materials need not be a difficult experience. Many ideas are readily available. They may come from literature.

We are told in one sentence, for example, that A. A. Milne's Winnie the Pooh (148) does ''Stoutness Exercises.'' All we are told is that he reaches up and then down to try to touch his toes. A simple conflict is implied because we know that Winnie has a protruding tummy that makes bending over a bit of a problem.

Elaborating on this idea, the leader might decide to write an activity focusing mainly on movement, going through an entire fitness program, doing all sorts of body-building activities. There might be some jogging, lifting weights, doing push-ups, and hitting a punching bag. The sense of completeness is the exercise program itself—starting and finishing it. The beginning might be slow warm-up exercising with just the paws. (After all, Pooh wouldn't want to overexert himself!) As the activities progress in intensity and difficulty, Pooh Bear will no doubt become tired and worn out and would finally need a rest—with the reward of a bit of honey perhaps.

The activity could be enacted individually. Or it could be played in pairs. Since Pooh Bear does his exercises in front of a mirror, a partner could play the mirror image.

Personal Experiences

One of the best sources for narrative pantomime is the leader's own personal experience. For many leaders work experiences have been a rich source. Grocery checkout cashier, construction worker, camp counselor, dental assistant, and tour guide at a cereal factory are just some of the many possibilities. Sports have been another popular topic for pantomime stories, including skiing, sky diving, scuba diving, and hiking. Pets such as hamsters, turtles, and guinea pigs have also had stories told about them that children have played.

Geographical areas and personal background lend possibilities also. Stories have been written about maple-sugaring in Vermont, selecting and cutting down a Christmas tree in Washington, being taken on a personal tour of the family's farm, visiting a local junkyard, or going through army basic training.

The detail and realism leaders can bring to these activities are a direct result of their own involvement in them. Usually the leaders also feel comfortable with these topics as well as enthusiastic about them. All of this adds to the playing experience.

Inanimate Objects

The leader may choose to create activities with inanimate objects if they are given enough action and involvement in the story to make them interesting to play. Consider the following example in which the children pretend to be a recliner chair.

T: Here you are all ready for the day to begin. You can hear the family getting up for the day. Here comes Mom to open up the curtains and let in the morning sunshine. Swish! . . . Yikes, that sun's bright . . . it makes your button eyes blink! Now she goes out in the kitchen to fix breakfast, and here come the kids and the dog. You hope they don't jump on you this morning . . . but they do! Zingo! All of them, all at once . . . they stretch you out flat in your reclining position. Ooh, for so early in the morning that's hard to take! Now Mom is calling them to breakfast . . . Good . . . Zingo! . . . You flip back into your upright position and now you ache all over. You just weren't built for this sort of thing. . . .

Now breakfast's over and the older kids and Dad have gone, and here comes Mom to sit down for the extra cup of coffee and the newspaper. Oh, you really love to read the newspaper. Mom gets all comfy and reclines you and opens up the paper. You have to read over her shoulder. . . . There's your favorite comic, "Peanuts." Oh, darn, she turned the page . . . and there's a furniture sale. Oh, boy, if there's anything that makes you nervous it's an ad for a furniture sale. Your stuffing gets tight and your nap stands right on end. Good, now she's turned the page again . . . and that's the end of the morning paper. She gets up and you pop upright again.

Now Mom's getting ready to clean. Here comes the vacuum cleaner and she's . . . oh, no! . . . she's going to clean you today. Oh, gosh, it tickles so . . . up at the top . . . and then your back . . . your face . . . arms . . . footrest . . . oh, oh, oh, it makes you giggle so. . . . Ah, now she stops and goes on with the rest of the cleaning. . . .

Now here comes Bobby the four-year-old to watch his favorite TV shows. Hey, Mom, look at that jelly all over him. . . . He's coming toward you and Mom doesn't even see him. . . . Yuck, jelly all over your arms . . . how uncomfortable. . . . Now Bobby turns on the TV set and watches a cartoon of a cat chasing a mouse. . . . Bobby starts to jump up and down on you. . . . He pounds your arms and kicks at your legs . . . ouch . . . ouch. . . .

Oh, boy, here comes Mom to chase him off you. There he goes and here she comes with some cleaner for you. She sprays the foam where Bobby put the jelly. . . . It makes you want to cough or sneeze or something . . . and you do, and again . . . Oh, boy, that's all you need . . . Now Mom finishes cleaning up the jelly. She takes Bobby upstairs with her and you are left for a little peace and quiet so you try to catch a little shut-eye while you can. Ah . . . how nice . . . sleep tight.

Using this format the leader can create many stories about different informational topics. Generally it is easier to create action if the inanimate object is going through some sort of process. For example, a tree may be cut down, the log sent to a paper mill where the bark is removed and the log chipped, blown, soaked, cooked, beaten, and finally rolled into paper. The children can react to these various processes and can pantomime the various shapes the wood is put through.

While it is fun to personalize the inanimate object as was done with the chair in the above story, one should be cautious of carrying fantasy so far that the original information is lost. A water molecule, for example, needn't have a name, wear a top hat, carry a cane, and tap dance through an adventure as it might in a television commercial. As much as possible, the leader should rely on the information itself to create the drama.

Additional topics with inanimate objects might be: the journey of an egg from an egg ranch through a modern-day processing plant, the recycling of glass or cans, the adventure of a tomato from the vine to the soup can, or the steps a letter goes through getting mailed.

Fantasy/Reality in Science Topics

Often subjects such as animals and plants have been personified and given human senses, feelings, and cognitive ability. There can be humor in a story about a crayfish who needs a squirt from an oil can to unstick a stubborn antenna. However, this is fantasy and cannot be passed off as a science lesson. Its literary value might also be in question.

There are writers of excellent literature who are also knowledgeable about scientific information. Writers like Jean George (*Vulpes, the Red Fox*) and Holling C. Holling (*Pagoo*), for example, have created nature stories that are accurate in their information and dramatically captivating as well. The leader would do well to select such literature for narrative pantomime and use it as a model for original narrative writing.

Compare the following two passages and note that even a few words can make a difference in writing that leans toward fantasy and writing that is more accurately stated. The story is based on the life cycle of a dragonfly.

A.

You spy a crack in your old skin and struggle to squirm through it. It's hard work and you're glad this is the last time you'll have to shed it. You push and push until you get rid of the clumsy thing. Now you admire your slim new body. But it's still stiff and your joints creak as you slowly try it out. The sun feels warm and you decide to unfold your wings . . .

The words "glad," "clumsy," "admire," and "decide" attribute human understanding and emotional feeling to an insect and therefore make the material less accurate than the following:

B.

You wiggle and squirm through the crack in your old skin. It's hard work, but this will be the last time you will have to shed it. You push and push until you are freed. Your slim new body is still stiff, and your old shell clings to the stalk below you. The sun is warm and your four wings start to unfold slowly . . .

Science Fiction

The combination of accurate information and a fictional setting is, however, a valid kind of writing and extremely useful for a number of curricular topics. Children frequently enjoy, for example, the idea of being made small in order to make explorations of various environments such as a bee hive, the workings of a watch, the inside of a tree, or the human eye. One leader took her class on an exploration of the ear, which they had been studying. Not only were they delighted to experience such events as bouncing trampoline fashion on the tympanic membrane, they also found it difficult to forget such an adventure and all the related information.

The following is an excerpt from an exploration of the parts of a flower:

T: Today we're going to look at the construction of a flower, but we're going to pretend that it is the year 3001 and scientists have developed some new ways to conduct scientific explorations. You are a special consultant who has been called in for this mission. But it is a secret mission, so you will be given your instructions at special points along the way. Let me know when you're ready for your mission by sitting at attention, saluting, and reporting for duty. (Children respond.)

Good. (Leader now speaks in an impersonal voice as if over an intercom.) *Good morning, scientists. Please check your equipment.* You notice that you've been issued a very tiny note pad, a very small pencil, and very tiny (handle them carefully!) special pollen-resistant goggles. There is also a capsule, but it is unmarked. Everything is encased in plastic to keep it clean.

Now enter the greenhouse. Inside you will be given additional equipment. As soon as you open the door you sense the cool, damp atmosphere. *In front of you there is a small box on the table. Add it to your equipment. In a moment you are to drink the contents of the vial, which will make you small enough to explore the flower from the inside. Now drink the special formula.*

You do and notice that it is a tasteless, clear liquid. Very quickly and painlessly your body shrinks. Your clothing shrinks with you. Your head swims and you feel the slightest bit of nausea. You look around and calculate that you must be about one inch high, the perfect size for this assignment.

Now open the box. Inside you find a laboratory coat, just your new size. *Remove any jewelry and anything that protrudes sharply or has a rough texture. You must leave the scientific environment exactly as you have found it: no marks, no telltale signs of human intrusion.* Inside the box you also find a pair of soft cloth slippers. *Put on the laboratory coat. Remove your shoes and put the slippers on. Now the goggles. Check that you have the notepad and pencil and you are now ready to begin. . . .*

Research

Through research, one can also find innumerable kinds of information that can be woven into interesting story lines. One might write "A Day in the Life of . . ." and then select an occupation, a child in another country, historical figure, animal, or insect to base the story on. Or one might consider "The Process of Making . . ." and select a product, food, shelter, or clothing. Another possibility is "Journey to . . ." for which one selects a particular building, historical site, city, country, or even another planet to build a story around.

In the following story, an unusual species of spider called "Argyroneta aquatic" lives underwater by building air-filled homes. He must struggle to keep the captured air bubbles anchored and to pull himself with guidelines. He is alert to the vibrations in the water and aware of his need to secure food. The story ends with the satisfying completion of a project and a deserved rest.

> **T:** You're in the process of building your web for the air bubbles you will soon capture. You move from one plant stem to another, throwing from your spinnerets silken web strands . . . .
>
> Deftly your legs secure the threads to the plants . . . and you carefully move back and forth from stem to stem until you have a finely meshed web. This web will become your summer bell home; later you'll build another for winter.
>
> Now for the air bubbles. . . . You swim to the top of the water. . . . Once there, you turn over and with your back legs you grab a bubble of air, pulling it gently toward you so that it covers the breathing pores around your abdomen. . . . Now your legs search for the silken guidelines you set earlier . . . there you are! . . . and holding securely to the line, you begin to pull yourself down to the new web. It's a difficult feat . . . for the air bubble is heavy and would rise to the surface if you didn't pull. . . . At the web you release your air bubble . . . and it rises into the web—captured!
>
> You take more trips to the surface for air . . . and soon your home contains several bubbles and is completed. Now it is time for a rest. . . . You carefully enter your air-filled home . . . and hang head downward. . . . As you rest, the water house sways to the rhythm of the moving water . . . its vibrations can communicate that danger or a potential meal is near. . . . It's vibrating!
>
> Your eight eyes signal food. . . . You emerge from your bell, carefully carrying an air supply with you. . . . A tiny fish swims near . . . you lunge . . . grab . . . sting with your poison . . . and carry the dead fish into your new home. You'll eat it in a while . . . but now you'll rest. The spider's day has been a busy one.

Space

As in all previous work, the leader also considers the use of space. The desk, for example, may be the box for a Jack-in-the-Box, which pops up on specific words in a brief story. Or it may be the frying pan or popper in which kernels of corn heat up and puff out into popcorn.

Or, as in the following example, the desk may become several things.

> **T:** Let's pretend you're going shopping. First drive your car, which will be your desk. Get out your key, put it in the ignition, give it some gas, and you're off. Back out

of the driveway . . . carefully . . . look to be sure you're not going to hit anything . . . Now stop, put it in "drive," and you head for town.
(Here one could include detail about traffic, safety, or the sights.)
Now you're at the department store. Get out of the car (at the side of the desk). Go
through the revolving door. Now up the escalator. Up to the second floor, where you
are going to shop for a bicycle. Ah, here's a nice-looking one. Try that one out. Oh,
you see some snowmobiles. Try one of those out. . . .

Pairs and Groups

Although it can present an additional challenge, the leader may also want to try
writing narratives for pairs and groups. Each character in the narrative, of course,
must have action to perform.

Topics which lend themselves to paired playing are tasks that require more
than one person, such as dentist and technician; pilot and flight attendant; or disc
jockey and radio engineer.

Other two-person topics might be a scientist building and testing a robot, a
plant competing with a weed, or red and white corpuscles working together in the
blood stream.

The following is a narrative for paired playing:

A PLANE RIDE

T: Today we're going to pretend to be Amelia Earhart or Charles Lindbergh flying
our planes. The desks will be the airplanes. You'll be playing with partners. One
partner will be the pilot; the other will be a student who is learning to fly. We'll play
twice so each person will have the chance to play both parts. Choose a partner and
decide between you who will be the pilot first. (Pause for organization.)

Now, in our plane, the Stearman biplane, the pilot sits behind the passenger-student.
So arrange yourself accordingly. (Pause again.)

You're going to take a ride across the mountains and land on the other side. This is
going to be a dangerous trip because of the bad weather through the mountains, and
the landing will be very difficult, owing to the rugged mountains surrounding the
landing field. Because this is a dangerous trip, you will have to listen to directions
carefully.

The Stearman biplane needs its propeller twirled to help the pilot start the engine.
Student, you need to learn this, so you stand at the side of the plane by the propeller.
Now, pilot, fasten your seat belt and shoulder harness. Make sure they're on tight.
You'll have to take your signal from the control tower. I'm operating the control tower
and you will get your signal from me. Put on your earphones so you can make contact
with the control tower and make sure everything is all set for takeoff. (Children pantomime earphones. Teacher holds hand to mouth to make a rather muffled sound as if
speaking over the radio transmitter.) "Biplane NC 211, cleared for takeoff."

OK, pilot, adjust your engine controls. Student, spin the prop to start the engine.
Whoops. Guess the old plane will need several spins to get started. You'll have to try
again. (Pause.) There! The engine throbs to life. Pilot, apply the brakes. Student, pull
out the wheel chocks. Now climb aboard. Fasten your seat belt and harness.

Student, listen carefully, in front of you is a stick that controls the plane's directions. It
is connected to the pilot's control stick. By placing your hands lightly—I repeat,

lightly—around it, you will be able to follow the pilot's sensitive control. In this way, you can get the "feel" of controlling the plane.

Both of you be sure your goggles are in place. Now let up on the brake and taxi down the end of the runway. You'll have to zigzag so that you can see beyond the nose of the plane.

You're almost at the end of the runway now, so quickly pull the stick toward you. Remember, student, when the stick is forward, it makes the plane go down and when the stick is pulled toward you, the plane goes up. Now the plane is rising off the ground. Up you go! Check your compass to make sure you're going north toward the mountains. Look down below you. The airport is small and far away.

You're going through the mountains now. It looks like you're going into a storm. Be sure to bank the plane so the wings don't tip too much one way. They should be kept level with the body of the plane. It's starting to rain hard now. Reach up to the top of your control panel and press the blue button on the right to start the windshield wipers.

If you look over to the left you'll see the flash of lightning. Don't look too long. Keep your eyes on the altimeter to be sure you stay well above the mountains.

Keep watching for the mountain tops so you can be sure to pass over them. Careful! There's a peak right in your course. Quickly bank the plane or you'll hit it. Whew! That was a close call.

It looks like you're passing through the storm safely. You're almost on the other side of the mountains now, and the landing field is coming up on the right. Pick up your radios and let's make contact with the control tower and let them know you're coming in for a landing. (Teacher as control tower.) "Flight NC 211. Cleared for approach to landing. Approach from the southeast." Now check your seat belts and prepare to circle the landing field until we can come in for a safe landing.

Now let's bring the plane down easy. You have to go slow because the fog is thick and you might miss the field. There it is! You're right on course. Stand by for a landing. Check the air-pressure meter next to the lever control. Now get ready to pull back the brake lever when you touch ground. You're down. That was a good landing. Pull back on the brake lever and let's bring it to a stop. A perfect three-point landing! Congratulations!

Narratives can also be designed for groups. Again, tasks that require input from several persons are useful topics: an operating team; a group of elves in charge of certain tasks in toy making; the expedition team in Thor Heyerdahl's *Kon Tiki* adventure. Group narratives might also be based on the workings of a car engine or the human heart, with children playing the various parts of each.

In the following example, based on a scene from Washington Irving's "The Legend of the Moor's Legacy" (35), there are parts for four children in each group: Peregil, the Moor, and the two enchanted persons who also play the stone entrance to the cave.

(Two players have their backs to Peregil, forming the cave's entrance. Peregil stands at the entrance of the cave, waiting for the Moor to arrive.)

It is chilly this evening, and Peregil shivers and wraps his cloak a little more tightly around him. As he waits, he thinks about his unhappy lot—being so poor and with so many mouths to feed.

And now he examines for the hundredth time the sandalwood box left by the Moor. Are the Moor's words true? Does the box really hold secrets? He opens it up and carefully takes out the small candle and the fragile piece of paper with the strange Arabic writing on it. He looks at the words, but they mean nothing.

He begins to become impatient for the Moor to arrive. Now a form can be seen through the trees in the distance. Ah, it is the Moor. You greet each other silently, and now you hurry quickly to test the power of the box. Peregil lights the candle and holds it while the Moor reads the incantation on the scroll. The perfumes from the candle send a sweet odor through the damp air.

Then suddenly there is a distant rumbling like thunder. ("Cave entrance" gives sound effects.) Suddenly the cave entrance opens and reveals a long winding stairway. ("Cave entrance" now becomes two enchanted guards.) You huddle together as you descend below. Shield the candle light, for if it goes out, you will be entombed forever in the cave. As you reach the bottom step you see a large trunk with huge bands of steel encasing it. At each end of the trunk you see two motionless men—enchanted, they are—and their eyes stare straight ahead.

Around the trunk there are many treasures, and you realize that you have indeed found wealth. You slowly and cautiously examine it—pick up a coin, try on a bracelet, examine a precious stone. Yes, it is real. And it is yours. You each take as much as your pockets can hold. There is more than enough and you are not the greedy sort.

You hurry to finish because the candle is small and may burn out. You climb back up the long, steep stairs. You take one more look at the enchanted men, wondering if they saw what you did. They have such a knowing look about them. But you must hurry; there is no time to waste.

You blow the candle out, and the cave entrance closes. (Guards become entrance again.) Peregil keeps the paper and the Moor takes the candle. You part, each happier and wealthier—for the moment, at least—than you have ever been in your whole life, and disappear into the shadows of the night.

Leader in Character Role

Often it adds to the fun as well as the meaning of the playing if the leader plays a character role. Generally the character is an authority figure or one who can legitimately direct and guide the actions of the children.

For example, in the Winnie the Pooh exercise activity mentioned earlier, the leader might have been Christopher Robin and said:

T: Now, Pooh Bear, I know you have good intentions, but sometimes you need a little help. It's time for your exercises, and I shall watch to see that you do them. In fact, I'll even count for you. We'll begin with the first one . . .

Often the children get more enjoyment out of following the character's rules and comply with them more willingly. Being Pooh following Christopher Robin's directions is more fun than doing what the teacher says.

Other roles might be as Zeus, who gives the cues for the thunderstorms; an inventor who designs and tests out robots; the captain of an expedition; the oldest and wisest member of a tribe; or a tour guide. For example:

T: Ladies and gentlemen, now that you are settled in your two-person outboard motorboats, let me introduce myself. I'm John Tiesman, your guide for the study of sea lions off the coast of Alaska. This tour will have its splendors, and there may be times when my trained senses will discover various sights which I shall quietly call to your attention. I trust our attempts to explore and study the life of this magnificent animal will be successful. Bon voyage!

Because the role is that of an authority figure, it usually brings with it control and discipline. If necessary, the leader can use the role to make and enforce rules when they are needed along the way.

> **T:**   As your tour director, I must ask you not to touch any of the stalactites or stalagmites in the cave. They have been growing for centuries, and one careless move from a tourist could cause inestimable damage. From this point on, you must walk through the passageways with extreme caution. Anyone who cannot abide by the rules will be asked to return to the entrance—with no refund of admission charge, I might add. Are we ready?

Usually it is helpful in playing a role if the leader changes voice or mannerisms in order to separate the role from one's everyday self. If this is a bit difficult, perhaps a small prop might help. A tourist guide, for example, might have a special hat or a badge. A control tower operator might use a chalk eraser as a microphone.

FLEXIBLE NARRATION

With experience, the leader will be able to be more flexible in narrating, ad-libbing, expanding, or condensing the material, according to the children's responses. The experienced leader may even be able to create a drama experience incorporating the children's ideas during the playing.

This technique is a useful one in recreating experiences the children have had, such as going on a picnic, or visiting a farm, or for learning about new adventures. The following is an excerpt from a wagon-train trip with a third-grade class:

> **T:**   It looks as if most of the families have finished packing their covered wagons. Now, before we roll out, there may be some crucial questions we need to answer. Let's gather by the fire here. (They all sit.) Now, do we have sufficient medical supplies?
> **C:**   We have some brandy and some bandages in our wagon.
> **C:**   Don't worry; Mary and John and I have already checked the medical supplies.
> **C:**   I have a question. I want to know how many days it will take us to get to Nebraska.
> **T:**   Well, we'll be lucky to make twenty miles a day. How long will that be? (The group takes a few seconds to compute the time.) Are there any other questions? All right, we've got a long journey ahead of us. Let's get started. Which family did we decide would lead? Bring your wagon over here, and the rest will line up behind . . .

With small classes or with those that are very socially cooperative, such drama experiences can evolve with little difficulty. However, the leader must bear the responsibility for planning the various events, conflicts, and resolutions for the activity. The leader must also keep the group organized in its discussions and in its playing in order to keep the dramatic excitement strong throughout.

FOR THE COLLEGE STUDENT

1. Write a 300–500-word narrative pantomime on any of the following subjects. Underline the action words. Label the conflict. Use descriptive language. Consider appropriate beginning and ending.
   a. Select a short folk or fairy tale and rewrite it as a narrative pantomime.
   b. Select a topic from social studies or science or another curricular area appropriate for narrative pantomime.
   c. Select a personal experience you have had that you can describe realistically and in detail suitable for narrative pantomime.
   d. Choose an inanimate object that can be personified and write a story about it.
   e. Write a story specifically designed for pairs or groups.
   f. Write a story specifically designed for the desk area.
2. Narrate your story for your classmates to act. Discuss together its strengths and weaknesses.
3. Practice flexible narration. Outline or write in detail a 300-word story on a topic you will narrate for your classmates to enact. As you lead the activity, concentrate on expanding or condensing the story, according to your classmates' input. Discuss afterwards.

SELECTED BIBLIOGRAPHY OF LONGER
MATERIALS FOR NARRATION

The following materials are suitable for narrative pantomime, but will need to be adapted or edited. In some cases dialogue will need to be edited also. The materials are arranged alphabetically according to title. The majority can be used for science and social studies units. The following symbols are used to indicate the age level the material might be best suited for:

Y   young children in kindergarten, first, and second grades

M   middle-grade children in third and fourth grades

O   older children in fifth and sixth grades

M—O   *Akavak (An Eskimo Journey)*, James Houston. New York: Harcourt Brace Jovanovich, Inc., 1968. Akavak and his grandfather undertake a journey that almost ends in tragedy. Possibilities for paired playing.

M   *All on a Mountain Day*, Aileen Fisher. Nashville, Tenn.: Thom. Nelson, Inc., 1956. A chapter about each of the wild animals on a mountainside, from rabbit to bobcat.

M   *All Upon a Sidewalk*, Jean Craighead George. New York: Dutton, 1974. A yellow ant has an important mission to carry out.

M　*Amelia Bedelia,* Peggy Parish. New York: Harper & Row, Pub., 1963. Amelia, a housekeeper, takes all her instructions literally.

M—O　*And Then What Happened, Paul Revere?* Jean Fritz. New York: Coward, McCann & Geoghegan, 1973. An accurate and amusing story of a national hero.

Y—M　*Ants Have Pets,* Kathy Darling. Champaign, Ill.: Garrard, 1977. Description of the life of Pogo, a farmer ant. Could be played in pairs to include the cricket pet.

M　*Babar, the Little Elephant* (The Story of), Jean de Brunhoff. New York: Random House, 1933. Classic story of a young elephant who is reared by an elderly woman who buys him clothes and an automobile.

Y—M　*The Bakers,* Jan Adkins. New York: Scribner's, 1975. Detailed description of bread making.

Y—M　*The Bears on Hemlock Mountain,* Alice Dalgliesh. New York: Scribner's, 1952. Jonathan finds out that there *are* bears on Hemlock Mountain and discovers a unique way to hide from them.

M　*Beaver Moon,* Miska Miles. Boston: Little, Brown, 1978. An old beaver is forced out of his lodge and searches for a new home.

M—O　*The Black Pearl,* Scott O'Dell. Boston: Houghton Mifflin, 1967. Ramon tells of his adventures with Manta Diablo, a fearsome fish, and of the search for a black pearl in Mexican waters.

M　*The Blind Colt,* Glen Rounds. New York: Holiday House, 1941. A blind colt must learn of the world, its joys, and its dangers.

M　*Brighty of the Grand Canyon,* Marguerite Henry. Skokie, Ill.: Rand McNally, 1953. The story of a burro who spends his winters at the bottom of the Canyon where it is warm and his summers on the North Rim, where it is cool.

M—O　*Broderick,* Edward Ormondroyd. New York: Parnassus Press, 1969. A mouse becomes a famous surfer.

Y—M　*Burt Dow, Deep-Water Man,* Robert McCloskey. New York: Viking, 1963. A fisherman and his giggling seagull pet have a unique adventure with whales.

M—O　*Call it Courage,* Armstrong Sperry. New York: Macmillan, 1940. A South-Sea island boy, son of a tribal chief, has many fears of the sea and sets out to conquer them.

Y—M　*Cosmo's Restaurant,* Harriet Langsam Sobol. New York: Macmillan, 1978. A typical day at a family-owned Italian restaurant. Black and white photos.

M　*C. W. Anderson's Complete Book of Horses and Horsemanship.* New York: Macmillan, 1963. Many descriptive passages including a chapter on riding techniques.

M　*Dancing Cloud,* Mary and Conrad Buff. New York: Viking, 1957. Many descriptive passages of life in a Navajo hogan.

Y—M　*A Day in the Life of a Veterinarian,* William Jaspersohn. Boston: Little, Brown, 1978. Documents a vet's many duties. Black and white photos.

M—O　*Doctor in the Zoo,* Bruce Buchenholz. New York: Viking, 1974. Fascinating account of the many duties of a zoo doctor. Black and white photos.

Y—M　*Elephants of Africa,* Gladys Conklin. New York: Holiday House, 1972. The adventures of a little elephant within the herd.

Y—M　*Emilio's Summer Day,* Miriam Anne Bourne. New York: Harper & Row, Pub., 1966. Emilio tries to amuse himself on a hot summer day in the city.

Y—M   *Evan's Corner,* Elizabeth Starr Hill. New York: Holt, Rinehart & Winston, 1967. Evan wants a place to be lonely in, a place to waste time in his own way. He fixes up a corner in his crowded apartment for himself and then learns that helping his brother fix his corner is also a rewarding experience.

M   *Fox and the Fire,* Miska Miles. Boston: Little, Brown, 1966. A young red fox searches for food and is interrupted by a barn fire.

Y   *Henry the Explorer,* Mark Taylor. New York: Atheneum, 1966. Henry, an imaginative little boy, decides to go on adventures outdoors.

M—O   *How a House Happens,* Jan Adkins. New York: Walker, 1972. Steps in the process of building a house complete with diagrams.

Y—M   *How Animals Sleep,* Millicent Selsam. New York: Scholastic Book Services, 1962. Descriptions of sleep habits of several animals.

M—O   *i am the running girl,* Arnold Adoff. New York: Harper & Row, Pub., 1979. Rhonda trains for a running meet. Told in poetic form.

M—O   *Indian Hunting,* Robert (Gray-Wolf) Hofsinde. New York: Morrow, 1962. Description of Indian weapons and hunting methods, and the ceremonial rites of the hunt. Other books by this author may also be of interest.

M—O   *Island of the Blue Dolphins,* Scott O'Dell. Boston: Houghton Mifflin, 1960. An Indian girl is left alone on an island in the Pacific and manages to survive.

M—O   *John Muir,* Charles Norman. New York: Julian Messner, 1957. The story of a famous naturalist and founder of the American national park system.

M   *Jonathan Livingston Seagull,* Richard Bach. New York: Macmillan, 1970. The struggles of a seagull who dares to perfect his flying skills into an art.

O   *Julie of the Wolves,* Jean Craighead George. New York: Harper & Row, Pub., 1972. An Eskimo girl must choose between the world of her ancestors and the world of the modern white man.

Y—M   *The Little Old Woman Who Used Her Head,* Hope Newell. Nashville, Tenn.: Thom. Nelson, 1935. A little old woman lives alone and is very poor but is always able to solve her problems, even though in unconventional ways.

Y—M   *Lone Muskrat,* Glen Rounds. New York: Holiday House, 1953. An old muskrat survives a forest fire and makes a new home for himself. His preparations for winter and his encounters with an owl, eagle, and other dangers make a dramatic nature study.

M   *Lone Seal Pup,* Arthur Catherall. New York: Dutton, 1965. A seal pup loses his mother and must fend for himself.

M—O   *The Long Ago Lake,* Marne Wilkins. New York: Scribner's, 1978. Fascinating data on outdoor life in the Wisconsin north country in the 1930s.

M—O   *Lumberjack,* William Kurelek. Boston: Houghton Mifflin, 1974. The author describes his personal experiences as a lumberjack in Canada as a young man.

Y—M   *Maple Harvest: The Story of Maple Sugaring,* Elizabeth Gemming. Coward, McCann & Geoghegan, 1976. Detailed description of the steps in the process of maple sugaring.

Y—M   *Mr. Charlie's Chicken House,* Edith Thatcher Hurd and Clement Hurd. Philadelphia: Lippincott, 1955. Mr. Charlie likes eggs so much he decides to build a chicken house.

M   *The Moon of the Winter Bird,* Jean George. New York: Thomas Y. Crowell, 1970. The dramatic experiences of a sparrow trying to survive in northern winter weather.

M—O *My Side of the Mountain,* Jean George. New York: Dutton, 1959. The various adventures of a young boy who tries his hand at living by himself in the Catskill Mountains.

M *Nobody's Cat,* Miska Miles. Boston: Atlantic-Little, Brown, 1969. The adventures of an alley cat in the city and his struggles.

Y—M *Octopus,* Evelyn Shaw. New York: Harper & Row, Pub., 1971. An octopus needs to find a new place to live.

Y—M *Paddy the Penguin,* Paul Galdone. New York: Thomas Y. Crowell, 1959. Paddy the Penguin gets to fly with the help of an airplane and a parachute.

Y—M *Pagoo,* Holling C. Holling. Boston: Houghton Mifflin, 1957. The growing and adventuring of a hermit crab.

Y—M *Pete's House,* Harriet Langsam Sobol. New York: Macmillan, 1978. Details of building a house. Black and white photos.

M *The Pine Tree,* George Maxim Ross. New York: Dutton, 1966. A pine tree struggles for survival.

M *The Plymouth Thanksgiving,* Leonard Weisgard. New York: Doubleday, 1967. Simply presented detail of the events leading up to the first Thanksgiving. Numerous characters for groups or entire class to play.

Y—O *A Prairie Boy's Winter,* William Kurelek. Boston: Houghton Mifflin, 1973. (Sequel is *A Prairie Boy's Summer,* 1975.) Picture book with separate descriptions of the many rigors and pleasures of living on the Canadian prairie in the 1930s.

M—O *The Printers,* Leonard Everett Fisher. New York: Franklin Watts, Inc., 1965. One of a series of over a dozen handsomely illustrated books on colonial craftspersons, including glassmakers, wigmakers, cabinetmakers, and homemakers.

Y—M *Red Legs,* Alice E. Goudey. New York: Scribner's, 1966. The story of the most common grasshopper in the United States.

O *Robinson Crusoe,* Daniel DeFoe. Many editions. A man is shipwrecked and lives for years on a lonely island.

M—O *Shaw's Fortune: The Story of a Colonial Plantation,* Edward Tunis. New York: Collins Publishers, 1966. Data on all facets of plantation life. Beautifully illustrated.

Y—M *Skunk for a Day,* Roger Caras. New York: Windmill & Dutton, 1976. This book starts out, "Today you are a skunk," and is illustrated with black and white drawings.

M *Sound of Sunshine, Sound of Rain,* Florence Parry Heide. New York: Parents', 1970. A young boy's experiences in a sightless world.

M *Tarantula, the Giant Spider,* Gladys Conklin. New York: Holiday House, 1972. Explanation of tarantulas as useful insects which need not be feared.

O *Thor Heyerdahl and the Reed Boat "Ra,"* Barbara Beasley Murphy and Norman Baker. Philadelphia: Lippincott, 1974. Description of the two Atlantic crossings made in papyrus boats. Black and white photos.

M—O *Tiktaliktak,* James Houston. New York: Harcourt Brace Jovanovich, Inc., 1965. An Eskimo boy is trapped on a rocky island and must make it back to food and safety.

Y—M *Time of Wonder,* Robert McCloskey. New York: Viking, 1957. A sensitive description of a summer's experiences in Maine.

M—O   *"To Build a Fire,"* Jack London. Many editions. A man in the Yukon, after a brave struggle, loses his battle against the 75° below zero temperature.

M   *Vulpes, the Red Fox,* John and Jean George. New York: Dutton, 1948. The descriptive and sensitive story of the life cycle of a fox.

Y—M   *The Web in the Grass,* Berniece Freschet. New York: Scribner's, 1972. Colorful picturebook of a little spider's dangerous and friendless life.

Y—M   *What Can She Be? A Police Officer,* Gloria and Esther Goldreich. New York: Lothrop, Lee & Shephard, 1975. Tells of the day's work of law enforcement. Others in the *What Can She Be?* series include such occupations as farmer, geologist, and film producer. Black and white photos.

M   *The White Palace,* Mary O'Neill. New York: Thomas Y. Crowell, 1966. Beautifully illustrated story of a salmon's life.

Y—M   *Window into an Egg,* Geraldine Lux Flanagan. Reading, Mass.: Addison-Wesley, 1969. Detailed account, with black and white photos, of the development of an egg which has had a "window" cut in it.

Y—M   *Who Needs Holes?* Sam and Beryl Epstein. New York: Hawthorn, 1970. A simple book to illustrate some basic science concepts.

M—O   *Wolf Run: A Caribou Eskimo Tale,* James Houston. New York: Harcourt Brace Jovanovich, 1971. Rather than face certain starvation, a young Eskimo boy sets off to find caribou against almost hopeless odds.

O   *Wrapped for Eternity: The Story of the Egyptian Mummy,* Mildred Pace. New York: McGraw Hill, 1974. Fascinating information about a fascinating subject, particularly for older children.

Chapter Five

Strengthening Concentration and Involvement

Up to this point we have introduced beginning activities and narrative pantomimes. Before going further with additional types of drama activities, however, it is important to stress the need for encouraging children's concentration and involvement so that they may go beyond a superficial level of playing to more meaningful experiences.

Identifying Involvement

The importance of aiding in-depth involvement cannot be overemphasized. Generally speaking, the success of drama experiences, as measured by both the teacher and the children, is dependent on the degree of involvement of the players. In discussing the expressive power of play, Maureen Mansell suggests that there is an aesthetic dimension which distinguishes many play activities and is crucial to validating the claim that creative drama develops the whole person. "At the moment of doing," she states, "when nothing outside the situation matters, there emerges a sense of ultimate integration: a fusion of the person with his or her surroundings."[1] It is this aesthetic experience the leader constantly looks for in the children's playing and assists them in achieving.

Usually the leader measures a child's involvement by observing certain

---

[1] Maureen Mansell, "Dimensions of Play Experience," *Communication Education*, 29, 1 (1980), 48. The poem we have reprinted on p. xiii of this text also describes this experience.

Involvement means believing what you are doing.

behaviors. Generally one is sure of involvement when children are so absorbed or engrossed in their playing that they are unaware of anyone observing them. Perhaps they enjoy the material so much that they forget about everyone else, or perhaps they are able to block out distractions successfully.

When children are involved in dramatizing they often demonstrate a detailed awareness of the experience. For example, a child pretending to walk a tightrope may step very carefully, exactly placing one foot ahead of the other, balancing the body with outstretched arms. The child may stop momentarily, gently swaying, eyes fixed straight ahead, arms moving as if in an attempt to regain a loss of balance, and then slowly move ahead. All these movements demonstrate that the pantomimer is very much aware of the narrow rope suspended high above the ground and of the skills required of one who performs on it.

Another clue of involved playing is the spontaneous addition of details that the leader has not specified. For example, the child pretending to walk the tightrope might also pretend to hold an imaginary umbrella for balance and bow and throw kisses to an enthusiastic but imaginary audience.

Involved children concentrate intently and are usually highly pleased with their work. Frequently they ask to repeat the material and seem to be revitalized with each playing.

Behaviors indicating a lack of involvement might be: showing off, hesitant looking at other classmates to see what they are doing, moving aimlessly, or appearing to be puzzled by the activity. They may also involve embarrassed giggling, whispering to others, crowding together, and other indications of insecurity.

There are times when the entire classroom seems to respond as one person, all with the same depth of involvement or lack of it. There may be times when some of the class is involved while others are only superficially involved.

The teacher can be very instrumental in making an experience and the playing of it as meaningful as possible. From the time the leader selects the material itself until the time the material is being replayed for the third or fourth time, the leader has the opportunity to affect the involvement the children will have in it. We shall discuss those steps and some of the considerations that will help the leader assure involvement each step of the way.

SELECTING MATERIALS

The first consideration the leader must make is in the selection of appropriate, enjoyable, and meaningful material. Children work best when they are intrigued. No one can respond to or concentrate on an idea that seems to be a waste of time.

Obviously the material should also appeal to the leader since his or her own involvement is usually contagious. The leader should select an idea to which he or she can be committed and feel confident and interested in it. The leader may need to be enthusiastic about the idea in order to sell it to a group who needs proof that the activity is worth its attention.

Materials that capture the children's attention may be subjects that thoroughly entertain, or they may be subjects that encourage intense discussions and stimulate sincere concerns. The leader usually has to learn from the group what kinds of situations and materials it finds most appealing. Many listings of materials will specify which age groups they are suited for. However, these are only guides and not sacred rules. One should learn which material is most interesting and meaningful for a particular group, regardless of its age level.

Groups also vary in personality. Some groups are satisfied only when the material tickles their funny bones and contains a joke they can enjoy together. Others want to be involved in more serious situations. Some groups enjoy romantic themes; others will reject any hint of a love element. Some groups like anything and everything; others are very finicky. Tastes and interests can be expanded, but that may take time and some careful planning.

Leaders' choice of material will naturally reflect their personalities and values. For this reason, leaders should periodically examine the nature of their favorite materials to see if they are meeting the needs of the children. One may discover that the children have other interests, values, and concerns. Leaders may have to reach beyond their own sphere of interest in order to keep alert to

When you're involved, no one can distract you.

new materials and to listen with a sensitive ear to both the spoken and implied interests of the children.

PRESENTING THE MATERIAL

All material, whether it is music, props, pictures, literature, or simply an idea, is only as good a stimulus as the leader's presentation makes it. As one tells a story, leads a discussion, or even gives directions, one's overall attitude can establish the appropriate atmosphere for the eventual playing.

Establishing Mood

All material has some general categorization of mood. For example, a story may be exciting, music may be peaceful, a picture may be humorous, or a prop may be curious. When presenting the material the leader can reinforce its mood by reacting appropriately. One may smile and laugh along with a humorous story, or tell it tongue in cheek. In playing recorded music, the sensitive leader will carefully fade music in and out rather than dropping or lifting the needle abruptly. Reaction to a curious prop may convey surprise in the voice when the leader poses the question, "Who do you suppose owns this? Have you ever seen anything like it before?"

Vocal quality, pitch, timing, or loudness and softness of voice are all tools the leader can use in contributing meaning and understanding. For example, the leader's voice can become quiet and convey a soft quality when referring to the feel of a kitten's fur. One can say the word "warm" and make the children feel it; or say "tangy, crisp apple" in such a way that they can almost taste it. A voice can creak like the door of the haunted house, moan like the wind, or boom like thunder. The voice can also convey feelings. The word "lonely" can be drawn out; sorrowful passages may need a low voice; or anxiety can be conveyed when telling about someone trapped in a mine shaft.

Presenting Literature

The leader should always be thoroughly familiar with the material. This is especially important in presenting literature. Even if the poem or story is well known or the teacher has used it several times before, it should always be reviewed before it is presented again. Familiarity with material eliminates the irritating tendency to omit crucial points, to mispronounce words, or to be halting and hesitant. It also allows the teacher the ability to establish rapport with the children and to judge the effect of the material on them.

It also helps concentration if the leader does not begin presenting the material until the children are ready to listen. Some leaders are particularly adept

A good story well-told will capture attention.

at captivating children's attention with storytelling. They begin a story and allow the first sentence or two to calm down or to entice a wiggly or listless group. Most teachers have to establish the rule that the material will not be shared until the children show they are ready to listen. Then they patiently and objectively wait a moment or two until the children settle down. They may also ask children to put their heads on their desks or close their eyes to aid listening.

Finally, it is helpful if the room and the children are arranged in a way that accommodates both the presentation of the material and the playing. For example, if the children are to play at the desk area, there is no need to have them sit on the floor in a circle to hear a story and then move back to their desks to play it. This can break the mood of the material and the children's concentration on it.

UNDERSTANDING THE MATERIAL

Children cannot play experiences they do not understand. There are several techniques the leader can use to aid understanding.

Stimulating Awareness

Understanding and involvement are reinforced when children are given materials related to the activity that they can touch, taste, smell, listen to, and carefully examine. For example, before playing an experience on scuba diving, the teacher may have available some objects associated with the activity: fins, a mask, an oxygen tank, and perhaps some shells and a piece of dried seaweed. These are shown to the children, and they talk about them and handle them. For some children these materials may be new experiences that acquaint them with the topic for the first time.

Or before children role-play young Helen Keller, the teacher may have the children close their eyes and examine various objects with their fingers. A film such as *Dream of the Wild Horses* can illustrate the beauty of slowed movement.[2] Or the pictures in a book such as Edward Steichen's *Family of Man* can demonstrate the universality of human emotions.[3] These materials can create images and awareness that words alone cannot communicate.

Discussion of Ideas

Discussions can be very useful in promoting greater understanding of the material, in clarifying perceptions, and in bringing the experience closer to the children's own.

Sometimes the language of material needs clarification. For example, in the poem "Foul Shot" (p. 122), the basketball player is said to be "squeezed by silence." He also "measures the waiting net." It may help to talk about these phrases; the children may need to explain them in their own words.

> **C:** "Squeezed by silence" means you feel cramped because it is so quiet and everyone's watching you.
> **C:** He "measures the waiting net" by sizing it up and aiming the ball real good.

Sometimes the use of analogies is helpful in dealing with unfamiliar subjects. For example, before pretending to explore the moon's antigravity environment, the teacher might help the children recall the floating sensation of wading in deep water.

Children can think of their own analogies also.

> **T:** We already know some things about a desert, even though none of us has ever been there. Can you think of something you have seen or experienced that would be like something in the desert?
> **C:** It would be hotter than it was in here the day the heat was turned on too high and we almost suffocated.
> **C:** My grandpa says when it gets really hot you can fry an egg on the sidewalk.
> **C:** It would be even hotter than it was this summer when we had the hottest day ever recorded.
> **C:** Those chameleons the first grade has look like the gila monsters in our book about the desert.

Discussion of Character

Children can become more involved when they discover the similarities between their own feelings and the feelings described in the materials. Discussions are an important process for identifying with emotions and motivations for behavior.

---

[2] Contemporary Films. McGraw-Hill. Nine minutes, color.
[3] New York: Museum of Modern Art, 1955.

T: In Maia Wojciechowska's *Shadow of a Bull* (129) there is one scene when all the boys merrily jump from a wagon of hay. All but Manolo; he's too afraid. What thoughts do you think are in Manolo's head when the boys suggest jumping? How do you think he feels? Have you ever been afraid of doing something the way Manolo is afraid of jumping?

The children may need to discuss how people express their emotions:

T: The story doesn't tell us, but I wonder how "Gertrude McFuzz" (p. 65) has her temper tantrum? What does she do, do you suppose?
C: When my brother has one, he pounds his fists on the floor and screams.
C: I think she goes to her room and slams the door.
C: She gets real angry. My dad, when he gets angry, says he could "spit nails."

Sometimes it is necessary for the leader to acknowledge that various children may have different perceptions and that it is important to respect each other's ideas. It may be helpful if the teacher openly and sincerely acknowledges the difficulty and concern everyone has when talking over and planning sensitive material.

T: As we talk about this idea we may hear answers that surprise us—answers we may think are silly or wrong. But we all have our own opinions, and it's important to be able to talk about them without anyone making fun of us or criticizing us.

In discussing emotional feelings it is helpful to ask, "What do you think?" This allows children to express their feelings and interpretations in their own way and from their own background of experience.

T: How do you think Johnny Tremain (101) felt when Isannah screamed that his scarred hand was "dreadful"?
T: Before we dramatize some sections from *Call it Courage* (p. 68), let's talk about courage. What is courage to you? What are some things you think a courageous person might do?

Children can sometimes feel more comfortable about discussing topics if teachers share their feelings also.

T: The "Star-Bellied Sneetches" (32) don't play with the Sneetches that don't have stars. They don't invite them to their wiener roasts. I remember how I felt when a girl in my class at school didn't invite me to her party. I think I know how those Sneetches without stars must have felt . . .

Through discussion, children have the opportunity to discover that others share their ideas and their powerful and often overwhelming feelings. While children may not say it, they often think to themselves: "So that's your idea, too! I thought I was the only person in the whole world who felt like that."

Discussions may be necessary if the experience is a culturally different one for the children.

T: James Huston vividly describes a very critical moment when the Eskimo Tiktalik-tak (p. 90) gives up hope for living and builds himself a coffin. Why did he do that? What are his last thoughts as he carefully arranges his weapons by his side? Why does he want his relatives to understand the reason for his death?

C: He had to build a coffin; he thought he was going to die.

C: If they didn't find his weapons, they might not ever know what happened to him.

C: I think he wanted to tell his family that he didn't commit suicide. He just starved to death.

In addition to clarifying the material to be played, preparatory discussions can begin to establish the mood necessary for involvement during the playing. They help to set the stage for the eventual enactment.

PLAYING THE MATERIAL

One of the questions teachers frequently ask is, "How do you keep the kids from acting silly?" Silliness or "goofing off" behaviors are usually the result of uncomfortable feelings. Rarely will anyone be silly for the sake of being silly. But without understanding the causes of these behaviors, the teacher may lose patience. And that adds to rather than solves the problem.

Humorous Material

As the children and the inexperienced teacher begin work in creative drama, it may be helpful to start first with materials that are humorous. Gay and lively situations relax everyone and build group rapport. If the characters are funny, there is less pressure on the child to play the part in a suave, polished, and formal way. Also, if the material is humorous, a little silliness or laughing does not destroy the mood as easily as it does with sensitive material.

Dramatic Material

Playing material rich in dramatic tension or conflict is often the most rewarding experience children can have. There is no question that it is worth the time it takes to understand the material and to work at becoming involved in it. Sometimes it is a surprise to find that the most unlikely children are the ones who lead in the requests for challenging material once they have had the experience of being involved in it. Working with highly dramatic material does, however, take additional and special considerations.

First, the leader must create an appropriate climate for beginning the work. Sometimes teachers assume that children will know the material is of a serious nature and that they will automatically respond appropriately. Many times this is not the case. It may be helpful if the teacher simply alerts them immediately to the fact that the material may be demanding.

T: We've been talking about the relocation of Indian tribes, and I thought we might be able to understand these tragic moments a little better if we enact the march along the Trail of Tears. This may take some effort on our part. . . .

Brief Playing

For initial attempts at in-depth involvement with dramatic material, it is helpful to keep the playing fairly brief. If children know the experience will be short, they may be more apt to participate in it and may be less anxious. They can be assured that the experience will be over before they have time to be embarrassed by it.

Brief playings are also easier on leaders. They too will not have to work so long and hard at creating and sustaining the mood. An initial success will also bolster both the teachers' and the students' confidence for a longer playing another time.

Concentration

Concentration usually needs to be encouraged. Although the leader will be tempted to caution the children to "think" or "concentrate," these admonitions by themselves will serve little good. Unless the children know what they are to think about or to concentrate on, or indeed what they are supposed to do when they think or concentrate, they cannot possibly oblige.

As we have suggested earlier, organizing the playing so that children work separately and privately can lessen distractions and aid concentration. In countless experiences the authors have observed that this technique alone can stabilize children and help them focus on their ideas. In addition, the leader can dim the lights in the room so that isolation and privacy are further aided.

Another technique is to ask the children to close their eyes. (Particularly

Checking for concentration.

Closing your eyes helps you think.
(Photo courtesy of Jon Vander Meer.)

when they are playing individually and are in limited space, having their eyes closed will not pose a problem.) By closing their eyes, the children are able to block out distractions and visualize their ideas. Some children adopt this aid on their own, even after they have become experienced in drama, judging for themselves when such a technique will make the playing more involving and hence more satisfying for them.

Often it is helpful if the leader discusses with the children what aids and what interferes with their concentration. Usually children know what distracts them. It may be other children just being near them, touching them, or purposely trying to distract them. Or they may be bothered by just being aware that others are near by. After playing, the leader can ask the children to evaluate the conditions under which they were working and find ways to make them better.

Particularly after children do give behavioral evidence that they are involved in the material, it is helpful to have them describe it.

T: There was one moment when most of you seemed to be very absorbed in what you were doing. At the moment when Jonathan Livingston Seagull (p. 89) was desperately trying to perfect his diving skills, what were you thinking and feeling? Why do you think you were the most involved at that moment?
C: I really felt like a bird instead of me.

C: I remembered what it was like when I was trying to learn to ski.
C: Flying was the only thing he cared about, so he put everything into it. I tried to do that too.

Selecting Volunteers

While it is true that the leader will want to have all children participate in the playing, it is always a wise precaution to begin with just a few of the children who can be most easily involved. Particularly when one is trying out new material and the group's response cannot be predicted, there is no point in taking chances with an entire class.

The first playing of the material is experimental; the first players are a model for subsequent playings. The mood set by the first playing is also easier to build on. Involvement may also be aided if the leader allows the children to judge for themselves when they are ready to participate.

Handling Problem Behaviors

If some children cannot follow the rules for playing, particularly when dealing with something as concrete as the use of space and a rule about no talking, the leader may have to ask them to remove themselves from the playing. This is important in keeping the climate of playing orderly and the mood of the material strong. If some children are becoming a distracting element, they are getting little from the experience and may also be hampering others.

Removing a child from playing can be done very quickly and privately in order not to cause embarrassment. The leader need only say:

T: I think the rule to remain in your own space and not distract others must be too difficult for you just now. When you think you can follow the rule, you may return.

It should be pointed out that when a child does not follow the rules, removal from playing is only a symptomatic solution to the problem. A more thorough analysis may be necessary in order to discover the real cause of the problem.

Even though children may need to be removed from the playing, they should be allowed to watch the others. Many children need to see others involved in an activity in order to understand it.

Throughout any handling of problem behaviors, the leader should remain objective. If the activity has been made intriguing and challenging, the fun of playing it will often be the drawing card for the child to comply with the rules.

Side-coaching

Side-coaching is a technique indispensable to the leader. In side-coaching, the leader "talks the children through" the activity, suggesting actions and ideas they might consider playing.

Sometimes side-coaching is needed by all the children, and sometimes only a few need such help. Generally the teacher does not know whether or not the children will need side-coaching until they have begun playing. It is not unusual for children to discuss an idea with great enthusiasm and appear to be very ready to enact it, and then during the playing suddenly become unsure of themselves. Side-coaching can often guide these children through a successful playing.

Side-coaching can also fill in what might be awkward silences. Just the sound of the teacher's voice can give security to those children who need it and can guide and encourage through moments of hesitation. Frequently, a group's lukewarm response to an idea changes to excited involvement with expert side-coaching from the enthusiastic leader.

Music, Lights, and Sound Effects

The use of music, lights, and sound effects can also aid involvement. They can add to the mood, create a wealth of pictorial images, and stimulate the imagination.

For example, it is much easier for children to pretend to be plants growing during warm spring rains when they are accompanied by Grieg's "Morning" from *Peer Gynt*. Or with an energetic tune such as Herb Alpert's "Whipped Cream," the children may find it easier to imagine visiting a bustling city department store, trying on hats and shoes, sampling display cologne, and snacking at the stand-up counter.

Lighting can lend very special effects. It is surprising what children can imagine with the simple technique of flashing the classroom lights on and off.

In a semidarkened room with the accompaniment of somber music, children pretend to be the Eskimo Tiktaliktak lifting the stone cover of his coffin into place.

Lightning and electrical storms, movie spotlights, neon signs, or the sparkling sights in outer space are only some of the possibilities. When the lights are off and the room dimmed, children can more easily imagine dark tunnels, mysterious underwater worlds, ancient ruins, the Arctic.

Sound effects have a similar influence. They can add to the mood, stimulate the imagination, and aid the involvement. For example, in some social studies books it is noted that the sound of fife and drum accompanied Nathan Hale to his place of execution. If the children were to dramatize this moment, it might be intensified by the ominous sound of drumming on the desk tops.

Leader's Participation

In some activities the leader's participation in a character role can be very helpful. It can set the scene, create the mood, and highlight the dramatic tension. With this technique, the leader gives the children something to respond to emotionally. It helps avoid the awkwardness of "feeling the situation."

For example, there is a strong moment in the story "Knights of the Silver Shield" (49). Sir Roland, a young knight, is told by his commander to guard an isolated castle. He wants very much to fight, and he is bitterly disappointed over the assignment. It is this dilemma that creates an interesting emotional moment. Although he obeys his commander, the temptation to leave his post is ever present.

The leader might initiate the experience by pretending to be Sir Roland's commander, who gives him his orders.

T: Sir Roland, being the youngest knight here, you have been chosen to stay behind and guard the castle. You must not allow anyone to enter until the battle is over and we all return. We are leaving, Sir Roland. Report to duty.

After saying this to the children the leader could then turn away as if he, the commander, were going off to battle. Sir Roland is left alone to wait, to guard, to pass the time, and to think about his feelings in that moment. The leader may end the experience by narrating a sentence about the return of the wounded knight.

After speaking the words of the character, the leader can pause and then play along with the children. This technique is helpful when children are bothered by the teacher's observation or need assistance in feeling that they are truly alone in their experience. By playing with the children, the teacher is also demonstrating a willingness to accept the challenge the activity presents.

REPLAYING

If an idea is worthwhile, it is worth taking some time to experience it. The best of creative thinking and understanding may be impossible to achieve in a first playing. Even the most experienced leader with experienced children may not achieve in-depth involvement with one try.

Some leaders, when guiding for greater depth of involvement, play the activity three times. The first playing may be treated as a run-through to give everyone a total perspective and a chance to see its potential. A second playing allows for adding new ideas, dropping ineffective ones, refining, and polishing. The third playing becomes a final synthesis of ideas.

When the first playing is experimental, it can be helpful to share this plan with the children. For example, it can be extremely comforting to the children if the leader says, "We've never done this before. Let's just try it and see what happens." Such a statement can be equally comforting for the leader.

EVALUATION

When the leader and the children evaluate the playing, there is increased possibility for in-depth involvement in subsequent playings. When the children are asked to think about what they have accomplished and to state what they liked about it, they are positively reinforcing themselves.

When the leader makes evaluations, they must be specific enough that the children know how to duplicate what is successful. Simply saying "good" is probably not helpful, since the children do not know what is being identified as good. But if the leader is more specific and says, for example, "Good; your puppets are walking very stiffly, just as if you were made out of wood," then the praise is for stiff movements, an action that can be observed and described.

Believability is also a key concept to consider. Something about the dramatizing should look real. In the above example the leader might have said, "I really saw puppets moving, not second graders."

Drama experiences without the children's self-evaluation and the leader's evaluative guidance will probably be superficial ones. Only when careful attention is given to all aspects of playing will in-depth involvement be achieved.

Example from *Venture for Freedom*

The following is an extended example of a thirty-minute activity with a fifth-grade class during their fourth session of creative drama. It demonstrates many of the techniques discussed in the chapter.

Noteworthy is the fact that there was lengthy preparation in order to guide the understanding and to establish a strong, serious mood and a sense of deep involvement. The physical activity itself involved walking only about six feet. The drama event was focused literally on only about three sentences of text. But the understanding of the event as well as the emotional feelings involved required much discussion and work.

The leader guided the children through three discussions and three playings. After thirty minutes of work, all the children had become involved in what developed into a very moving experience.

The slaves disembark from the ship.

The children and the teacher grouped themselves on the floor at one end of the room. The teacher introduced the book *Venture for Freedom* (145), explaining that it was a true story based on the experience of a captured African tribe and of an African king's son whose English name was Venture Smith. She read short, specific episodes describing the fatal beating of Venture's father; the day Venture sneaked down to the ship's hold to find his mother; and the moment the Africans disembarked into the blinding Barbados sun and slavery.

Then the teacher and the children discussed the following questions:

What kind of people do you think they must have been to have a king who died rather than betray his tribe?

The story gives us some idea of the grim condition in the ship's hold, but expanding on that with your imagination, what do you think the hold was like?

How must Venture have felt, knowing his mother was in that hold?

His mother told him to go back on deck and stay alive. How do you think she felt, saying that? How did Venture feel?

What do you think it was like to come out of the ship's hold, after so many weeks in the dark, into the blinding sun? What thoughts and feelings do you think they had?

How must Venture have felt, knowing that this would be the last time he would see his mother and his people?

After the discussion the leader played a recording of "Sometimes I Feel Like a Motherless Child." She explained that the song grew out of and reflected the sorrow of the slave-trading days.

The teacher asked the children to put themselves back into this time and into the lives of these Africans. The lights were turned off. They were to imagine that they were in the ship's hold and that the two chairs she had placed close together in the middle of the room represented the ship's disembarking plank. Slowly, one at a time or in pairs, they were to come out of the hold, walk the plank, and then sit and wait for their brothers and sisters.

She told them to think about who they were, their physical condition, their attitudes about seeing the earth again, about the slave seller who would bark his orders to them as they slowly emerged into the day, their feelings about each other, and their feelings about slavery.

In order to help establish a mood, the teacher asked the children to close their eyes and softly hum "Motherless Child" as they thought about their characters. After a few

107

moments the teacher stood and in a rough and callous voice growled, "All right, look lively! Come on out!"

As the first children reached the plank, the teacher threw open the curtains to reveal the very bright sunlight. The children slowly walked between the chairs, some seriously involved in the activity, some snickering to their partners. After they had all assembled, the leader turned on the lights.

She talked to them for a few moments, commenting objectively. Quietly, and in the mood of the material she said, "As we played this the first time, some of you were involved in the moment and some of you found it difficult. It's not easy to play something as serious as this, but I think we can do it if we work at it some more. Let's try it again. Now that you know what it's about, let's have you decide if you think you can remain involved in it this next time. If you think you cannot, you may sit and watch."

Six children sat down. The activity was repeated. The involvement was stronger this time, but the leader noted that the children might be able to create an even more believable moment.

"What do you think? Shall we try it once again?" she asked.

They all agreed they wanted to try the experience again, and the leader offered them the choice again of playing or watching. All the children got up to play. This third playing was the most successful; and the children spontaneously expressed their satisfaction with it.

When children have once experienced in-depth involvement in a drama experience, often they will not be satisfied with superficial playing again. However, they may still need much assistance in arriving at that goal. With the leader's guidance and with the children assuming their share of the responsibility, everyone will enjoy most those experiences made more enriching through in-depth involvement.

FOR THE COLLEGE STUDENT

1. Select some material suitable for dramatization. Have in mind a particular group of children who will play it. Consider the following questions.
a. What do you personally like about the material? What is your commitment to it?
b. How will the material serve the interests, needs, and concerns of the group of children who are to play it?
c. What will be important for you to consider in presenting the material?
d. What methods might you use to assist the children in understanding the material? Be specific.
e. What considerations might be necessary for the group and/or for the material in playing it? Outline your plan for playing the material.
f. What special effects might be used for the playing of the material?
2. Lead the children (or your classmates) in playing the above material. Analyze the effectiveness of your plan for playing. What changes might you make to improve your plan?
3. Select some material rich in dramatic conflict. Practice reading it aloud, using your voice to convey the mood. Select music appropriate for the material. Rehearse the music with your reading until you can smoothly operate the phonograph as you read. Share this with your classmates.

4. Treat humorous material following the procedure suggested above.

5. Brainstorm with your classmates all the techniques the leader can use to increase psychological security and positive evaluation.

6. Using the extended example on pp. 106–108, analyze all the techniques used by the leader to aid involvement. What other techniques might have been employed?

Chapter Six

Developing
Creative
Pantomimes

In the previous chapters we focused mainly on narrative materials which the leader selected, adapted, or wrote for the children to interpret creatively. Creative pantomimes encourage the children to imagine and develop their own ideas for playing.

Some children can create with ease. The teacher can suggest an idea and then simply observe their self-confident and original responses. Many children, however, will need assistance and guidance. This chapter is devoted to topic suggestions and to techniques for encouraging children in the development of creative pantomimes.

TOPICS

Creative pantomimes can take many forms and may be based on a variety of topics. Because these are pantomimes, notice the emphasis on having the children think about what they will do and what actions they will perform.

The pantomime may be brief and based on a favorite story.

T: Let's pretend that you are a Gingerbread Boy and you've just come to life in the oven. The door is still closed and you're waiting to get out. I'll be the Old Woman who baked you, and when I open the door, you jump out and do *one* thing you think the Gingerbread Boy would do in his first moment of life. . . .

T: The story *Horton Hatches the Egg* (p. 209) doesn't tell us, but I wonder what

"Be as small as you can be . . . what are you?

Maizie-Bird does all day long before she manages to convince Horton to sit on her egg. Let's pretend we're Maizie. Think of three things you might do to help you pass the time and to help you forget that you're bored and tired and have kinks in your legs. When I say "one," do your first idea. . . .

Or, perhaps in a history lesson, the leader might want the children to put themselves in a famous person's situation, if just for a few minutes, doing, thinking, and feeling like that person might have.

T: According to our studies of Columbus, it seems that this man had great determination. One early historian, who talked with some of the great men on that famous voyage, recorded that it was Christopher Columbus who persuaded the captains of the *Pinta* and *Nina* to continue sailing for three more days. At the end of three days, Columbus said he would turn back if land were not sighted. The day this promise was made was approximately October ninth; land was sighted on October twelfth!

We know that mutiny was always a real possibility. Yet Columbus kept the sails at full spread even though his men were afraid of the strong gales. He offered rewards for sighting land. We also know that Columbus felt he had divine guidance.

In view of what we do know, let's imagine that you are Christopher Columbus. Put yourself back in time to the evening of October eleventh, a few hours away from the moment land was sighted. Where do you think Columbus would be during those hours? What is he thinking and feeling? What are some of the things he would do?

Creative pantomimes may be more extended and may also be played in pairs and groups. Note in the following examples that the leader gives a framework within which the children work out their own ideas:

T: Decide between you who will be the shadow and who will be the person the shadow is following and imitating. You'll have to decide who the person is, what he or she does, perhaps the kind of job he or she has while going through a day's activities. . . .

111

T:　Now that you've heard the little story behind the music "Danse Macabre" by Saint-Saens, let's divide into groups for the different graveyard scenes. You'll be the skeletons rising from your graves and dancing until dawn for this one night each year. . . .

T:　In your groups, plan your version of this story: You are stagecoach travelers, all with a particular destination. The stagecoach is loaded and you begin your journey rather uneventfully. But as you are out in a desolate area, you are attacked by two desperadoes. You're able to hold them off and arrive at your destination safely, though some of you may be wounded.

Initial Material

In beginning creative pantomimes it is often helpful to use stimulus material that contains some specific ideas. The more ideas the stimulus provides, the more ideas there will be for the children to try out first or to fall back on if their own imagination needs assistance. The ideas contained in the material help "prime the pump" of creative thinking and can also be of use to the leader in side-coaching.

For example, a little book called *I Need a Friend* (Putnam's, 1971) tells of a number of things one can do by oneself, but says that friends are needed for doing other things. One can pack a picnic basket alone, but it's nice to have someone with you on a picnic, the book tells us. Partners can play the first half of the idea solo and the second half together, alternating just as the book does, with a number of similar ideas. Building on this idea, the leader could ask, "What else can you think of that you can do alone—and what are those things you need a friend for?" The children who can think of additional ideas are free to play them, while the children who have trouble thinking of different ideas are free to repeat those contained in the original material.

It may also be useful in initial work to use humorous characters, such as "clumsy workers" or "mischievous monkeys," which are easier for the children to enact. They needn't be afraid of not being able to give a polished performance because the characters themselves aren't that sophisticated. Mechanical movements such as those made by robots or toy soldiers may also be easier (if precision isn't demanded) because these characters have stilted and abnormal kinds of movements the child can hide behind, if necessary.

Another useful idea for beginning work with creative pantomimes, particularly with older children, is to play music at a very fast speed and have them move to the tempo as in an old-fashioned movie. This way the children are so busy moving that they won't have time to be concerned about their movements and how they look.

However, this can become a bit hectic, particularly when the entire class is playing simultaneously in small groups. Therefore, it's a good idea to add some control by telling the children they must freeze when the music stops. Rehearse this a few times before letting them all break loose on a pantomime of any length.

TECHNIQUES FOR PLAYING CREATIVE PANTOMIMES

Brief Playing in Unison

The playing time of the pantomimes will vary according to the number of ideas the children have. At first the leader may want to keep the activities as short and as simple as possible in order to help the children feel comfortable. Children are usually willing to risk inventing if they're asked for only one or two ideas.

As another aid, the children should play the ideas in unison for their own satisfaction and self-evaluation rather than for audience evaluation. Later, children will probably enjoy sharing their work with classmates.

Private Response

It may also be important in beginning attempts to keep the work anonymous, with private responses. In order to do this the children can play a brief idea and then freeze. While they are frozen, the leader can move around to a few children quickly and quietly and ask them to whisper their ideas, *if they wish.*

Usually it is fun to try two or three ideas in this way in succession. Then the leader may quickly check on the ideas of five or six children. For example, the ideas may be based on a well-known story such as "Cinderella."

T: Okay, here's the first one. You are Cinderella and you are cleaning the house. Your stepmother says, "Get to work, Cinderella!" What will you do? One . . . two . . . etc. Freeze. I'll just come around to a few people, and you whisper what you are doing at this moment if you care to. (Teacher moves around to five children.)

Here's the second one. You are one of the stepsisters getting ready to go to the ball. You think you are very beautiful and elegant, but you have to work hard to make yourself even presentable. One . . . etc. Freeze. (Again talks quickly with a few children.)

And here's the third idea. You are someone attending the ball, and there are so many marvelous things to do and see. Think about who you are. I wonder what you will do. One . . . etc.

The leader listens appreciatively to a child's pantomime idea.

In listening to the ideas, the leader encourages and appreciates without making judgments. For example, one might say simply, "That's interesting," "Yes," or "I see." Or one may respond nonverbally with a smile and a nod.

For some children, however, it may be important to convey an even higher degree of interest and enthusiasm in order to encourage their further efforts. The leader's response should be genuine and not a forced one, or the children will see through it and perhaps feel as if they have been exploited.

After hearing children's answers, the leader may share some of the ideas with the entire group, making certain not to identify children with their responses.

> **T:** Some stepsisters were putting on lipstick getting ready for the ball. Someone was putting on a corset. And one poor man said he couldn't find his false teeth, and didn't know if he would be able to make it to the ball in time! And another person was crying because her false eyelash kept sticking her in the eye!

When the leader repeats the responses, two goals are accomplished. By stating them aloud, the leader shows acceptance of the ideas. And if there are a variety of responses, the children hear different ideas which they may want to try in repeated playings.

Brainstorm Discussion and Playing

In stimulating creative thinking, another technique is to *brainstorm*. Brainstorming may be done either in discussing or in the playing of the ideas. With brainstorming the children are encouraged to think of as many ideas as they can, as quickly as they can, without anyone evaluating them. The children have a full reservoir of ideas waiting to be tapped; early evaluation can squelch the flow. For example,

> **T:** Now that we've heard Paul Simon's song, "Feelin' Groovy," can you tell us what are some of the things you do when you're feeling groovy?

The children's answers might include eating, sleeping, playing baseball, reading, playing the guitar, baking, and so forth.

If the children have a number of ideas immediately, the leader may dispense with discussion and go to a "brainstorm playing." For example,

> **T:** Let's act out as many of our "feelin' groovy" ideas as we can. Whenever I say, "Now," you change what you're doing and try something else. If you get stuck for an idea, don't worry. Just repeat something you did earlier. . . .

A second step in brainstorming is selecting one idea and developing it in more detail. In a replaying, children can select their best idea and play it in depth. For example,

> **T:** Now pick one idea you like to do the most. What if you had a whole day to do just that one thing? . . .

Another type of brainstorm playing can be done by quickly playing a number of different ideas. Here are some useful ideas from magazine ads:

There are 84 Things You Should Do Before the Movers Arrive . . .
How to Stay Young . . .
The Great Experiment . . .
The Best Minute of the Day . . .
They Said It Couldn't Be Done . . .
Introducing—the Most Famous Person in the World . . .
Around the World—in 80 Minutes . . .
We'll Give You 60 Minutes to Catch up on all your Paperwork . . .

These ideas are best played quickly, with discussion saved until several have been tried. The activity is good for a physical warmup and to jog the mind for ideas. Again, to follow through with the idea of brainstorming, the children's best or favorite idea could be elaborated on in a replaying.

Side-coaching

Whenever the leader encourages the children to create their own ideas, he or she should be prepared to side-coach. In side-coaching, the leader reminds the children of the different ideas they mentioned in discussion, notes the ideas played by the more confident children, or suggests additional ideas. The wording of the side-coaching, however, should be tentative, since the leader is often making guesses about what is happening. Also, the leader will not want to impose ideas on the group.

> **T:** I can see you have a lot of ideas for saving energy. It looks as if some people are putting insulation in the attic. . . . Hmmm, I wonder if someone bought a wood-burning stove? I think I see someone busily chopping wood, . . . I wonder if anyone has thought about putting up storm windows?

The amount of side-coaching the leader gives will depend on how much help with ideas the children need. Generally the children who have their own ideas will not be distracted by the teacher's side-coaching. The children who need help are the ones who listen to it.

Musical Side-coaching

The playing of recorded music while the children are pantomiming performs many of the same kinds of functions as the leader's verbal side-coaching. It also makes movement seem more logical. The leader will probably find side-coaching much easier to do with musical accompaniment.

For this reason, many creative pantomimes are based on musical selections which readily stimulate movement ideas. The leader can play a small segment of a particular piece and then say, "Let's suppose someone or something is moving about in a certain way. Who or what is this person or thing, and what is it doing?" If appropriate, the leader might also ask, "How does the person or thing feel about what it's doing?"

Then the children can try out their movement ideas. If they are to work in pairs or small groups, they will need to briefly talk about their ideas before playing.

There are many helpful musical selections which can be used for this activity; however, it is best not to give their titles to the children or it may limit their thinking. Classical selections might include Moussorgsky's *Pictures at an Exhibition* ("Ballet of the Unhatched Chicks," "Catacombs," or "Gnomes") or Saint Saens's *The Carnival of the Animals* ("Aquarium," "Elephants," or "Fossils"). More modern selections might include the music of Herb Alpert ("Tijuana Taxi," "Whipped Cream," or "Mexican Corn") or the compositions of Leroy Anderson ("The Typewriter Song," "The Syncopated Clock," or "Jazz Pizzicato").

CONTROL AND ORGANIZATION
IN CREATIVE WORK

In initial work, the beginning and ending of the activities usually must be carefully defined. The signals can simply be "Begin" and "Freeze." Or if music is used, the leader may say, "When the record begins, you may move. When the music stops, you stop."

The leader may be more inventive with the signals. Often the material itself can provide the idea. In the earlier example of the "Gingerbread Boy" (p. 110), the leader pretended to be the old woman in the story and gave the signal, "When I open the oven door . . ." For the musical pantomime "Danse Macabre," (p. 112) the leader may say, "When the lights go off, it will be midnight, and the skeletons will rise up and perform their dance. When the lights come on again, it will be the approach of dawn, when you must return to your resting place once again."

If the leader wants the children to time their own length of playing, they may be instructed to freeze when they have finished and wait quietly until all the other players have finished. To help sustain everyone's involvement and thinking, the leader may ask those who have finished to close their eyes or be seated. This also helps the teacher assess the number who are still playing.

Mechanical Movement

Another technique for control is to use *mechanical movement*. It is orderly, predictable, and organized. The leader can be the operator of the machines and can control the beginning and ending of the activity with an "on" and "off" switch.

For individual playing, the children may be robots with the leader as the inventor in control of them.

T: Robots, when I sound the buzzer, you will prepare yourselves for your work. First, you will be self-cleaning and self-oiling.
Now, robots, do your work . . .

For group work, the various parts of the machine might be created. For example:

T: The doughnut machine in one of the *Homer Price* stories (94) plays a very important part. If we were to create that doughnut machine, we'd have to understand what different parts it has and how they each work.

The children will probably mention the "part that squeezes out the dough," "the flipper to turn the doughnuts over," "the paddle that keeps pushing the doughnuts along," "the chute they come out of." Usually the parts the children mention are the parts they would like to play.

College students create a machine with their bodies.

Perhaps six children become the machine, and several go through the machine as the doughnuts while appropriate music is played. Then, the entire class may be divided into groups to create their own doughnut machines. On replays they can switch parts.

Imaginary machines can also be invented. The children might have ideas for creating machines that will solve all sorts of problems, from doing their homework to changing personalities.

Additional Ideas

1. Create clocks with characters that move as the hour strikes, or a music-box scene with characters that move as the music plays. What little scene do they enact? Leroy Anderson's "Syncopated Clock" and Frank Mills's "Music Box Dancer" can be the accompaniment.
2. Be robots going on a picnic or other activity. Perhaps rain causes them to rust into position for the ending.
3. Create a mechanical circus with Aaron Copeland's "Circus Music" from *The Red Pony*.

Setting the Picture in Motion

Another orderly, structured format might be to create a picture that comes to life and then returns to a still picture once again. For example:

T: When the music begins, your idea of "slithy toves" will come to life and "gyre and gimble in the wabe." When the music stops, the still picture of the Jabberwocky's (4) home will return.

T: In this short poem, "The Shopgirls" (30), the idea is presented that when the shopgirls leave the stores and the working day is over, certain things in the store come to life. What might some of these things be and how do they move? What position might they freeze into at daybreak?

T: This picture shows five people in a crucial moment. There seems to have been an accident of some sort. In your groups decide how the situation might have begun and what events led up to this moment. Think of another still picture to begin with; then you'll act out the moments leading up to this picture and freeze.

Another way to set a picture in motion in a dramatic way is to do it in sequence. Each child in the group is assigned a number. After they have all decided what part they are to play and what they are to do, they all take their places and freeze into position. Then the leader calls out "one" and all the ones begin moving. The leader calls "two" and all the twos move along with the ones. When everyone is moving, the action is reversed until everyone has stopped moving and is frozen again.

This organization may be used for various subjects. For example, the children are studying early railroad-building in the United States. The leader divides the children into groups of five. In each group there will be those who lay the ties or "sleepers," "shakers" who hold the spikes, those who hammer, those who carry the water, and one supervisor. The teacher assigns numbers for each role, and as the numbers are called, the children perform their action.

A variation of this idea might be to create "pictures" of railroad life: a group of people scouting new territory, a "gandy dancer's" ball, and so on. The leader may think of other topics for this orderly structure.

LEADER PARTICIPATION

The leader's playing a character role continues to be a useful device for organizing and guiding drama activities.

In the following example, the leader plays the part of a chief, and continues that role in the discussion that follows. Notice also how the mood of the moment is built.

T: We've learned that a guardian spirit, a "Wyakin,"[1] was very important to a number of Indian tribes. It was important to have a supernatural force that had power to protect. For the Nez Perce Indian his spirit could appear in a number of shapes, and each shape had a particular meaning. A grizzly meant power. A deer brought speed. We're going to imagine that you are all Indian youths involved in the sacred search for your Wyakin. Listen to my questions; think about them.

If you were an Indian youth, where would you go for your sacred experience? It will be important to note what's around you, for something in that environment may be your guardian spirit.

The Nez Perce's custom was to build a pile of stones and wait for the sign. What will you do to prepare for your spirit? What will you do as you wait for the spirit to appear? What thoughts and feelings might go through your mind as you wait? In what form will your Wyakin appear? What power will it bring?

When you have thought about these questions and have some idea in your mind, come over here and we'll sit on the floor in a circle. (The children arrange themselves.) I'm not certain what ritual preceded the young Indian's vigil search, but let's imagine that it is time for you to begin your search. I'll pretend to be the Indian chief giving you your final instructions.

(The teacher stands, walks slowly around the circle, softly and rhythmically clicking two hard sticks together, then sits.) My children, your moment has come when you must seek your guardian spirits. Go search for the place where your spirit will come to you. Prepare for it. Follow the customs, keep your vigil. You will know when the Wyakin appears. . . . When it does, return home and speak to me of your spirit. (The children leave the circle, all at their own pace, prepare for and discover their Wyakin, return, and describe the Wyakin to the "chief.")

CREATING FIGHTS AND BATTLES

Fights and battles are of extreme interest to many children, but such activities need a special word. Since they involve exciting action and physical contact, it would be foolhardy to let a group of children enact a fight scene without some

[1] Adrien Stoutenberg, *People in Twilight: Vanishing & Changing Cultures* (New York: Doubleday, 1971).

previous preparation. The leader should show the children how to "stage" fights as, in fact, they are handled in movies, in the theatre, and on TV.

Children are usually intrigued and impressed with the fact that the "realistic" fights they see in dramas are really artful pretense. They like to learn, the way actors and stunt people do, how to throw a punch without making actual physical contact with the partner. They like the challenge of pretending to receive a blow in a convincing manner.

For the first step in staging, the children should probably work alone, imagining their foe. They must practice and perfect their skill in stopping the blow at the precise moment before contact. The point of contact they aim at may be imagined. Or the children may aim at a wall, their desk, or the palm of one hand.

Next, they pretend to receive the blow. Again, the foe could be imagined. It is a good idea to direct the punches by counting or beating on a drum. The teacher may say, "You will hit (or be hit) three times. Ready? One... two ... three." The teacher may want to say *where* the hits will be. "The first will make contact on the left shoulder, the second in the stomach, and the third on the chin."

The teacher may be the imagined foe and respond to the punches or pretend to throw them.

(Receiving)   "Ya got me there.... Ooh!... Ugghh! Whew! I've had enough!"

(Giving)   "Take that!... And that... Zingo! That'll teach ya, ya ornery varmint!"

When the leader is assured that the children do understand the staging of fights, they may work in pairs. They must decide who throws punches and who receives them. It would probably be wise to limit them to five blows for the first time. Again, the leader can control it by counting or drumming the beats as above. The leader should go slowly with the counting, quickly assessing what is happening before proceeding further. The speed is increased only when the children exhibit skill and sensitivity to each other. If any children find it too difficult to control themselves in pairs, they may need to work solo for a while longer. If problems occur, the activity must be stopped immediately.

Further help is given when the leader reinforces the challenge of skilled, artful pretense.

T: All of you could actually hit someone, but it will take skill and concentration to come close and *not* touch.

When the children have shown real skill and care in their work, they may want to try some scenes of fights and combat from different materials: social studies, science, or literature. The fights may be between people or animals. Along with these dramas might be valuable discussions on historic weapons or animal armor. For example:

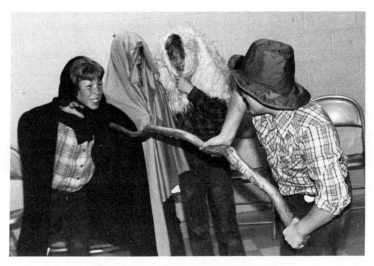

Fight scenes require careful rehearsing.

T: Now that we've read the Robin Hood episode with the miller (35), let's divide into groups of five and pretend to be the miller, Robin, and some of his men. We'll just do the part beginning with the miller opening his bag as he pretends to search for the money, continuing with the blows he gives the flour-covered men, and ending the scene when Robin gives three blasts on his horn. I'll give those blasts. Get into your groups now and plan who will play what part, and how Robin and his men react when the joke they have planned backfires. Also, you need to plan who will get hit first, second, and so on.

A lively instrumental tune played during this episode of a would-be joke can help keep the brawl lighthearted.

Example from "Foul Shot"

When the leader becomes more experienced, creative pantomimes can evolve from the efforts of the leader and the group together. As the leader assesses the group's response to a given activity, it is possible to build and improvise on the idea as sudden insights appear.

The following is a description of two one-hour periods with a class of fifth-graders. It was the first time the majority of the children had experienced creative drama and the first time the children and the teacher had worked together. The leader began with a narrated poem, and by the end of the second hour, the children had progressed to creative activities involving group planning.

The leader began by reading the poem, "Foul Shot," by Edwin A. Hoey:[2]

[2] Special permission granted by *Read Magazine,* published by Xerox Education Publications, © 1962, Xerox Corp.

With two 60's stuck on the scoreboard
And two seconds hanging on the clock
The solemn boy in the center of eyes,
Squeezed by silence,
Seeks out the line with his feet,
Soothes his hands along his uniform,
Gently drums the ball against the floor,
Then measures the waiting net,
Raises the ball on his right hand,
Balances it with his left,
Calms it with fingertips,
Breathes,
Crouches,
Waits,
And then through a stretching of stillness,
Nudges it upward.
The ball
Slides up and out,
Lands,
Leans,
Wobbles,
Wavers,
Hesitates,
Exasperates,
Plays it coy
Until every face begs with unsounding screams –
And then
     And then
          And then,
Right before ROAR-UP,
Dives down and through.

After a brief discussion of the poem to make sure the children understood it, the leader narrated and the children pretended to be the player. On the second playing, they became the player and then the basketball. This second playing was done in slow motion to focus on the intensity of the moment. When someone suggested that the crowd should cheer at the end, the leader suggested a silent, slow-motion scream to fit the pantomine. A third playing of the poem then took place.

During these repeated playings the leader worked for involvement by the use of her voice, particularly timing, when she read the poem; positive feedback on what she had observed the children pantomiming; and the children's self-evaluation of their involvement in the material.

Because of their response, the leader suggested that the children might like to expand the poem even further and asked them to invent the other players. Where were these players while the foul shot was being thrown? What was their attitude about the shot? Then the leader divided the class into groups. Each group was to decide who would be the player making the shot, who would be on his or her team, who would be on the opposing team. The children suggested having a referee who would hand the imaginary ball to the player and blow a "whistle." Desks were rearranged to give more space for the basketball teams. After the groups were organized, the leader again narrated the poem while the children enacted their ideas.

When the children returned for a second drama session, they were still talking about the "basketball poem." Although the leader had another lesson planned, she asked if they had any additional ideas about how they might like to play the poem. They thought they'd like to add the spectators. The leader and the children together discussed such questions as: What kinds of people would attend that basketball game? While the game is going on, what would they do besides sit and watch? The children were given some time to do any group planning and organizing they needed.

After this planning time, the leader gave each group of five a number. When the leader called a group's number, members of that group were to pretend they were spectators. They could talk, use the classroom space they needed, and do anything they felt was appropriate for their characters. All the other groups were to freeze and watch. The leader called the numbers randomly and varied the time each group performed its activities.

The final experience based on "Foul Shot" was initiated by the children. The groups decided that they wanted to do the half-time entertainment for the game. The leader gave them time again to plan and rehearse. When all the groups were ready, they shared their ideas with the rest of the class. There were tumblers, trampoline artists, a Scout drill team, and a marching band.

FOR THE COLLEGE STUDENT

1. Select several stories on which creative pantomimes could be based. Design a creative pantomime on one story you find particularly interesting. Remember to consider individual, pair, and group playing.

2. Make a list of ten popular and classical records that could be used to stimulate creative pantomimes. From this list, choose five and briefly describe the pantomimes the music could stimulate. Lead your classmates in a creative pantomime activity based on one of your selected records.

3. Make a list of poetry especially suitable for stimulating creative pantomimes. Design a creative pantomime activity on one of these poems.

4. Keep a file of your original ideas for creative pantomimes.

5. Practice giving encouragement during creative pantomimes. Select a story and

design three creative pantomimes. Lead your classmates in these three pantomimes. Discuss with your classmates the positive techniques you used and their effectiveness.

6. Design a creative pantomime using the brainstorming technique. Lead your classmates in this activity. After the experience, guide them to select their best ideas, and in a replay, encourage them to explore those ideas more fully.

7. Design a creative pantomime activity using the "Mechanical Movement" or "Setting the Picture in Motion" format. Base the activity on a curricular topic. Specify the signals for beginning and ending the activity.

8. Design a creative pantomime in which you will play a role to stimulate the children's involvement. Select a curricular topic and a topic based on literature.

9. Outline a plan for staging a fight or battle scene. These may be from literature or they may be based on historical events or science (for example, animals and insects).

Chapter Seven

Creative
Story-Building

Many children are capable of creating stories on their own that they can enact with little assistance from the leader. Other children, however, are dependent on the leader to give them an idea to work with and guidance through plot outline. In this chapter we will discuss some ways the leader can guide children to create and play dramatic stories on their own.

When children create their own dramatic stories, the challenge is greater and they have the chance to express themselves in more diverse ways than in the previous activities. While the leader still presents an idea or a topic as a stimulus, the children have a great deal of freedom within that framework to develop a plot that is meaningful and satisfying to them. As they work with conflict and resolution in their stories, they often experience problem solving.

Although the stories are action based and expressed in pantomime, the leader frequently continues the playing by stimulating verbalizing in a character role. These dialogue experiences clarify and develop the children's stories further, as well as laying a foundation for more comprehensive verbal work later.

Overview

For this activity the leader first finds an intriguing idea. Then a carefully worded plan of discussion questions is developed to guide the children in creating their story ideas. The children prepare their ideas individually, in pairs, or in groups. Then the ideas are played simultaneously, with the leader side-coaching, if needed. For follow-up, the leader can extend the experiences by playing a character appropriate to the topic and questioning the children about their adventure.

The following is an example of how one teacher guided a class of second-graders through a creative pantomime story based on Mary Norton's book *The Borrowers* (62).

The children were not familiar with the book, so the teacher told them briefly about the tiny people who live under the floorboards of the house and who search around the house for things to use in their own miniature world. The book's illustrations were shown so that the children could see a number of ordinary objects such as postage stamps, thimbles, and pins being used in unique ways.

Each child was to pretend to be a Borrower who would go searching for new objects to use in redecorating his or her own little house. To stimulate ideas about what could be used, the teacher brought three objects to class to discuss: a small gold pillbox, a fancy beaded ballpoint pen, and a small decorative mirror. What might they be used for? Where would the little Borrowers find them? How could they get these objects down from tables or out of drawers left ajar? Since the children were to be tiny people working in a giant world, what equipment might they need in order to get and transport the objects back to their home under the floorboards?

The children discussed using string and safety pins to hook various objects and pull them to where they were needed. They also thought of the possibility of hooking the pin in a drape and climbing up the string. The pillbox they thought of using for a baby bed, the pen could be used for a decorative column, and the mirror, they thought, would make a neat skating rink.

The leader also focused on the problems the Borrowers might meet. The children commented on the problems posed by household pets, the dangers of getting too near a bathtub filled with water, and the difficulty of walking on shag carpeting.

The discussion of all these ideas took about twenty minues. The first playing was done individually, and the children were allowed to find their own space to work in. The lights were dimmed to indicate nighttime—the working day for Borrowers.

The children settled in their working spaces and were to pretend that they were listening to be sure when all the household had retired. Their cue to begin playing their story would be the ''clock'' striking one o'clock. For this signal, the leader hit a stick on a metal platter. The children knew they had to be as silent in their work as possible since discovery by the homeowners would mean great trouble for them.

With the accompaniment of the somewhat mysterious ''Arabian Dance'' from Tchaikovsky's *Nutcracker Suite,* the children began their borrowing. The leader side-coached their playing.

As the musical selection neared completion, the second signal of six bongs for six o'clock was given. The children were reminded they would have to return home again quickly since the household awakened at that hour. While the clock was striking, the children hurried to finish their story and made their way home. Then, because they had worked so hard all night long, the leader side-coached by saying, ''You fall exhausted into bed,'' as the music faded out and the lights were turned on again. After telling their experiences, the children were given a few moments to plan a second borrowing episode with a partner.

After the drama experience, the leader chose to have the children write a story and draw a picture about it. The following is a written account of one child's experience:

My partner, Don, and I pretended to be borrowers. We waited until 1:00 A.M. *We crawled through a tunnel. We met face to face with a cat that cut me two times and rolled over on Don. The clock started to ring 6:00* A.M., *and we heard someone getting up. So we got out of there! Don forgot to take something back so he tore back, put the things right outside our tunnel, and tore back just as somebody went by our tunnel. (Jim, age 8)*

Now let's examine each of the steps in the creative story-building in more detail.

CHOOSING AN IDEA

The topics for these creative stories, whether fact or fiction, can come from a number of sources. And because they are to be pantomimed, the topic should have a heavy emphasis on movement. Ideas can come from literature.

T: The little boy in *Harold and the Purple Crayon* has such interesting adventures with his magic crayon. Let's pretend that you have a crayon like his and you're going to draw an adventure you'd like to have. . . .

They can come from social studies.

"In a creative story, I make up and act out my own ideas."
(Photo courtesy of Jon Vander Meer.)

> **T:** Imagine that you are members of a conservation crew working with wildlife in Africa. It's your job to catch the wild animals and tag them so you can learn more about them. . . .

You can get ideas from science.

> **T:** As the world-famous team of Dr. Pinna and Dr. Lobe, the ear experts, you will need to use your secret invention to make yourself small enough to travel in your patient's ear in order to find the source of the problem. . . .

Or you can use music, a picture, or a prop.

> **T:** Listen to this electronic music from *The In Sound From Way Out!** If you were to make up a story about this music, what would it be? Who's in the story? What's happening? . . .

The sources of ideas are limitless and restricted only by the leader's imagination.

Topics with Built-In Control

It might be wise, particularly for first attempts, for the leader to select topics with built-in control. For example, children are usually more motivated to play quietly if they are secret agents doing undercover work, museum statues which come to life when all is dim and quiet, or elves secretly doing good deeds or slyly making mischief.

DISCUSSION

Discussion questions essentially focus on character, environment, plan of action, conflict, and resolution. In other words, the children need to plan who they are, what they are going to do, what problems they might have, how they will solve them, and how the story will end. However, the specific wording of these questions will depend on the topic and on the leader's objectives in using the material.

With individual playing the children plan their ideas in a large group discussion. With pair and group stories, obviously, the children will have to discuss their ideas together. It is also possible for many ideas to be played individually first and then as pair and group work in replayings.

Discussion Outline

The discussion format usually involves five questions. Generally the first question introduces the topic; the second and third build the adventure; by the fourth question, conflict is introduced; and with the fifth question, the story is brought to a close.

* Recorded by Perrey-Kingsley, Vanguard Recordings for the Connoisseur.

The following are three examples of discussion outlines:

INDIVIDUAL PLAYING

T: Now that we've read *Harold and the Purple Crayon* (p. 65), it might be fun to go on our own magical adventure. Let's suppose you have a crayon like Harold's that will draw anything you want.

    a.   Where would you like to go on your adventure?

    b.   How will you get there? Do you need to take any supplies with you?

    c.   What are some of the things you'd like to see and do? What unusual things might happen to you?

    d.   Harold's trips are not without some problems. What kinds of problems could happen to you on this adventure?

    e.   But with a magical crayon Harold usually figures a way out of any problems and gets back home safely. How do you think you could solve your problems and how will you return home?

PAIRS

T: It's Halloween. You and a friend have decided to visit a haunted house. At least, you think it's haunted.

    a.   What might be some of your reasons for going?

    b.   You're going at night and it's a bit chilly. What things will you need to take with you? What route will you take?

    c.   How will you go about investigating the house? What are some things you want to check? What do you think you might find?

    d.   What problems might you run into in a haunted house? At least there will be the two of you to face them together—maybe you'll even be able to help each other out. What do you think could happen?

    e.   Anyone who visits a haunted house is probably confident enough to survive anything. Let's suppose your venture turns out all right. Bring back a souvenir, though, to prove you were really there. We'll find out what your souvenir is after you return.

SMALL GROUPS

T: Let's suppose that it's 1773 in Boston and you are the group of people called The Sons of Liberty, who object to the high tax on tea. You disguise yourselves as Indians, board a tea freighter at night, and throw the tea overboard.

    a.   Now, what are your plans for disguising and arming yourself for tonight? Your disguise should be good enough to fool the British.

    b.   Next you need to plan your strategy for getting down to the harbor and out onto the ship without being spotted. How will you do that?

    c.   Once you get to the harbor and get on board the ship, how will you take it over and get to the tea? How will you take care of the crew?

    d.   It's always good to be prepared for problems. What sort of problems do you anticipate, and how will you solve them?

    e.   After the mission is completed, you'd better lay low—maybe even go into hiding. How will you do that?

Wording the Questions

There are several points to remember in asking questions:

1. Try not to ask more than five questions or the discussion may last too long. You might telescope several short or related questions into one longer question.
2. Be sure the questions follow the story line format. There must be a beginning, middle, and end to the stories, with a conflict and resolution.
3. The questions should help the children think of *action* they are to pantomime. Avoid situations where characters interact, particularly with dialogue, or the children may have nothing to pantomime.
4. Keep the questions moving in chronological order. Once you have progressed along a story line, you usually can't go backwards in time.
5. Ask questions that are open-ended. Avoid questions that the children can answer with "yes" or "no." Such questions build a minimal story line. Open-ended questions encourage embellishment of ideas.
6. Ask questions in the most intriguing way possible. Ideally, each question should be so fascinating that the children bubble over with ideas. Some hints to consider:
   a. Give the children importance. A discussion might open, for example, with the leader saying that Paul Bunyan has the flu and has called on them for help feeding the hungry lumberjack camp. Children might become expert goblin catchers, called upon by the person in the poem "The Goblin" (3) to rid his home of this noisy creature. Or, the President might send them on an important mission back into history to discover needed answers to pressing problems.
   b. Add tension to the questions to build interest. The zookeepers in Palmer Brown's poem "The Spangled Pandemonium," (4) for example, might be in danger of losing their jobs if they can't find this unique animal who has escaped from its cage. Or, those who go on adventures with the Half-Pint Jinni (88) must always be sure to double their wishes since he can grant only half ones.
7. The questions should be worded in the future tense since the children are planning what they will be playing after the discussion is ended.
8. It is helpful to word the questions tentatively so the children can change their story as they hear more ideas discussed. "What *do you suppose* you'll do next?" for example, leaves the way open for flexibility.

Discussion should continue only as long as it motivates and helps the children formulate their ideas. Some groups enjoy discussion immensely, while others prefer to proceed to the playing as soon as possible.

What is most exciting about the discussion is the evolving of numerous ideas, the cross-fertilization of thinking, and the expanding and elaborating of ideas. During discussions children may hear ideas they particularly enjoy; some they may like even better than their own. They may decide to put several ideas together in their stories—their own ideas as well as those of others. Discussions are most valuable when they encourage this kind of creative process.

Discussions are as useful to the leader as they are to the children. They help forecast the ideas the leader can expect to see. With this information, the leader can better organize the playing. For example, some children may comment on possibilities for fierce combat in their adventure. The leader may then decide to preview the fight scenes or to control space so that the ideas can be played safely and successfully.

Discussions also help the leader recognize what is happening in the playing. Because a child mentions in discussion that her balloon ship will develop a leak, the leader can more readily understand why the child is swirling and sinking during the playing. The leader also knows what to use for questions and feedback in the discussion afterward.

Some very creative children will have ideas on almost any topic posed. As soon as the leader asks the first question, there may be a buzz of excitement from them and an energetic waving of hands. One may then limit the length of the discussion by telescoping the questions and announcing them for private consideration.

> **T:** If you have your ideas about what you will be investigating on the moon's surface, what kind of equipment you have, the problems you will encounter, and how your trip begins and ends, raise your hand. It looks like we're ready to go ahead without discussing it.

Particularly when children are excited about their own ideas, it may be more important to let them play them rather than waiting to listen to the ideas of other children. Some children are more interested in talking about their ideas *after* they have played them.

PLAYING

Preview Playing

As a helpful measure, the leader may want to have the children *preview* a part of their ideas before playing the entire drama. For example, how will you get into your armor before going off on your adventure as a knight? Or before a story drama is created on sky diving, for instance, the leader may want the children to check out the procedures and maneuvers a diver goes through in order to have a safe fall. The children might practice the "stable" fall with both arms and legs apart. Such maneuvers must be understood so that they become automatic for the sky diver. Practicing before enacting the story thus simulates actual conditions.

Signals to Begin and End Playing

The length of playing time for these dramas can vary. Initially the children may be able to create only short stories; gradually they may be able to increase their playing time to several minutes.

Even though the children have thought about their own beginnings and endings for the stories, it may still be necessary for the leader to give signals for both. This is particularly important for first playings or for groups who have trouble sustaining involvement. Whenever the leader observes that the involvement is decreasing, a signal to end may be given.

When the children have had some experience, the leader will want to let them finish their stories at their own pace. The advantage of this is that not all children will have the same involvement in or as many details to their stories as others. Those who finish early can simply be instructed to sit and wait quietly until everyone is finished.

It will add more to the mood if the leader is descriptive and gives the signals in imaginative ways.

> **T:** When you hear the clanging of pots, you'll know the cook's signaling you cowboys for the new day of driving cattle on the open range. You'll know the day is ending when you hear the soft strums of the guitar by the campfire.

SIDE-COACHING

As before, music will play an important part in encouraging the children's ideas and provide a background for their dramas. Therefore, it must be carefully selected beforehand.

Verbal side-coaching* for a creative story should essentially remind the children of the various stages of their plot: the beginning, the action, and the problems they may be encountering and the ways they may be solving them. It is important not to be too specific in side-coaching since the children's ideas are all different and they are probably not all moving through the various stages of the story at the same speed. The wording of the side-coaching, therefore, must be somewhat tentative. Note this in the italicized words in the following example:

> **T:** It *appears as if* this is really going to be an exciting adventure. I can feel it in the air. *Some* people have already left on their mission and *others* are in the final preparations. . . . I *hope* everyone will be able to accomplish the goal they've set for themselves. . . . *Some* people *seem* to have run into a problem . . .

It is crucial not to interject any sort of new idea in the side-coaching. The leader may remind the children of ideas that were expressed in the discussion, but it will only confuse the playing to add ideas such as, "Look out for that shark!" or "Suddenly you discover gold!" Such statements will turn the playing into a narrative pantomime rather than the children's own creative story.

LEADER ROLE FOR DIALOGUE

In creative drama it is important for the teacher to be able to stimulate dialogue. One of the first ways that this can happen is for the leader to create a role to play and then interact with the children in this role, commenting and asking questions to stimulate thinking and talking.

---

* Verbal side-coaching will probably be needed more for individual playing than for pair and group playing. When children interact with each other, even in pantomime, they rely more on each other than on the leader for assistance.

In-service teachers enact a solo adventure about diamond mining.

The character role may be set up at the beginning of the playing, if desired. In the following example, note how the mood is set, the conflict is enhanced, and the signals for playing are all given with the leader's opening remarks before the children begin their acting.

A.

The adventure is based on Miles Standish and a party making the first trip to the shore of their new land. The children are divided into several small exploring groups. The leader has chosen the role of one of the pilgrim fathers who stays behind on the *Mayflower*.

T: Goodman Standish and friends, be at rest about those of us who would remain on board ship. We will be safe. But, good brothers, be vigilant. The shore looks peaceful, but dangers would lurk. Do not tarry.

B.

The children are creating dramas about child labor in the dangerous and unhealthy factories of the 1900s. The class has decided that everyone's story would begin during the early morning hours at the factory. The leader plays the role of a supervisor.

T: All right, you ragamuffins, get to work! And make no mistakes! There'll be no pay for the sloppy and lazy. Get started, and be quick about it!

C.

In the Spangled Pandemonium adventure mentioned earlier, the leader might be the mayor of the town who is concerned for everyone's safety. ,

T: As the mayor of this town, I want you to know we're all counting on you. Our fair city has never had a problem like this before. I'll be in my office waiting to hear from you when this adventure is over. Be careful, and good luck!

Side-coaching in a Character Role

Although it is always possible to side-coach in a quietly objective voice that is the leader's own, it may be particularly appropriate to side-coach in a character role, as in the following example. The children are creating story dramas about race-car driving. They are in groups that include the drivers and crews. The leader lends an air of excitement and authenticity in the role of the official announcer.

> **T:** It's a great day for the races, all you fans out there! The cars are lined up for the beginning of this day-long race. The excitement here is great—the atmosphere is tense. The engines are roaring, and the race is about to begin. At the wave of the flag, each team is on its own. Good luck! . . . And they're off! What will be the outcome of this race is anybody's guess. . . .

Other techniques for side-coaching in character are also possible. The pilgrim father mentioned in example A, for instance, might write in his diary and say the comments aloud.

> **T:** On this day we have made the momentous decision to explore this new land. We know not what dangers lie ahead. . . . Several of our people have been sent out to explore and we can only hope and pray that all will be well with them. . . .

Follow-Up in a Character Role

Even if the leader does not choose to play a character role early on in the creative story, one should not miss the opportunity to extend the story in a verbal interaction in a character role afterward.

As the leader becomes more experienced, it will probably be easy to improvise comments and questions as one is stimulated by and reacting to the children's responses. However, it is always helpful—and crucial for the beginning leader—to plan some of the questions beforehand.

Again, it is useful to think of the wording and tone of voice for the character. For example, how would one speak if one were playing the role of a salty sea captain? And while it isn't necessary to dress up or use actual props for playing a character, there might be some references to costume or props. For example, what commentary and questions could the sea captain build around a sword, a treasure chest, or a parrot?

The questions are most stimulating and challenging if they extend the story and build on the children's earlier ideas. Note the following example:

> The creative story has been based on Mary Ann Hoberman's poem, "The People of Backward Town" (28). The children's stories have centered on a day in the life of one of these people who "take their walks across the ceiling," and who "only eat the apple peeling," among other unusual behaviors. The leader plans to play the role of a visitor to the land, and the questions which have been planned are:
>
> "I'm afraid I'll have a problem during my visit, and I always like to be prepared. What are some things I should be especially careful about?" (The leader is prepared for the fact that some children may give their responses in backward sentences.)

"I understand you've had a recent campaign to find a slogan for your town. What were some of the suggested slogans?"

"Say, here's a sign I just found over there. I can't read it, and I wonder what it's for. Can anyone tell me? (The sign could spell DANGER backwards and perhaps could be held upside down. The children have to read it and then explain its importance.)

"I have a gift here (hold imaginary box) from the mayor of my town to the mayor of yours. Where's the mayor? (Someone will probably volunteer.) I don't know what it is, Your Honor, so I guess you'll have to open it to find out. I hope it's something you can use. (The child opens the gift and tells what it is. If this proves popular, there can be more gifts and more mayors—or council members.)

"I'd like to take back some photos of your town to show my friends and neighbors. Have we got some people who wouldn't mind having their picture taken? I like action shots, so you'll need to be doing something. Who'd like to be first?" (Can do in groups to go more quickly.)

It is particularly important in the questioning to introduce new ideas or problems to be solved. One might also ask for opinions, evaluations, descriptions, or other similar categories of creative thought. Such questions stretch the children's imaginations and thought processes beyond just simple conversational questions.

The following are examples of questions from a variety of topics:

a. Reporter talking to the survivor of a plane crash: "The rescue team said they had no trouble finding you. You were a big help to them. What exactly was it that you did to help them find you?"

b. Head elf to apprentice elves who have done good deeds: "I have to write your good deed down in this record book and then evaluate its importance on a scale of one to five, with five being the highest. What was your deed and how important would you say it was?" (Can be negotiated.)

c. Government official to secret agent: "There's one expenditure here in your report that I can't quite figure out. It's listed as 'miscellaneous,' but the amount you've given is $1,035.74. You'll have to justify that."

d. Dr. Timepiece talking to children who have just gone through a time machine to another period of history: "I'm trying to perfect my machine. What improvements would you suggest?"

e. Wizard whose lost wand the children have found: "You deserve a reward for your efforts. What would you like—within the power of my wand—to have as your prize?"

f. Royal monarch to early discoverer: "This is the map we have of the country you have just explored. In what ways should it be changed?"

Highly Verbal Children

Generally it's best to ask the questions to the group as a whole and then call on volunteers. When the children are highly verbal, the leader will have to move quickly from child to child to give many a chance to speak. Another alternative is to have one, two, or even three children join as questioners along with the leader. It may be appropriate to give these children other character roles; sometimes they will suggest characters themselves. In the Backward Town adventure, for example, the children could be the potential visitors and the leader could then become a travel agent introducing them around.

If the majority of the class is highly verbal, the leader might proceed with other dialogue ideas, dividing the class into pairs and groups. These will be discussed further in Chapter Ten.

Reticent Children

When the creative story idea has been an intriguing one and the follow-up questions are particularly captivating, even the shyest child will want to become involved. But it is a good idea to be prepared with easier questions that can be answered "yes" or "no" for children who find it difficult to talk up in the classroom. Even nodding or shaking the head in answer to a question can be a big undertaking for some.

As another precaution, it is sometimes helpful for the leader to have an "out"—a reason one can give for the child who appears ready to speak and then freezes at the last minute. For example, a reporter might say to an inventor, "I can understand your not wanting to talk to me; this invention of yours could be top secret stuff."

REPLAYING

Once the children have tried a creative story idea they like, they may ask to play it again. Some children may want to incorporate ideas they have heard from others. They may want to work with a partner or in small groups. And they may have their own ideas for changing the format outline. Before replaying, the leader should encourage the children to evaluate their previous playing, perhaps asking what they would like to repeat in the second playing or what they would like to change.

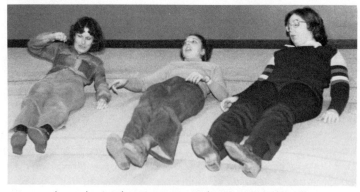

In-service teachers try a group adventure as astronauts.

If sharing of ideas is desired, it is best to have several children playing at a time. Even with small groups, two or three can play at once. This minimizes the idea of performance and its disadvantages.

Verbalizing

Sometimes in the small-group stories, children will see verbalizing possibilities. Naturally, when the groups play simultaneously, this verbalizing must be held to a minimum.

When small groups share their ideas, however, and ask to include dialogue, they should be allowed to do so. Of course, only one group at a time will be able to share.

Children who desire to verbalize in these stories are probably ready for the challenge of dialogue work which will be covered further in Chapters Nine and Ten.

FOR THE COLLEGE STUDENT

1. Outline lesson plans for two separate creative pantomime stories. One is to be based on fiction or fantasy; the other on fact. One should be for individual playing; the other for pair or group.

a. Introduction

Write out the exact words you will use to introduce the material and the idea to the children. Or if the children have already studied the material, outline the information covered previously.

b. Discussion

Form five carefully worded discussion questions to help the children get a story line for their ideas. For each question, give three possible answers (speculative on your part) which three children might give you. When you have finished this section, check the five answers you have received from each child and see if each child has a completed story outline. If not, examine the questions again for possible problems.

c. Organization of Playing

Indicate whether any and what kind of preview playing is necessary.

Give the directions (use exact wording) for the children to get organized for playing. Also give exact wording of directions for beginning and ending the playing. Specify if you are in a character role.

d. Side-coaching

Write out in exact wording five or six side-coaching comments appropriate to the story idea. If you are side-coaching in a role, specify your character.

List music being used.

e. Leader Role

Explain your character for the final discussion.

In words as your character would say them, write out five open-ended questions appropriate to the story and your character that you could ask.

Explain how you would encourage other roles for highly verbal children. Include an "out" for the reticent child.

List materials needed for this lesson.

2. Lead your classmates in one of your lesson plans for a creative pantomime story. Discuss afterward the effectiveness of the plan. What were the strengths? How might it be improved?

3. Keep a file of materials that would be appropriate for creative pantomime stories. Be sure to include both fictional and factual ideas. In addition to literature and textbook information, you might also want to consider newspaper clippings, pictures, props and costumes, music, slides, and films.

Chapter Eight

Pantomimes for Guessing

In the previous chapters, the methods of playing were designed primarily for private communication. The children played their ideas mainly for their own satisfaction. As often as possible, all the children played in unison so that no audience was created. There were opportunities for voluntarily sharing experiences with each other, but there were no obligations on the part of the children to present their dramatizations to their classmates.

Even though there was no intent earlier for public communication to be the goal, anyone watching the playing would probably have been able to understand what many of the children were doing and "saying." In fact, the leader has been translating nonverbal ideas in side coaching.

T: I see some happy people.
Something very dangerous must be happening to some people.
I can tell by your movements that some of the animals in our zoo are very big and some are very small.

In order to encourage children's abilities to send and receive nonverbal messages, the leader can involve the children in pantomime games. In pantomime,* the players enact ideas while the audience watches and guesses. They base their guesses on the players' actions and facial expressions.

---

* It should be pointed out that pantomime can be a highly skilled art form as practiced by an artist like Marcel Marceau. It is not our aim to have children learn to pantomime in this stylized manner.

An audience must watch carefully for clues.

There are benefits enjoyed from audience situations for both player and observer. The audience gains practice in watching and interpreting as accurately as possible the ideas of others. The player has the opportunity to communicate ideas to an audience. For some children, having their classmates watch what they are doing is an incentive for them to concentrate. Often the player is stimulated and challenged to communicate as clearly as possible and to polish and refine the expression of ideas so that they can be more clearly understood. It is this performer/audience situation that will require some considerations in order to make the learning situation as valuable as possible.

Although it is a common procedure to have one child at a time pantomime an idea in front of an entire class, we prefer to avoid it. It places undue pressure on the performer, which is usually unjustifiable. And if the plan is to have everyone in the class perform a solo pantomime, the audience may become bored and tired before the ordeal is ended. There are a number of other methods we find preferable.

TYPES OF PANTOMIME

Team Pantomime

One kind of pantomime activity, *team pantomime,* is based on a popular children's game called by various names: "New Orleans," "Trades," or "Lemonade." Two teams line up and face each other. Team 1 decides on an occupation to pantomime for Team 2. It walks to a designated line near Team 2 and chants the following:

Team 1: Here we come.
Team 2: Where ya from?
Team 1: New Orleans.
Team 2: What's your trade?
Team 1: Lemonade.
Team 2: Show us if you're not afraid.

Team 1 then pantomimes the trade or occupation it has decided on. Team 2 calls out its guesses, and when the guess is correct, Team 1 must run back to its original place without being tagged by anyone from Team 2, which chases the first group. Tagged members must join the opposite team.

This game can be played acting out topics other than "occupations." The rhyme may also be changed. The topic for the following chant is seasonal activities.

Here we come
Where ya from?
Kalamazoo
Whadda ya do?
Depends on the weather
Well, give us a clue.

The game may also be played by more than one group at a time. The chasing and tagging, of course, are optional.

Sequence Games

Another method is called *sequence game*. For this game, pantomime activities are written or pictured on cards. Since the pantomimes are to be played in sequence, the cue is also on the card. The cards are distributed at random to the children. There should be enough so that each child has at least one card. Or there may be two players to each card. Each player's pantomime has to be interpreted correctly before the next player can participate. Suspense is created in the quiet and careful watching and waiting for one's cue.

The first card might say:

You begin the game. Pretend to mount a Harley-Davidson 750. Rev it up and cruise around the room once. Then sit down in your seat.

Another player will have the card that reads:

Cue: Someone pretends to ride a motorcycle around the room and then sits.
You: Turn off the lights and then go back to your seat and sit.

The next player will have the card:

Cue: Someone turns off the lights. Sits.
You: Stand and clap five times. Then sit.

It is helpful to the children to write the cues in a different color than that used for the directions for the pantomime. For example, the cue may be in red (stop and look) and the pantomime in green (go ahead). Having the children stand to pantomime and then sit down helps also.

The individual pantomimes in the game may be unrelated to each other, as they have been in the above example. Or they may tell a simple story. The following is an example of a modern Eskimo seal hunt.

You: Stand and pretend to put bundles of heavy clothes, sealskin boots, and boxes of food into the umiak in the middle of the circle. Sit.
Cue: Someone pretends to put supplies in the umiak.
You: Go to the center of circle and pretend to step carefully into the umiak. Then sit in the umiak.
Cue: Someone sits carefully in the umiak.
You: Sit down behind the person in the umiak.
Cue: Two people sit in the umiak.
You: Pretend to start the small motor that propels the boat. After a few moments, pretend that the motor catches and then sit down, ready to steer the boat. . .

A sequence game might give practice in learning directions: Fly south; swim east; roll a ball northwest; and the like.

Pictures can also be used in place of words for sequence games. For example, pictures of animals, of people performing various tasks, or of different

"You stand and pretend to be a patriot sneaking on board the ship to
dump the tea."

emotions are all possible. One teacher used pictures of various body parts (head, hand, leg, ear) the children were learning. The children were to move the body part pictured on the lower half of their card after someone performed the cue pictured on the upper half of their card.

Sequence games work particularly well for activities which follow a step-by-step procedure such as performing a task, following a recipe, or tracing the path an object such as a letter takes.

Various ways of using the alphabet are possible with sequence games. An "A" word (perhaps an animal or verb) is followed by a "B" word, and so forth (anteater, bear, cat).

The leader should prepare a master sheet which contains all of the pantomimes in their proper sequence, in case the group gets lost. In order to involve as many children as possible and as frequently as possible, the leader can make three sets of each game and three master sheets and divide the class into thirds for simultaneous playing. A child from each group can follow the master sheet.

Once children are familiar with sequence games, they can either help transcribe the material on cards or even create their own games. One group of sixth graders worked diligently on a sequence game based on the process of preparing an Egyptian mummy, while another created its version of a Spanish bullfight.

Add On Pantomimes

Add Ons are played similarly to the sequence game. As before, one player's nonverbal message must be understood before another player can participate. In this game, however, each child invents a pantomime to fit the topic.

The activity begins with one person pantomiming an idea while the audience tries to guess *silently*. The guesser (checked by the leader) joins the first player and assists. For example, one child may pretend to cook dinner. The second player may decide to set the table, another may make a salad, and so on. The players add on until a specified number, perhaps twelve, is reached.

A variation of this game might be to pretend to be various people at an event, adding on to the scene. Try, for example, the Indianapolis 500 (pit crew, drivers, fans, owners, flagpersons, and so forth).

Older children might like to add on in pairs. For example, the activity might be "cooking breakfast." One player fries the eggs while the partner *becomes* the eggs. Other partners for cooks might be oatmeal, bacon, pancakes, toast, and the like.

Another variation of this method is creating an object, with each pantomimer becoming part of the object. For example, if the object is a clock, one player may become the hands, another might form the face, while another may be the alarm. Other parts might be the second hand, legs, knobs, gears, and springs.

Building a Place

In still another variation of this game, children may create a room or location, equipping it with appropriate furnishings or objects. A space is marked off on the floor, with doors or entryways indicated. The players bring one item at a time into the specified area. The object is to create a complete imaginary environment; therefore, the players must remember where each item is placed so that they do not walk over or through it. Children can furnish a modern living room, a covered wagon, an Egyptian tomb, a science lab, Heidi's grandfather's Alpine hut, or a grocery store.

For an added challenge, the children may be required to use a previous item in some way after they pantomime their new item. For example, after bringing in test tubes to the scientist's laboratory, the player then lights the Bunsen burner brought in previously.

A variation of the game is to build an entire shelter, following the appropriate steps. For example, children may build a log cabin, wigwam, igloo, or modern-day house, constructing walls, roof, and windows, in addition to the furnishings.

Even a city, state, or country can be created by the players pantomiming actions appropriate to the various locations (for example, Paris: the Louvre, the Metro, the Eiffel Tower, Napoleon's Tomb). Another requirement might be to place the locations as if on a map, observing appropriate directions and distance relationships between each.

Intra-Group Pantomimes

For another way to pantomime, the leader may divide the class into several groups of five or six persons. In each group three or four members pantomime ideas for two members to guess. The instructions might be, "Pantomime all the words you can think of that begin with the letter *r.*"

The three pantomimers do not confer with each other; each thinks of his or her own ideas and enacts as many of them as time permits. The two guessers work as quickly as possible and write down the ideas. If an idea cannot be guessed, the pantomimers or the guessers may say, "Pass," and the pantomimers go on to another idea.

A time limit of one or two minutes for each topic may be imposed. Afterward, the children might like to discuss the ideas that were the "most humorous," "most difficult to guess," or "those that appeared on every group's list." Avoid introducing competition by counting the number of words on each list.

Other topics might be rhyming words (*at:* bat, cat, and so on), verbs, household chores, toys, ways we use water, consonant blends (*st:* stand, street, stop, and so forth).

The advantage of this method is that the audience is small and the time limit encourages the children to pantomime quickly. Even the most reticent children will find it difficult not to get caught up in this game, since attention on them will be minimal.

A hint: Caution the children to work quietly so other groups won't hear their ideas. This reasoning usually makes more sense to them than just being quiet, and this game can get a little noisy.

Count-Freeze Pantomimes

Another kind of pantomime, the *count-freeze* method, is to select six or eight volunteers to pantomime simultaneously in front of the rest of the class. They may pantomime individually, in pairs, or in small groups. This method is useful when the space is limited or when the leader wants only a few children at a time to play.

This method has the largest audience. Therefore, the playing should be kept moving as quickly as possible. The children pantomime their ideas while the leader counts to five or ten. The counting may be as slow or as fast as is necessary. Sometimes when the performers are having a difficult time, a fast count is more comfortable. If the players are truly involved in their pantomimes, and the audience is interested in watching, the counting can be slowed. Usually it is helpful to say "Hold" or "Freeze" until the guessing is completed. The players may sit down when they are guessed. Here are two examples:

> **T:** We've been talking about connotations of words. What if I said the word, *adventure?* What does that word mean to you? What would you act out? (Other words might be discovery, sacrifice, freedom, dreams, happiness, invention, or serendipity).
>
> **T:** Let's pretend you're packing something to take on a camping trip. However, the first letter of what you take should be the same as either the first or last initial of your name.

Another variation of count-freeze is to have the groups spell out words. For example, children might spell out a city by acting out simultaneously animals whose names begin with the appropriate letters. "New York" might be spelled

Eating different foods in a count-freeze pantomime.

College students spell out "Lansing" using occupations: librarian, airplane pilot, nurse, secretary, ice skater, nurse, and golfer. (Photo courtesy of Jon Vander Meer.)

out by seven children pantomiming *n*anny goat, *e*lephant, *w*alrus, *y*ak, *o*rangutan, *r*hinoceros, and *k*angaroo.

As a variation of charades, several children at a time might act out words of a title (omitting the articles a, an, and the). For "Row, Row. Row your Boat," three people could pantomime rowing, a fourth might point to the audience ("your") and the fifth might mime seasickness.

Syllables of longer names or titles might be acted out by groups also. "Washing-ton," "Indian-apple-us," and "Robin-son Crew-sew" are some possibilities.

Frozen picture of Washington crossing the Delaware.

Frozen Pictures

A simple, fun way to do pair and group pantomimes for guessing is to create *frozen pictures*. The children work out their ideas, decide what parts they will play, and then freeze into position.

Pictures may be titled, "The Night the Ghost Visited," "Pony Express Ride Breaks Record," or "Napoleon Defeated at Waterloo."

Art masterpieces can be recreated: *Sunday Afternoon on the Island of La Granae Jatte,* by Seurat, *Accident at the Zoo,* by Daumier, or Picasso's *Guernica.* Statue or museum groupings are also possible.

Scenes from favorite stories and books or scenes of historical or current events might also be created.

One-liners (See Chapter Nine) may be added to these frozen pictures to aid the guessing; or the pictures could be set in motion, perhaps to a count of five.

GUIDING PANTOMIME GUESSING

Since pantomimes for guessing require an audience/performer situation, it is the leader's responsibility to encourage appropriate audience behaviors as well as to emphasize the goal of conveying and interpreting nonverbal messages as accurately as possible. In order to achieve these ends, the leader should keep several points in mind.

Limited Guessing

There is usually little justification for allowing more than three guesses for each pantomime idea. When the children know that the guessing will be limited, they are challenged to perform and guess more carefully. In beginning work, the leader may even want to limit the guessing to only one guess. If the idea cannot be guessed, the child should simply state what was being pantomimed. So that the child won't feel unsuccessful, the leader might say:

T: You have us stumped, George; would you like to tell us what it was?

If the leader allows guessing to go past three guesses, there can be problems. Some children can perform interminably.

One little second-grader was performing something extremely elaborate. The directions were for the children to continue to pantomime until their idea was guessed. The little boy went on and on, saying "no" to each guess. Yet he continued pantomiming interesting actions.

Finally the teacher asked, "I guess you'll have to tell us what your idea was, Billy." Billy thought for a moment and then answered somewhat sheepishly, "I forgot."

Some children enjoy the audience's attention, and they keep their actions vague in an attempt to trick the guessers. Limiting the guessing can help avoid this problem.

Sometimes children also become upset with the audience when their idea is guessed. They think they have failed to trick the audience. To reinforce the goal of communication the leader might say:

T: You pantomimed your idea so well we were able to guess it right away.

Sometimes children do not realize that their idea cannot always be guessed with total accuracy, and they hold out for specific guesses, as the kindergarten girl did in the following example:

Audience: You're a lion.
Sally: No.
Audience: You're a tiger.
Sally: No.
Audience: You're a panther.
Sally: No. I'm a *lioness with green eyes.*

Evaluation

The leader may reinforce the goal of communication through verbal feedback to the performers.

T: Sandy, I knew immediately that you were a tiny spring in the clock. You stretched, and then relaxed and jiggled. And each time you did exactly the same movement.

T: I can tell you have really been studying that book on armor. All five of you were pantomiming so believably I could practically feel the weight of each article of clothing you put on.

It is helpful to discuss particularly careful pantomimes, pointing to the details that help the audience accurately receive the messages. For example,

T: What do you suppose Cliff was doing when he moved his hands like this? (Leader demonstrates.)
C: Taking the cap off a tube of toothpaste.
T: How did you know it was toothpaste? Couldn't it have been hair cream? Or first-aid cream?
C: No! He squeezed it on his toothbrush and brushed his teeth!
T: Cliff used a special kind of toothbrush, didn't he? What kind was it?
C: Electric.
T: How do you know?
C: Cause he plugged it in and jiggled.
T: What was Orlando doing?
C: That's easy. Peeling an onion.

T: How could you tell?

C: Because he peeled it and cried.

T: Cliff and Orlando were very careful in their actions. They added details that helped us know what they were doing.

The leader should, of course, be careful about implying that a child is unsuccessful in pantomiming. Some children *will* be more successful than others, but it is important to encourage continued work. The more the children have the opportunity to pantomime, the more skilled they will become.

To stress the importance of close observation, the teacher might ask the viewers to try to guess silently what each person is doing and then write it down on paper. After the pantomiming is over, the teacher can call on one volunteer to guess everyone's ideas while the other members of the audience check their lists for accuracy.

The children may also be challenged to see if they can guess and *remember* each person's idea without writing the answers on paper. This method can give them an exercise in recalling details.

The discussion should not be allowed to become boring or overly critical. Again, the greatest improvements will come about through practice and through doing rather than through the extended evaluation of others.

ADDITIONAL TOPICS

The following additional topics for pantomime may be used with one or more of the methods discussed in the chapter.

Who am I (are we)? Players choose someone from history, literature, science. current events, and so on, to pantomime.

What am I (are we)? Children can pantomime certain animals, inanimate objects, machinery, toys, plants, and the like.

What am I (are we) doing? This may be as simple as acting out verbs, or may cover topics such as making a cake, driving a car, or milking a cow. Pantomimes may be more challenging, such as buying a waterbed, washing an unwilling dog, or setting up a tent in a windstorm.

What am I (are we) seeing, hearing, tasting, smelling, touching? Pantomimers react to various sensory stimuli which may cover such topics as seeing a ghost, listening to a symphony orchestra, tasting unsweetened lemonade, smelling ammonia fumes, or touching a hot iron.

What's the weather? Players enact clues for audience to guess the seasons or the climatic conditions. It may include acting out seasonal sports or chores, putting on appropriate clothing, or demonstrating various types of natural disasters.

What am I (are we) feeling? Children act out various emotions. They may use whole body or the leader may limit the children to using only their hands, feet, face, or back, for greater challenge. They may combine emotions with "doing" pantomime by showing an action as well as how one feels about doing it. The pantomime may be extended even further by having something happen to change the mood. For example, you happily prepare for a picnic, but it begins to rain and plans have to be cancelled. Now you are disappointed.

Where am I (are we)?   Children pantomime being in various locations such as an elevator, a desert island, haunted house, or circus midway.

Let's get ready to go.   Children pretend to pack supplies for various adventures such as going on a fishing trip, preparing for a hike, loading a covered wagon, or equipping an explorer's ship.

Transportation.   Players pretend to journey via various modes of transportation, which may be broken down into categories such as modern (electric car, space ship), historical (horse and buggy, high-wheeler bicycle), foreign (rickshaw, camel), or fantastical (flying carpet, seven-league boots).

Family portrait.   Members of a family prepare for and pose for their portrait. It may be an historical family, a royal family, literary family, an animal family, a vain family, cartoon or television family.

Dress up.   Players pretend to be certain characters dressing in their appropriate garb, such as Pippi Longstocking, a knight, an astronaut, a desert nomad, or an Egyptian priest.

Foods.   Children pretend to grow, harvest, or prepare and eat familiar and foreign foods: lobster, spaghetti, wild rice, coffee beans, peanuts, coconut, and the like. Or pantomime foods from the four basic food groups.

Health and hygiene.   Players can demonstrate various good (or bad) habits such as brushing teeth, getting fresh air and exercise, and eating healthy foods.

Energy Conservation.   This involves demonstrating various ways to conserve energy at home, school, in business and industry.

Occupations.   Children can act out various occupations of their choice or may focus on groupings such as community helpers, circus performers, and occupations in colonial times.

Tools.   This would entail a demonstration of various tools people used in the past or presently use to perform certain occupations or tasks: doctor's stethescope, blacksmith's bellows, carpenter's level, scientist's microscope, and so on.

Machines.   This is a demonstration of simple tools such as levers, wedges, and pulleys, as well as more sophisticated machines such as electrical appliances or construction equipment. Children may operate the machinery or become the machines. This topic can also include human organs, such as the heart, lungs, or stomach, since they resemble machines.

Sports.   Children enact favorite sports or act like favorite athletes. The sports may be categorized into team sports, Olympic events, winter sports, and so forth.

Animals.   Different groupings of animals might be enacted: pets, zoo animals, circus animals, mammals, farm animals, amphibians, and four-footed animals.

Biography: Children enact a famous or historical person performing a typical activity or acting in a famous event. They may focus on various categories such as Famous Women (Rachel Carson, Barbara Jordan, Maria Tallchief), Black (or other minority) Heroes or Heroines (Martin Luther King, Frederick Douglas, Mary McLeod Bethune), or Famous Scientists (Albert Einstein, Marie Curie, George Washington Carver).

Inventions. Inventions are pantomimed and the class guesses the inventor as well as the invention.

Musical instruments. The children pantomime the instrument of their choice or one from a category such as orchestral instruments, marching-band instruments, percussion, woodwinds, and brass.

Safety. This involves pantomiming the do's and don'ts of various activities: bicycle riding, water sports, camping activities, household or school activities.

First aid. Children demonstrate techniques for removing a foreign body in the eye, aiding a choking victim, treating frostbite, giving first aid for burns, and the like.

Festivals and holidays. Children act out various activities associated with holidays in the United States (Fourth of July, Halloween, Christmas, Hanukkah, Thanksgiving) or other countries (Chinese New Year, French Bastille Day, a Mexican birthday). The audience guesses the custom and the country.

Word pantomimes. Several games can be played using categories of words or parts of speech. For example, in an *Opposite Game* the audience guesses the opposite word of the one pantomimed (for example, hot—cold). This game may also be played with homonyms. For example, the group pantomimes the word "weigh" and guesser must spell "way." Other words to be acted out might be words with a long vowel sound, spelling words, and vocabulary words.

Countries and customs. Children enact a custom and the audience must guess both the custom and the country, as, for instance, British afternoon tea, a Mexican siesta, a Japanese preparing a tatami mat, and a Spanish bullfight.

PANTOMIME SKITS AND STORIES

More elaborate pantomimes can also be done. The children, individually or in pairs or groups, can plan and play lengthier activities which may develop into complete stories.

As the children become skilled in pantomime, it should not be necessary to have to guess each detail of a pantomime story, although evaluation of the effectiveness of the communication is still important.

What was the most understandable moment?
When did you have difficulty following the story?
Was it clear who the characters were?
Were the characters and their feelings believable?
Was there a satisfying ending?

Activities

Without saying a word. In groups the children must both plan and play a nursery rhyme or fairy tale without talking to each other the entire time. Writing notes or mouthing words is not allowed. This game is a real challenge, but the rewards make it worthwhile. To make it somewhat simpler, the children can verbally brainstorm titles and list them on the board. Then by pantomiming, groups select from the list (without going to the board and pointing!). When the stories are shared, do not be surprised if one or two people in a group are acting out a story different from that of everyone else in the group. It demonstrates the difficulty of accurate communication. It is useful for the leader to use pantomime too in conducting the group sharings.

Proverbs. Children are asked to develop a skit to illustrate a proverb.

"Make hay while the sun shines."
"A stitch in times saves nine."
"A friend in need is a friend indeed."

News story of the week! In groups, children illustrate a news event. Having a newspaper at hand for this activity can stimulate interest in reading further about the events as well as providing the ideas for the skits.

Television shows. Children can act out favorite television shows. They may combine TV shows with story commercials (those that can be pantomimed and do not require verbalizing).

Favorite stories. Children may act out some of their favorite stories for the class to guess. These might be short stories such as fables. Or they might be from a basal reading series, independent reading, or stories they've seen dramatized on television. This activity can also "advertise" books to the class or serve as book reports.

Your hit parade. Some years ago there was a television show called "Your Hit Parade." Each week the top songs were sung and dramatized in simple fashion. A song that remained in the top listings for several weeks had to be dramatized in a variety of ways. Some songs had lyrics and some didn't. Select some songs that can be pantomimed in groups while the music is playing, and see how many varieties there are. Children will enjoy using popular music.

You are there. Skits may be based on scenes of scientific or historical significance. Facts about the events may be listed on cards, or the children might do research work in preparation.

Test drive of the first automobile
When the Wright Brothers flew their plane
When penicillin was discovered
When land was opened in Oklahoma
Driving the golden spike for the Transcontinental Railroad
During the first heart transplant
When Jane Addams opened Hull House
Charles Lindbergh landing after his trans-Atlantic solo flight
Alexander Graham Bell making the first telephone call
When women were allowed to vote
Discovery of radium by Madame Curie
When the MIssissippi River was discovered
When King Tut's tomb was found

The invention. Children act out their version of the discovery of these inventions:

laughing gas	mirror	potato chips
suspenders	popcorn machine	snowshoes
rubber band	fireworks	bubble gum
fire	the wheel	

Charades. Players are given song, play, book, film, or television titles as well as common sayings to act out. Usually the words are acted out one at a time, although they need not be acted out in the order in which they appear in the title. Sometimes only one syllable at a time is acted out.

The pantomimers have several aids they can use:

(a) They may tell the guessing players, "This is a _____ (title or saying.) There are _____ words in it. I'm going to act out the _____ word."

(b) The player may say, "This is a short word." The guessers then simply call out as many short words as they can think of until the correct one is called. Words such as "a," "an," "the," or various pronouns and prepositions can be handled quickly in this manner.

(c) The pantomimer may act out a word that *sounds* like the original word if that would be easier to guess. The word "car," for example, might be easier to act out and guess than the word "far."

For additional curricular emphasis, story titles might be from basal readers or popular library books. Sayings might be historical quotes such as "Walk softly and carry a big stick" (T. Roosevelt), "Give me liberty or give me death" (P. Henry), or "A house divided cannot stand" (A. Lincoln).

In the classroom, charades is best played in small groups so that more children have a chance to pantomime and the audience is kept small.

FOR THE COLLEGE STUDENT

1. Play some of the pantomime activities suggested in this chapter. Afterward, discuss the special skills required of the pantomimer and the interpreter in encoding and decoding the nonverbal messages. How successful were you in doing each?

2. After playing some of the pantomime games, discuss which pantomime types would be most useful for different grade levels. Also discuss which curricular topics might be particularly suitable for the different types of pantomimes.

3. Create ten pantomime activities, using various curricular topics in each. Vary the types of pantomimes you use.

4. Now select one of the pantomime games you have written and guide your classmates in playing it. Consider the various techniques you can use to guide the playing, to help the audience interpret the pantomimes, and to evaluate the playing. Afterward discuss the activity.

5. Create your own type of pantomime, perhaps creating a variation on a type mentioned in this chapter. Teach it to your classmates.

Chapter Nine

Beginning
Verbal
Activities

In the previous chapters we have emphasized pantomime activities, encouraging the leader to allow verbalizing whenever it occurred spontaneously. The leader will also want to develop the children's skills in verbalizing, expressing themselves, and interacting with others in drama activities.

Children vary in their readiness to verbalize. Some children feel free about talking and expressing ideas, opinions, and feelings as they play; other children are more reticent.

By becoming familiar with a variety of activities and techniques for aiding children's verbalizing, the leader can design appropriate activities for a group.

SOUND EFFECTS

There are many simple verbal activities and games which can be played to help the children feel more comfortable with talking. At first the leader may want to begin with just sounds. The children do not have to use language, but can simply play with the voice, making *sound effects*.

Sound Effects from Literature

There are a number of stories and poems that focus on sounds. The leader can narrate these materials, as was done with pantomime. When the leader pauses in the narration, the appropriate sounds can be made, thus enhancing the children's listening and interpretive skills.

The literary materials that follow cover a broad range of topics and curricular areas. For example, poems like "The Sounds in the Morning" and "The Sounds in the Evening" give opportunities for making the sounds of dogs barking, wind whispering, cats mewing, and owls hooting. The story "The Devil's Pocket" contains echo sounds. Margaret Wise Brown's books challenge with such sounds as butter melting and grasshoppers sneezing!

"The Barnyard," Maude Burnham. (4)

"The Bed," Pura Belpré. (44)

"The Devil's Pocket," George Mendoza. (11)

"Hearing Things," Aileen Fisher. (39)

The Little Woman Wanted Noise, Val Teal. Skokie, Ill.: Rand McNally, 1943.

The Noisy Book, Margaret Wise Brown. New York: Harper & Row, Pub., 1939.

Noisy Gander, Miska Miles. New York: Dutton, 1978.

Noisy Nancy and Nick, Lou Ann Gaeddert. New York: Doubleday, 1970.

"Paul Revere's Ride," Henry Wadsworth Longfellow. (4)

Quiet Noisy Book, Margaret Wise Brown. New York: Harper & Row, Pub., 1950.

"The Sounds in the Evening," Eleanor Farjeon. (13)

"The Sounds in the Morning," Eleanor Farjeon. (13)

Too Much Noise, Ann McGovern. Boston: Houghton-Mifflin, 1967.

Why Mosquitoes Buzz in People's Ears, Verna Aardema. New York: Dial Press, 1975.

Original Sound-Effects Material

The leader can also create original materials for sound effects, emphasizing many areas of the curriculum. Activities can be based on the seasons, holidays, or weather sounds. The sounds might be in different locations or countries, such as a busy seaport, a factory, a zoo, a jungle camp, or an open market.

Certain sounds that younger children (and even older ones) have trouble pronouncing, such as "s," "sh," "th," "r," could be incorporated into a sound-effects activity. The "s" sound might, for example, be made by a rattlesnake getting ready to strike; "r" by the sound of a motor; "th," by air escaping from a leaky balloon; "sh" by the sound of running water.

The sounds may be combined into a story.

T: One dark night I was at home alone. I was reading a book in a chair by the window. Outside the wind was blowing softly. (Sound) The tree limbs were gently tapping on the roof and the windowpanes. (Sound) The tall clock in the corner ticked steadily. (Sound) Then it struck one o'clock. (Sound) Then strange sounds began . . . (The story proceeds with scary sounds and builds to a climax, with something being knocked over in another room. The narrator discovers a cat had wandered into the house and caused the accident; it wasn't a ghost or prowler after all!)

The following dramatic incident is based on the surrender of Lee to Grant at Appomattox from information in a social studies text:

T: Let's imagine it is the afternoon of April 9, 1865.
It's very quiet . . .
All eyes are looking down the dusty road to the court house.
A blue jay calls . . .
An annoyed squirrel answers back . . .
In the distance, young children shout and begin a game of tag . . .
The muffled sound of horses is heard . . .
And a gray figure riding a gray horse approaches . . .
All sounds cease . . .
Slowly the gray horse, Traveller, passes the line of waiting Northern soldiers . . .
He stops at the gate of the McLean house . . .
General Lee's footsteps on the wooden stairs are clear and brisk . . .
Now another figure on horseback rides into view . . .
And while the watching men softly sing "Auld Lang Syne" . . .
General Grant disappears into the house . . .
And the battle-weary country waits for peace.

Sound Effects Variations

Although it is fun and a challenge to make sound effects vocally, children may also want to experiment with other ways of making them. One fourth-grade class discovered the most realistic sound for rain was achieved by scraping their feet

"Follow the arrow to make the sound."

over the bits of gravel that had accumulated under their desks on a particularly muddy day!

Another way to create sound effects is to use instruments, sometimes assigning a particular instrument to a character in a story. The sound effect is made whenever the character is mentioned. Finger cymbals, for example, might be the sound for an Emperor; a drum might signal the villain, and so on. Don't overlook the fun of taping these stories after they have been planned and rehearsed a few times.

Controls for Sound Effects

Often children enjoy making sound effects so much that they get carried away. To control the sounds, the leader should use special signals. Some leaders use a pointer or arrow to signify a volume dial and indicate the directions for on and off and for varying degrees of volume. Some leaders have used a picture of a large ear on a stick. The higher the stick is raised, the louder the sound.

SEQUENCE GAMES

As in "pantomimes for guessing," a sequence game can also be made for verbal activities. The children have an opportunity to talk, but they read the lines written for them rather than having to invent dialogue.

Again, the cards are made up with a cue and a line to read (or perhaps a pantomime to perform). The cards are distributed at random, with each child receiving at least one card. The first card might say:

> You begin the game. You stand and say, "Good morning, ladies and gentlemen. Welcome to the Fourth Grade TV Personality Show!" Then bow and sit down.

Another player will have a card that reads:

> **Cue:** "Good morning, ladies and gentlemen. Welcome to the Fourth-Grade Personality Show." Bow and sit.
> **You:** Stand and say, "Brought to you by 'Multicolored Jelly Beans.'" Then sit.

The next card will read (there might be three of these cards):

> **Cue:** "Brought to you by 'Multicolored Jelly Beans.'" Sit.
> **You:** Stand and clap and clap and clap. Then sit.

Sequence Games from Literature

Sequence games may be made up from poems and stories which have interesting dialogue or statements in a series. Because they follow a question-and-answer format, riddles and jokes are also good to use. Alphabet and number books also follow a sequence. Following are some suggestions:

ABC's of Space, Isaac Asimov. New York: Walker, 1969.
A Big City, Francine Grossbart. New York: Harper & Row, Pub., 1966.
Ashanti to Zulu, Margaret Musgrove. New York: Dial Press, 1976.
"A Was Once an Apple Pie," Edward Lear.   (4)
Drummer Hoff, Barbara Emberly. Englewood Cliffs, N.J.: Prentice-Hall, 1967.
Fortunately, Remy Charlip. New York: Parents', 1964.
"The Gardner's Song," Lewis Carroll.   (3)
The Green Machine, Polly Cameron. New York: Coward, McCann & Geoghegan, 1969.
"I Can't," Said the Ant, Polly Cameron. New York: Coward, McCann & Geoghegan, 1961.
John Burningham's ABC. Indianapolis: Bobbs-Merrill, 1964.
The Last Cow on the White House Lawn and Other Little-Known Facts about the Presidency, Barbara Seuling. New York: Doubleday, 1978.
Let's Marry! Said the Cherry! N. M. Bodekker. New York: Atheneum, 1974.
Lucky Book of Riddles, Eva Moore. New York: Scholastic Book Services, 1964.
Magic Letter Riddles, Mike Thaler. New York: Scholastic Book Services, 1974.
One Was Johnny, Maurice Sendak. New York: Harper & Row, Pub., 1962.
"Peter Perfect, The Story of a Perfect Boy," Bernard Waber.   (26)
Pierre: A Cautionary Tale, Maurice Sendak.   (3)
"Say Something Nice," Bernard Waber.   (26)
"Sick," Shel Silverstein.   (48)
The Star-Spangled Banana and Other Revolutionary Riddles, compiled by Charles Keller and Richard Baker. Englewood Cliffs, N.J.: Prentice-Hall, 1974.
What Do You Do, Dear? Sesyle Joslin. Reading, Mass.: Addison-Wesley, 1961.
What Do You Say, Dear? Sesyle Joslin. Reading, Mass.: Addison-Wesley, 1958.

Original Sequence Games

Many curricular materials can be adapted fairly easily into sequence format. One leader reviewed characters from Greek and Roman mythology by giving each an appropriate statement to make. The cues, which in this case were read, were the names of the characters who had spoken the previous quote. For example,

Card 1   You begin.   "If Athena can weave better than I, let her come and try."
Card 2   (Arachne)   "I knew I should have used a super glue instead of wax!"
Card 3   (Icarus)   "The only man I'll marry is the one who can outrun me."

The following extended example is from a sixth-grade social studies lesson on exploration in the New World:

1. You begin the game. Stand and say, "The time is the late 1400s. The place is Europe. Curtain going up!" Then sit.

Interpretive reading skills are encouraged in verbal sequence games.

2. You stand, walk around the circle, and call out, "For sale, for sale, our latest shipment of spices, silks, perfumes, and gems! For sale, directly from the Indies. Come and get it while it lasts!" Return to your seat.

3. You stand and say (shaking your head sadly) "Too bad we can't have more." Sit.

4. You jump up and say excitedly, "Ah, but we could if we had a sailing route to the Indies." Sit.

5. You stand, clap your hands as if you're trying to get someone's attention, and say, "Children—recite today's geography lesson." After two people recite, you sit.

6, 7. (Two cards) You and another person will stand and recite together: "Roses are red, violets are blue. The earth is flat, and that's the truth." Then bow and sit.

8. You stand and say slowly, "Very interesting." Sit down slowly.

9. You stand and say, "But not true!" Sit.

10. You stand and say, "And it doesn't even rhyme." Sit.

11. You stand and say, "Mama mia, have I got an idea! I'll go west (point one way) to get to the east" (point the other way). (Wait to sit down until someone says, "Noooo!")

12, 13. (Two cards) You stay seated and yell, "Noooo!"

14. You stand and say, "Everybody knows the earth's flat as a pancake. And if you go too far, horrible sea monsters will get you." Then pretend to be a sea monster, growling and showing claws and teeth. Sit.

15. You walk slowly around the circle, pretending to be very tired and say, "Poor Columbus left Italy and finally went to Spain—to King Ferdinand and Queen Isabella. They gave him three ships and a crew." Return to your seat.

16. You stand and rock back and forth on your feet and chant, "Sailing, sailing, over the ocean blue. And when we arrive—if we get there alive—it'll be 1492." Sit.

17. You stand, look around, put your hand up to your forehead as if you are shading your eyes and shout, "Land, ho!" Sit.

18. You stand, pretend to be near death, and gasp out the words, "Thank goodness, I thought we'd never make it." Then stagger and fall down.

19. You stand, pretend to plant a flag in the soil, and say, "I name this island San Salvador and claim it for the King and Queen of Spain." Sit.

20, 21. (Two cards) You stay seated and cheer, whistle, clap hands, etc. (There will be two of you doing this.)

22. You stand and say, "Columbus and his crew stopped at other islands in the Caribbean Sea also." Sit.

23. You stand and say, "What do you know? We're the first ones to ever take a Caribbean Cruise! Think I'll go for a swim." Then pretend to dive into water. Sit.

24. You stand and say in a big, deep voice, "I have named this island Hispaniola and on it I have built a fort. Guard it well, men! I'm going back home." Then walk around the circle and sit back down.

25, 26. (Two cards) You stand, salute, and say, "Aye, aye, Sir." Sit. (Two of you will do this.)

27. You stand and say, "Now it's 1513 and I'm Balboa. I have crossed the Isthmus of Panama and I claim this body of water for Spain. I name it the Pacific Ocean—meaning peaceful—(Yawn)—boy, it sure is . . . (then lie down and fall asleep and snore once).

28. You stand, pretend to ride a horse around the circle, and then say, "I'm Cortes. I've spent the last four years conquering Mexico in the name of Spain." Sit.

29. You stand and say, "The year is 1532. Pizzaro's the name and exploring's my game." Then say in a loud whisper, "Listen! I've heard that there's lots of gold and silver down in South America. The King of Spain has agreed to help me get it. What do you say? (After DeSoto shakes your hand, you sit.)

30. You stand, go over to him, shake his hand, and say, "The name's DeSoto. I think we'd make a good team." Then return to your seat.

31. You stand and march to the center of the circle, and announce in a big voice, "They marched toward the heart of the Inca Empire." Then return to your seat.

32. You stand and say in a frightened voice, "Who are these men who steal from us?" Sit.

33. You stand and yell, "Our towns are burning! Run for your lives!" (Then pretend to be hit and fall dead.)

34. You stand and say, "The Emperor will save us!" (Then pretend to be hit and fall dead.)

35. You stand and raise your hands up as if asking for silence and calm, and say slowly and in a big voice, "I am the Emperor. I am God. I have thirty thousand soldiers, and the Spaniards have only a few men. Why is everyone so afraid?" Then fold your arms across your chest and sit down slowly.

36. You stand, cup your hands to your mouth, and call to the Emperor, "Hey, Emperor! How about dinner at our place?" (Then turn your head and laugh behind your hand.) Sit.

37. You stand and announce, "And so the Emperor and five thousand unarmed Inca warriors went to a feast. The Emperor came in a golden chair carried by slaves. The warriors were killed by the Spaniards." Sit.

38. You stand and shout angrily, "Why do you do this terrible thing?" Sit.
39. You stand and shout, "Gold! We want gold!" Sit.
40 You stand and say, "I will have this room filled with gold if you will let me go free." (Remain standing until you hear someone say, "What do we do now? Kill him." Then fall dead—but do it in slow motion.)
41. You stand and say, "Gold and silver came from all parts of the Inca Empire. At first the Spaniards were glad. Then they worried about what to do with the Emperor." Sit.
42. You stand and say in a loud whisper, "What do we do now?" Sit.
43. You stand and say very seriously, "Kill him." Sit slowly.
44. You stand and say, "Thus ends a sad chapter in history. Land and wealth gained but at the cost of human suffering." Curtain going down! (Music)

The leader should encourage appropriate interpretive reading of the lines in sequence games, pointing out the opportunities for variety in vocal inflection, pitch, dynamics (loud and soft), timing, pauses, and so forth. Often it takes a run-through reading first for the children to familiarize themselves with the material and to get into the spirit of it. Usually the children ask to repeat the game and to switch cards. After several playings, there is often a considerable improvement in their vocal skills. Sometimes they also enjoy the challenge of trying to improve their previous reading rate.

Once children are familiar with sequence games, they can help transcribe the material on cards themselves or even create their own sequence games.

ONE-LINERS

For initial work with verbalizing, it is often easiest to begin with what we call *one-liners*. For these, the children have to say or create only one line of speech. There are several kinds of activities that can serve this purpose.

To begin, the leader or the children can make a list of familiar one-line statements. Many of the one-liners are famous because of *how* they have been said, and children enjoy imitating them. The lines can be placed on cards and distributed. The following examples are from television and may need frequent updating:

"Sit on it!" The Fonz
"Let's get Mikey!" Life Cereal commercial
"COOKIE!" *Sesame Street's* Cookie Monster
"Good Morning, Captain." *Captain Kangaroo*

Other famous lines may come from well-known stories, such as "Who's been sleeping in my bed?" "Then I'll huff and I'll puff and I'll blow your house down!" or "It is I, Big Billy Goat Gruff!"

One-Liners from Magazine Ads

In flipping through magazines, the teacher (or the children) can select interesting statements and place them on cards. Here are some we've found.

Amazing!
I don't believe it.
Yeah, but station wagons are so dull.
Thank you, honey.

Cards are distributed randomly; children may read them in any order, pretending that they make sense following one another. Sometimes different voices can be used, such as robot/computer, witch, politician's campaign voice, and so on.

A variation of the game is to have the children stand and say their line when they think it's appropriate. Several cards may be distributed to each child.

For a third variation, the cards may be sequenced alphabetically, according to the first letter of the statement (*a*nnouncing something you may not want to hear, *b*e cool, *c*an you really manage without money?, *d*ecide for yourself, *e*xactly!, and so on).

One-Liners with Pictures

Pictures can stimulate ideas for one-liners. The leader selects pictures of people or animals in interesting poses with unusual facial expressions. The children think of what the person or animal might be saying. The line should be said as they think the person or animal would say it. Pictures which work well for this purpose are posters, large ads from magazines, and calendar art.

One-Liners with Frozen Pictures

In the last chapter, frozen pictures were discussed—scenes which contain several persons frozen in their interaction with each other. To aid the guessing, or as another variation, one of the characters might speak a line appropriate to the scene. Or the scene might be considered a photograph in a newspaper and an appropriate headline could be announced.

One-Liners with Props

One-liners can be combined with props. For this activity, the leader selects a simple but interesting prop. Volunteers demonstrate a use for it, saying one line of dialogue to accompany the prop's use. For example, a folding yardstick can be shaped into several things: (a) a fishing pole, (b) the letter *Z*, or (c) a triangle. One-liners that can accompany these uses might be:

(a) "Shucks, been here over three hours and haven't had a nibble."
(b) (Holding letter against chest) "Coach, I'm gonna get in there and win the game for old Zorro U."
(c) (Holding triangle around face as a picture frame.) "The family doesn't know it, but I can see everything that goes on around here!"

STORYTELLING

Storytelling can also give children opportunities to verbalize, as well as to imagine and create plots. The children may build their short stories in round-robin fashion, with each volunteer adding another line.

Storytelling with Wordless Picture Books

One of the easiest ways to begin storytelling is to use wordless picture books which have no text but tell a story in pictures. The children interpret what they see happening in their own words, sometimes even adding dialogue they think the characters might be saying. Some examples are: *The Adventures of Paddy Pork*, John Goodall. New York: Harcourt Brace Jovanovich, 1968. *The Bear and the Fly*, Paula Winter. New York: Crown Publishers, 1976. *A Boy, a Dog and a Frog*, Mercer Mayer. New York: Dial Press, 1967. *Bobo's Dream*, Martha Alexander. New York: Dial Press, 1970. *Changes, Changes*, Pat Hutchins. New York: Macmillan, 1971. *The Damp and Daffy Doings of a Daring Pirate Ship*, Guillermo Mordillo. New York: Harlan Quist, 1971. *Shrewbettina's Birthday*, John Goodall. New York: Harcourt Brace Jovanovich, 1971. *The Silver Pony*, Lynd Ward. Boston: Houghton Mifflin, 1973. *Who's Seen the Scissors?* Idem. New York: Dutton, 1975. *The Wrong Side of the Bed*, Edward Ardizzone. New York: Doubleday, 1970.

Storytelling with Pictures

Single pictures might also be used to stimulate storytelling. Unusual pictures work well, but the leader can make even an ordinary picture sound intriguing. For example, a story based on a picture of a man on horseback might be started by the teacher, "Once upon a time there was a man who owned an enchanted horse that could take him anywhere he wanted to go."

The leader may find it helpful to refer to the framework of questions presented in Chapter Seven as an aid to encouraging plot development in storytelling.

Storytelling in Character

Once children are accustomed to creating stories, another dramatic dimension can be added. Children can pretend to be characters rather than themselves doing the telling. In this way they can try out character voices, gestures, and attitudes through their stories.

There are numerous literary sources that show storytellers in action. For example, the children may pretend to be the poet mouse who shares his supply of beautiful stories with his family in the story *Frederick,* by Leo Lionni (Pantheon, 1967); or Mother Bear, who tells Little Bear stories about himself in the book *Little Bear,* by Else Holmelund Minarik (Harper & Row, Pub., 1957); or Pa Ingalls, who entertains his children with short adventures from his past in Laura Ingalls Wilder's series of "Little House" books.

Other characters suggest themselves in other areas of the curriculum: Eskimos of long ago sharing myths or stories of hunts during an Arctic night, hobos telling tales of dangerous railroad rides, or soothsayers reading signs and predicting the future.

Another variation is to select an incident from a picture story, the newspaper, or a fact from the *Guinness Book of Records,* and tell the incident as if you were the person involved. ("You want to know my recipe for the hottest chili in Texas? Well, it goes something like this . . .")

More Storytelling Variations

After children become skilled in storytelling, they will enjoy the challenges of incorporating certain words into their stories, such as new vocabulary words, spelling words, and foreign words. Or the first word of each new sentence in the story must follow the first word of the previous sentence in alphabetical order. (For example, *A* story about a cat. *B*oy, was he an ornery cat. *C*ats are often ornery, but this one was especially bad.)

Another variation is to stimulate stories from a series of sounds; say, five, for instance. The sounds must be incorporated into the story, perhaps even in the same order they are given. (Ring bell, tear paper, jangle keys, tap a pencil, whistle. What story does that suggest?)

Another possibility is the incorporation of particular characters, props, or settings into the stories. (For example, try making up a story including these three things: a magician, a single white glove, and a haunted house.) Older children may enjoy working in groups to create these stories and may even dramatize some of them. (See the next chapter for further discussion of this activity.)

Time Limits in Storytelling

As the children become more skilled in storytelling, the leader may need to establish a time limit for each person's contribution. The sound of a bell or the flash of classroom lights are possibilities. Some teachers use a ball of knotted twine, which they pass to storytellers sitting in a circle. As the storyteller spins a tale, the ball is unraveled; when the knot is reached, the ball is passed to the next person.

Older children, and some younger ones, love the idea of being stopped in mid-sentence, which forces the next storyteller to end the thought. This technique also challenges the children to listen closer and to mesh their creative thinking with that of another person.

VERBAL GAMES

Games in which children can pretend to be other characters are useful for stimulating verbalization. They are relatively easy to organize in the classroom and can involve the entire class. Groups of children can take turns being panel members.

Experts

For this game panel members are declared to be experts on a particular topic. The class questions them as a group on their subject. Areas of expertise might be owners and trainers of fleas for a flea circus, people who knit small socks for birds, people who believe that living in caves is superior to living in buildings, and people who have pigs as house pets. The purpose in using *unusual* expertise is that children can feel more confident about giving their opinions and ideas. After the panel members each speak briefly, the rest of the class may question them.

To Tell The Truth

As a variation of a popular television show, a panel of three children (or more) pose as a particular famous person: living, historical, or fictional. The rest of the class poses questions to determine who is the real person. All the panel members must research the character, but one is designated to be the true character and must give accurate answers to the best of his or her ability. Other panel members may give inaccurate answers occasionally. A time limit for the questioning is imposed.

Inanimate objects might also be used for this game. For example, children might play the role of a particular food, transportation, invention, and so forth.

What's My Line?

This classic television show presented contestants who had unusual occupations that the panelists tried to guess within twenty questions. A panelist could continue to question the contestant until he or she received a "no" answer. Each program also featured a celebrity mystery guest.

For the classroom, three contestants could have the same occupation or identity and take turns answering questions. Questioners could be volunteers from the class rather than a panel. The teacher serves as moderator.

Current-day occupations would be useful topics for career education. Historical occupations might be appropriate for social studies. Mystery guests could be living persons or persons from literature or history.

Liars' Club

Another television game show which older children find challenging operates on the premise that all the panelists know the true use of a particular object. Actually, only one panelist has been told what the object is; the others must create believable explanations. The objects are often antiques, unusual objects, or are new products on the market. Contestants vote on the most believable explanation.

For the classroom, instead of a panel, volunteers may present their explanation. No one is told the actual use of the object until the game is over. The class is allowed to ask questions of the volunteers. In the spirit of fun rather than competition, a vote might be taken on the most believable explanation before the object's true identity and use are told.

Other dimensions to the game can be given if the children pretend to be archaeologists and try to identify how an object was used by a particular culture the children have studied. Or they might be museum directors who must deter-

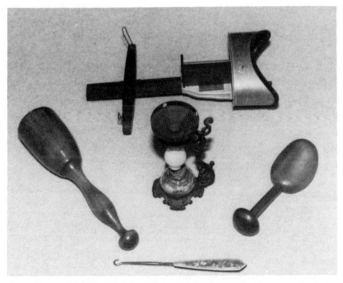

Props for "Liar's Club": (clockwise) stereoscope, darning egg, button hook, wooden potato masher, and (center) antique vaporizer.

A college student tries to identify an object while skeptical classmates
wait their turn (Liar's Club).

mine the true identity of an object in order to set up a display and label the object
appropriately.

Character Panel Discussions

This activity has many variations. Several children (usually four or five) comprise a panel. They are given roles to play or they may establish their own, usually with varying viewpoints. Members of the audience, who play themselves or a character role, question the panelists. If they play a role, they should identify themselves before asking their questions. The leader will need to play the role of moderator.

The goal of the game is to explore dialogue situations and to search for information and ideas. Final decisions are not necessary.

The following ideas are only a sample of the many possibilities:

A.

Panel members are various characters, real or fictional, who are known for their ingenuity. The audience poses problems it would like to have solved, such as personal problems ("My little sister won't stay out of my room") or national problems from current events. Answers should be appropriate to the characters' approach to other problems.

Literary characters might be Harriet the Spy, Tom Sawyer, Homer Price, and Pippi Longstocking. Animal characters and mythological characters are also possible. Historical characters such as past presidents, inventors, or explorers might be used.

B.

A variation of the above would be to assign characters to the panelists who answer questions anonymously. The audience tries to guess the characters' identities after a period of time.

C.

A panel of characters in a given story may be questioned by the audience as to their motivations for their actions or other details not answered in the stories. For example, Sleeping Beauty might be questioned about what it was like to be asleep for so long. Was she glad when the prince woke her up? Is he the prince she would have chosen? Another character might be the thirteenth fairy. Why was she so upset about not being invited to the christening? Why did she wish the princess to be killed—and by a spinning wheel?

The fairly simple activities in this chapter should help build the children's confidence in verbalizing and should lay the groundwork for the more challenging activities presented in the next chapter.

FOR THE COLLEGE STUDENT

1. Collect stories and poems suitable for sound-effects activities.
2. Create your own sound-effect story. Base it on a curricular topic.
3. Practice telling or reading a story while using the control of an arrow.
4. Adapt a story for a sequence game.
5. Write a sequence game; base it on a curricular topic.
6. Collect interesting pictures, props, and one-liners useful for stimulating verbalization.
7. Try round-robin storytelling with your classmates, using some of the techniques mentioned in this chapter.
8. Play at least one of the verbal games with your classmates. Can you think of others?
9. Create your own panel games or adapt some of the ones presented in this chapter.

Chapter Ten

Creating Dialogue

Thus far, all the verbal activities have been fairly simple ones. Any dialogue interaction between the children has been limited mainly to answering questions. It is also possible to create dialogue situations in which children improvise conversations at length. Eventually, older children will be able to develop stories and skits in groups. This chapter will cover some of the materials and methods a leader can use in helping children improvise dialogue.

SELECTING DIALOGUE MATERIAL

There are many sources for creating dialogue. Some may come from literature, such as the verbal guessing game between Rumpelstiltskin and the Queen when she reveals his secret name, or Toad's fast talk in *Wind in the Willows* (147) as he tries to get himself out of trouble spots.

Many stories revolve totally around a dialogue scene. The solving of a conflict through talk becomes crucial to the outcome of the story. For instance, Dr. Suess's "The Rabbit, the Bear, and the Zinniga-Zanniga" (p. 191) is a "trickster" tale in which a rabbit skillfully talks a hungry bear out of eating him.

Dialogue scenes may also be based on a variety of curricular topics and improvised out of the imagination and resourcefulness of the group. Children may create the dialogue that might have occurred when Governor John Winthrop tried to convince the people of Massachusetts that the water was pure enough to drink. Or they might enact the scene that could occur between a reluctant Thanksgiving turkey and a hungry pilgrim with a ready musket.

Amount of Dialogue

The amount of actual dialogue recorded in materials will vary. Sometimes a selection records exactly what the characters say. Sometimes the conversation is implied indirectly.

> Quietly Sid and Kim discussed their plan for escape. In the early morning Sid was to ring the bell as he always did. That would be the signal for Kim to release the heavy door latch . . .

Some passages only hint at a possible dialogue scene.

> Hardly anyone believed that a car could be a substitute for a horse.

Yet any of these passages could form a basis for creating a dialogue scene. The leader should be alert to the many possibilities for dialogue wherever they may be found.

Conflict

What makes dialogue scenes intriguing and dramatic is the conflict involved. Conflict encourages further explanation of different sides of an issue. When a conflict is resolved or a compromise is reached, the discussion is usually ended. As the leader selects and creates dialogue material, conflict should be considered. For example, a scene might be created in which old prospectors sit around a campfire and have a *contest* to see who can tell the tallest tale; Benjamin Franklin, busily inventing, might experience increased annoyance while being interviewed by a *persistent* biographer. Or a scene might be improvised from the tense moment in the story *Tomás Takes Charge* (139), when Tomás and Fernanda try to *convince* the landlady that their father has not left home and that the rent will be paid soon.

Accuracy of Dialogue

In creating dialogue, one point must be considered: How much freedom of interpretation does the leader and the class want to allow? When children make up their own stories or situations, they are at liberty to interpret the characters and the dialogue in a variety of ways. For example, it is fun to put historical people in a modern setting. Amusing scenes can develop if George Washington tries to converse with the Jackson Five, or if a cave man receives a call from a modern appliance salesman. Anachronisms by themselves provide humor. It is also an enjoyable way to make comparisons with different eras in terms of technology, language, and attitudes.

However, there may not be as much freedom when the characters are well defined in the literature or if the setting is to be an historically accurate one. For example, one group of children became upset with a classmate who pretended to ride a motorcycle in a dramatic story set in medieval times. They knew the motorcycle was inappropriate to the setting and that it introduced humor into a serious scene. As a group they decided that motorcycles should not be allowed.

Switching Roles

In dialogue scenes, there are often two or more sides to an issue. Playing out these situations shows children the various attitudes people have. They have the opportunity to see what it is like to hold a particular viewpoint.

It is important, then, that the children interchange roles frequently. One technique for switching is to break up the scene in the middle of the discussion. The two sides switch parts, or new players from the audience may step in. The latter technique often freshens up the scene with new ideas, as well as giving more children an opportunity to play.

TECHNIQUES FOR FACILITATING DIALOGUE

Some children can improvise dialogue readily and with little difficulty. They may be verbally sophisticated, or the leader may have progressed them to a point where they are ready to experiment with improvisation. Some children need much help and guidance. The leader's own participation in the scenes and careful planning may be crucial to their success in dialogue work.

Leader as Initiator

One common practice, particularly with younger children, is to set up a dialogue situation with individual children or with small groups. In this way the leader bears the responsibility for keeping the scene moving along. Usually the children remain at their desks.

In the following example, the teacher shows the class a picture of a space man and a moon creature talking with each other. To create conflict, the leader suggests that the moon creature wants to go back to earth and the astronaut is giving all the reasons why that would be impossible. The leader says, "Let's suppose I'm the moon creature and you're the astronaut. What reasons would you give me? Raise your hand if you want to talk to me."

> **T:** I've heard it's lovely there, and I want to go.
> **C:** But there's no room in the space capsule.

The teacher assists children with dialogue by playing a character role.
(Photo courtesy of the *Kalamazoo Gazette*.)

T: But I could squeeze myself up real tight and you'd never even notice me at all.
C: But there's no food for you to eat. You'd starve.
T: I'll have my mother pack a lunch. Etc.

When children are ready to try ideas on their own, the above technique may serve as a brief rehearsal, if needed.

Leader and Children as Initiators Together

Sometimes children accompany the leader in initiating conversation, all playing the same role. The plan works for both verbal and less verbal children. The leader urges the verbal children subtly to ask questions, make comments, and respond to each other. In this way, the leader gradually relinquishes the initiator role. For the reticent children, it gives them a chance to identify with the role, whether they verbalize or not.

In the following example, the leader is playing the mother in a third-grade class. The children are pretending that they have brought home an animal they want to keep as a pet. The leader has conversed with several children at their desks about the various kinds of pets they have, how they found them, and the advantages and disadvantages of keeping them. The children have been listening to each others' ideas with interest and have enjoyed the interchanges. One verbal boy suddenly says to the leader, "I want to do what you're doing." The teacher suggests that he might be the father. The child begins to repeat much of what has

already been said, so the leader gradually includes other children into a larger
scene and stimulates conversation when it's needed.

> **Father:** What have you brought home this time?
> **Child:** It's just a little kitten.
> **Father:** We can't keep it. (Pause)
> **Mother:** And, Father, Charles over here has a snake someone gave him. And
> Theresa has this rabbit. (Points to two other children who have already conversed
> with her)
> **Father:** Well, we can't keep any of them. Everything's got to go. We haven't got
> enough money to buy food for all these animals.
> **Theresa:** I could use my allowance money for rabbit food.
> **Charles:** This snake only eats mice. I can catch those for him.
> **Father:** Nope. They still have to go. (Pause)
> **Mother:** Well, I can't help but think of the mess they'll cause.
> **Father:** Yeah. They're really gonna stink up the place.

As the scene continues, a girl who has not spoken at all up to this point in
the playing, asks to play the mother. The leader relinquishes the role to the child,
but remains ready to step in if needed, perhaps as a neighbor who brings over a
free puppy from a new litter—another conflict to solve!

Double Casting

Another technique that aids in dialogue is *double casting;* that is, two (or more)
children are cast in the same part. Those children who feel confident can speak
out. And generally, what one child can't think of to say, the other one can. Those
who are more reticent can still be a part of the experience without having to bear
the total responsibility for the verbal exchange.

In the following example, the children have been divided into groups.
They have created the star-making machines in Dr. Seuss's story "The
Sneetches" (32). There are two owners of each machine with whom the leader
will initiate dialogue. The leader poses a problem: being afraid to enter the
machines. The children, as the owners of the machines, will lose money if they
cannot convince the Sneetches of the machine's safety. Note their creative approach to problem-solving.

> **T:** Let's suppose I'm a customer and you are Sylvester McMonkey McBean. Who
> thinks they could convince me? (Children volunteer and the leader walks over to
> one group)
>   Mr. McBean, I sure would like to have a star, but I'm afraid to go in that
> machine. It looks awfully complicated. How can I be sure it won't hurt me?
> **C:** Well, I'll go in first and you can see that I'm okay when I come out.
> **T:** That's a good idea. All right, I think I would try your machine. (Goes to another
> group) I'm afraid of the dark, Mr. McBean, so I don't think I'd like to go inside that
> machine of yours. I'll bet it's awfully dark in there, isn't it?
> **C:** Naw. You see, the stars inside are shiny, and they make it bright enough to see.
> **T:** Well, what do you know? That makes me feel a lot better.

Narrow and Broad Questions

The kinds of questions the leader asks in initiating dialogue can be modified according to each child's readiness to talk. One may ask either narrow or broad questions. *Narrow questions* require only "yes" or "no" answers, a short reply, or a choice between alternatives the leader poses.

T: Do you like your job? (yes or no)
C: Yes.
T: When do you think the rest of your crew will return? (short reply)
C: Tomorrow.
T: Is that difficult or easy to do? (choice of alternative)
C: Difficult.

Because these questions can be answered easily, the child is under minimum pressure.

Broad questions call for more reflective thinking. They ask for opinions, motivations, and value judgments, and require reasoning. They usually cannot be anwered in only a few words. For example,

How do you feel about your job?
What kind of working conditions would you prefer to have?
Why have you chosen to stay behind when others have journeyed on ahead?

Verbal children prefer the challenges of the broad questions, while more reticent children can feel threatened by too many of them too soon.

The following examples demonstrate the leader's use of broad and narrow questions while playing a scene based on the story, "The Peddler and His Caps" (35). The leader has asked groups of three children each to think of possible villagers they might be and the different reasons tney might have for not wanting to buy a hat from the peddler. Notice that the children in the following example are at ease in verbalizing, particularly Child #1.

T: Good morning. Isn't this a beautiful day?
C#1: Is It? I haven't noticed. I've been too busy.
T: Oh? What keeps you all so busy?
C#1: I'm an accountant and I have to add all the figures for the grocery store.
T: Oh, I'm sure you *are* very busy. And how about you?
C#2: We stack the shelves.
T: Well, I don't want to take much of your time. I have some fine hats and I wonder if you'd care to buy one?
C#1: Now, what would I do with a hat?
T: Why, couldn't you wear it?
C#1: I work all day long, from morning to night, and I never leave this house and I don't wear a hat inside. It's bad luck.
T: Well, how about you?
C#3: No, we don't want any, either. It's bad luck.

175

Another group of children in the same playing, however, are not as verbal. Notice how they give limited responses and the leader has to carry the scene. Narrow questions are used to continue the playing so that the children can still feel successful.

> **T:** Good morning. Isn't this a fine morning? (The three children giggle and only one responds.)
> **C#1:** Yes.
> **T:** What are you doing on this beautiful day?
> **C#1:** Cleaning.
> **T:** Ah, well, now, I have just the hat for you. It's the latest in dusting caps. Just the thing to wear when you're cleaning. Won't you buy one? (More giggling and finally:)
> **C#1:** No.
> **T:** Aw, shucks. Do you mind telling me why?
> **C#1:** (Pause and then whispers) I don't know.
> **T:** Would you like to look at any other hats I have here?
> **C#1:** No. (The other two shake their heads.)
> **T:** Well, thank you very much for your time. I guess I'll have to try someplace else. Goodbye.
> **All:** Bye.

There are times when children do not immediately answer a question the leader poses. They may lack knowledge and understanding of the subject, or they may simply need time to think. After allowing sufficient time, the leader can reword the question or continue the dialogue as if the unanswered question were not important to their conversation. Otherwise, the children may feel that they have failed in verbalizing. This could be detrimental to their future attempts at verbal interaction.

Simple Debate

With older children, an easy way to initiate dialogue with the whole class is to divide it in half and present each with an opposite viewpoint to uphold. An advantage of this technique is that the children all have a part they can identify with, whether they feel confident enough to voice their opinions or not. In some cases, the leader may wish to take "straw votes" from time to time to give children the opportunity to indicate their preferences nonverbally. These scenes can also be played at the desks, which simplifies organization.

For example, one-half of the room could make all the positive statements they can think of while the other half responds with the negative ones. The ideas can simply be called out by volunteers on either side of the room. The statements may be made in response to each other or they may be presented randomly. For example,

Yes.	No.
It's a beautiful day.	There's rain in the forecast.

Ice cream.	Spinach.
Vacation.	Schoolwork.
I love to watch TV.	The set's broken.

Other ideas may also be handled as simple debates, with the leader playing a mediating role. For example, in Roald Dahl's *Charlie and the Chocolate Factory* (68), Willy Wonka has difficulties with several children. One little girl, Violet, swells up like a blueberry and turns purple after disobeying orders not to chew the experimental gum. The Oompa-Loompas, or factory workers, have to take her away to the juicing room. Willy, the owner, is upset with Violet for disobeying his rules, but he would like to have her problem solved, also.

Although Violet really has no choices given to her in the book, a simple debate might take place if half the class are the Oompa-Loompas trying to convince the other half of the class, who all play the role of Violet, that being dejuiced is her only option. Violet, on the other hand, argues that there might be other solutions.

The leader, as Willy, moderates the discussion, calling on those who have ideas to express. To extend the scene further, Willy might also ask questions of each side. For example: What will happen to Violet in the juicing room? What sort of machines and equipment do you have in there? Violet, why did you disobey the orders? Has this ever happened to you before?

A similar arbitration scene might be played between the pilgrims and the crew of the *Mayflower* based on Wilma Hays's book (71). The captain wants to help the pilgrims get settled before leaving them to fend for themselves in a new country. But he is also worried about his crew. They are anxious to get home because it is December and the sailing will be difficult. Each day the crew members are becoming more hostile. Both the crew and the captain had wanted to be home for Christmas, but now it is impossible. The leader plays the captain and moderates the two sides of the argument, encouraging a discussion of the various reasons for going or for staying.

Character Panel Discussions

This technique, which was suggested in simpler form in the last chapter, may be used to present several viewpoints. Again, the structure is an orderly one and the children can remain seated at their desks throughout. The following are some possible ideas:

1. Leader hosts a talk show. All the panelists are the various stepmothers from folk and fairy tales. They tell their side of the story and try to convince the audience that they aren't so bad after all. The audience questions the details of their stories.

2. As a variation on searching for other viewpoints, take any folk or fairy tale and consider a reversal of character images. In Red Riding Hood, for example, is it

possible that the wolf might be a sympathetic character? Could his mother, or employer, or Boy Scout leader speak in his behalf and answer questions the audience poses? To keep up the tension, two other panelists could speak for Red Riding Hood and her Grandmother, too.

3. Historical events may also be played in this format. A panel of members of the Virginia Company might try to convince the audience to settle in the New World. The audience knows about the hardships and failures of the earlier colonies, however, and is reluctant.

4. The leader may also assign characters and viewpoints to the panel and the audience. For example, a town meeting is called; the leader is the mayor. Two panelists present the side of those who want a new factory built. One might be the president of the company and the other, a local contractor who will do the building. Both emphasize the number of jobs that will open up in the community, which has an unemployment problem. The other two panelists might represent environmentalists. One has data about the company's past record of waste disposal abuse, and another believes the plant location will pose unsolvable problems. Members of the audience are the citizens of the community. Some are unemployed; some work for the construction company which will do the building. Some live next to the plant site. The remainder are not sure how they feel about the issue.

Pair and Group Scenes

When children are comfortable with verbalizing they may want to handle pair and group scenes on their own. The leader may present a situation such as, ''You are a real estate agent trying to sell a ramshackle house to a doubtful client,'' or ''You are Cyrus McCormick trying to convince a skeptical farmer that the reaper is safe and workable.''

For a group scene the leader may suggest, ''The scene is a lost and found department. Different people enter with various objects they have found or to claim lost objects.'' Another possibility might be: ''The scene is a park bench. A wallet with money in it is lying on the ground. Who enters and what do they decide to do with the wallet?''

Variations

Pair and group conversations might also be turned into guessing games. The children can pretend to be fictional or historical characters, or even animals or inanimate objects, carrying on a conversation. The scene is stopped periodically so the conversationalists can be identified from the clues given. Here are two examples:

> I don't want you coming around here again!
> But what harm did I do?
> Harm? What about the food you ate and the furniture you broke?!
>
> Goldilocks and Papa Bear

I know you can do it; I have a lot of faith in you.
Well, I've sewn a lot of things, but this is a real challenge.
Here's the design we have in mind.
Ah, but five points are just as easy to make as six.

George Washington and Betsy Ross

Another variation is to let pairs and groups pantomime their conversations while audience members speak the dialogue for them.

Sharing Conversations

When children are comfortable with verbalizing, they may like to work out their ideas and then share them with the rest of the class. One helpful technique for sharing is to select several pairs or groups to converse. They are labeled pair (or group) 1, 2, 3, and so forth. The leader calls out the numbers randomly, and that pair or group is then given several seconds to share their conversation. The children do not know when their number will be called, which delights those who like challenges. The leader can also cut off the conversation at any time—even in mid-sentence. This control can limit those who might go on forever and eases those who are less verbal out of any embarrassing pauses. Some children like the additional challenge of carrying on the conversation of the previous pair or group, rather than taking up their own train of thought.

Conclusions for Dialogue Scenes

In all of the above dialogue scenes, there has been no concern for bringing the conversations to a conclusion. They can be left as exploratory ventures in which different points of view and various ideas and solutions are offered. In a sense, it is a similar process to brainstorming—searching for a number of ideas and possibilities before final decisions are made.

If the leader wishes the children to come to a conclusion—to settle on a decision—this should be set out for them at the beginning as a goal. While not all children may be able to achieve it, the teacher might say, "Try to find an answer to your problem to end your scene," as a challenge for those who can. Or the leader might guide the group to discover compromises so that both sides are satisfied.

In the next section we will discuss group stories and skits which usually do have solutions and endings.

Example from "Taper Tom"

In working with group scenes the leader and the children may play a scene several times. In the course of guiding the group through replayings, several of the techniques just discussed may be employed.

The following is an account of a leader's participation with a class of third-graders in the story "Taper Tom," or "The Princess Who Couldn't Laugh" (35).

After she told the story, the leader focused on the situation where numerous contestants offered to try their skills in attempting to make the Princess laugh. Initially the leader felt that the group would want to be the contestants. She would be the Princess, and through this role help carry the conversations when necessary as well as the organization of the various entertainments.

In the role of the Princess, she established that each contestant would announce himself or herself to the audience and bow upon entering and leaving the courtroom. (In character) "State your name, my good man (or woman), and bow before the court."

The children had suggested a variety of antics to make the Princess laugh, but when the ideas were enacted, they were all variations on the theme of pratfalls. During the first playing these ideas were accepted by the teacher. For the second playing, however, the leader suggested that they think of new ideas, omitting any falls.

For the replaying, the children suggested adding a panel of Princesses, some servants, and a guard. The leader felt that her participation might be necessary for organization, and she created the authority role of Queen.

During this experience the children's ideas for making the Princess laugh included tickling feet, telling jokes, flipping pancakes, playing in a musical band, dancing, and acrobatics. The Queen actually had very little to do this time. The children duplicated much of what she had established in her role as Princess. The children easily carried conversations, and the "Princesses" were particularly adept at keeping the entertainment progressing from one act to another. "Servants, give this man some money for his show; but we're still not laughing! Next!"

The teacher's leadership was necessary, however, when the musicians pretended to drink liquor. The leader initially chose to ignore the drinking, but when other children decided to imitate it, the "Queen" calmly and quietly told a servant that there would be "no drinking on the job." With no rancor, the servant obeyed, and the scene proceeded smoothly.

PAIR AND GROUP SKITS

With older groups and with classes that have had some dialogue work, the children may be ready to create their own stories and skits utilizing dialogue. Skits can be created in a number of ways and with a number of kinds of stimuli.

Improvisation

Skits are usually played *improvisationally*. Sometimes they are created on the spot, with very little planning; sometimes the children will work for a longer period of time on their ideas and even rehearse them before sharing them with others. However, unless dialogue is actually written out and memorized, the scene is said to be played improvisationally. The children may have their plot and some dialogue in mind, but neither they nor the audience know exactly how the scene will actually be played. The spontaneity of improvisation is what captures everyone's attention, even the players' themselves. It is also more like a real-life situation.

In some cases, children will want to work on improvisational ideas several times. The goal, then, is to keep the best features in the scene and drop out the less effective moments. The scene is then considered a group creation, and when it is finished to the group's satisfaction, everyone is usually ready to move on to another challenge.

Endings for Skits

It is helpful to suggest to the children that as they plan, they should work out an ending to their scene. This is necessary so that they will all know when they have reached the point when their scene is over. Even so, they may forget to do this. What happens then is that a scene can reach an argumentative stage, and fist-icuffs and wrestling seem to be the only way out. And often they cannot even bring that to an end.

In these cases, the leader may walk over to the group and ask quietly, "Do you have an ending?" If it does not have an ending or cannot think of one, then one might be narrated by the leader.

In the following example, the children have developed skits based on returning an item to the complaint department. One group could not settle its argument, so the teacher intervened.

> **T:** And so the complaint manager and the irate customer never got a chance to find out who would win the argument for the bell sounded for the closing of the department store. And to the strains of the Muzak playing "We Wish You a Merry Christmas," they all went home.

The leader might also have stepped in as the store manager, who could help them work out an agreement.

EVALUATION

Audience Behavior

As before, the leader may have to guide for sensitive audience behavior. Some classes are not unduly critical of each other. They may, in fact, identify with the children who falter and be very sympathetic.

Sometimes children will become impatient with their friends when they are having difficulty. *They* know what to say in the same situation, and so they may call out a line. "Mae! Tell him you don't want to go on the picnic!" "Psst, George, you're supposed to say . . ." Sometimes just a quiet reminder to anxious audience members will suffice. They sometimes need to have it explained that prompting from the audience interrupts the players' thinking and does more harm than good.

After the children have played their scenes, it is useful to have them evaluate their efforts. Self-evaluation continues to be important.

> What did you like about your scene?
> In your scene, what moments were the most enjoyable for you? Why?
> If you could do it over again, what would you want to change? Why?
> In your opinion, how successful was the ending to your scene? Why?

When children have a great deal of confidence in their ability to create dialogue scenes, the leader may want the audience to give its evaluation of each scene. Positive evaluation is paramount; the leader's wording of the discussion questions is crucial.

> What did you *like* about that scene?
> What were the things that were said by certain characters that were *especially believable?*
> What lines of dialogue were *especially typical* of the characters?
> During what moments did people *help each other?*

The leader's own feedback to the children will also be important. This may be particularly true if the children in the audience insist on being overly critical. Or if the scene could benefit from additional challenges, the leader may need to suggest these. As in previous work, however, it may be that continued playing of the material, more than anything else, results in more involving and believable dramatization.

SKIT IDEAS

Familiar stories. An easy beginning for group skits are reenactments of familiar material such as favorite television shows, television commercials, and simple folk tales. After brainstorming for topics as a class, children are divided into groups to plan their dramas.

Silent movies. Children can create dialogue for old silent movies or films in which the sound has been turned off. Check the school media center for filmstrips of wordless picture books that could be used for this purpose.

Sunday funnies. Select Sunday funnies with enough action that the basic plot of the story is understandable. Block out the dialogue and have the children create the story in their own words.

Talking pictures. Select pictures which show several people (or animals or objects) in a problem situation. Children may plan a solution to the scene, freeze into the picture, and then improvise the ending. It may even be appropriate to begin the scene prior to the conflict situation, too.

Proverbs. Children develop skits to illustrate a proverb.

"Two heads are better than one."
"All that glitters is not gold."
"A fool and his money are soon parted."

News story of the week. Children recreate their version of a news event. Having newspapers at hand can stimulate interest in reading further about the events as well as providing ideas for the skits.

Stories from advertisements. Check the newspaper ads for possible recreation of stories behind them. Items that are for sale or messages in the "Personals" section might pose possibilities. For example: "House for sale. Furnishings included. Vacating immediately. Best offer." "Learn to speed-read in one week. Success guaranteed or your money cheerfully refunded."

Opening lines. Skits can be based on opening lines, such as the following:

1. It seemed a perfect day for the event. Crowds were gathered for the momentous, historic occasion. One person in the crowd, however, seemed out of place.
2. Silently and without warning it seemed to come upon them like a thief in the night. Not until the following morning were they aware of what had happened.

Famous last words. Create skits that focus on "famous last words" such as:

"I have an idea that will revolutionize the world!"
"I know exactly what I'm doing!"
"I told you we should have called the police!"

Commercials. Create commercials for products not usually seen on television.

1. Sell yourselves as a group. What skills do you have? Who would you like to have hire you? What will you charge? Services guaranteed?
2. Recycle what might be considered junk. How might it be recycled for other uses? (Examples: One large oversized glove, used bubble gum, cracked mirror, one old tennis shoe)
3. Sell products from the past. How might a guillotine, a suit of armor, a covered wagon, or a spinning wheel have been marketed in their day?

If persuasive techniques of advertising have been studied, children might be asked to focus on a particular type of appeal such as the bandwagon approach, testimony, appeal to status, and so on.

Stories from unrelated words. Prepare a set of cards with *places*, another set for *things* (props), and another for *characters*. Groups select one card from each set. Shuffle cards to produce an infinite variety of combinations.

Settings	*Characters*	*Props*
elevator	Miss Piggy	treasure chest
Island of No Return	good fairy	magic wand
museum at midnight	prehistoric monster	flying carpet
airport	statue that comes	diamond necklace
abandoned mine shaft	to life	poison apple
lost & found department	Snoopy	singing harp
junkyard	miser	velvet cape
information desk	Superman/-woman	sneezing powder
haunted house	spy	seven-league boots
tower with revolving	detective	candelabra
restaurant	genie in a bottle	

Role-playing situations. There are a number of situations children can dramatize in order to explore various ways of handling personal and social problems. Sometimes the dramatizations will demonstrate unacceptable behaviors. but these can serve to illustrate the consequences of such behaviors. Searching for the most appropriate solutions becomes the goal.

1. Children have the habit of crossing an elderly woman's lawn. She confronts them one day. What happens next?

2. A group of children are throwing hard-packed snowballs at passing cars and shatter a windshield. The car stops and the driver starts shouting at the group. Then what happens?

3. A group of friends are bored and looking for something to do. A couple of them suggest shoplifting for the fun of it. Others are not so sure. What does the group finally decide to do?

4. A group of friends are playing. Two children, new to the neighborhood, enter the scene and ask to play. Some of the children don't want to include the newcomers. How does the scene end?

Prop stories. Collect a number of interesting props, bits of costume, pieces of material, and the like. Brainstorm some ideas for several of them. Who might have owned this jewel box? What does this key unlock? Where is the treasure buried according to this map? Then select three or four props from which each group of children can create a story. *After* the children have planned their stories, they may use any of the leftover props to add to their play.

For example, a scarf, candlestick, pocket watch, and mallet might suggest this story to a group: A woman (wearing the scarf) and her husband (carrying the pocket watch) are robbed. The only clue is the candlestick, which was dropped by the thief. A courtroom scene evolves, with the mallet as the judge's gavel. The thief, the butler in disguise, is apprehended when his fingerprints are found on the candlestick.

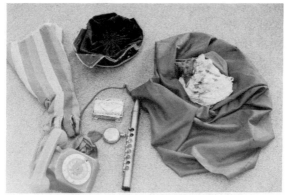

Props can stimulate story ideas.

"Who's got an idea about this strange-looking pitcher? Where do you suppose it came from? What was it used for? Who owned it?"

"We think and think . . . new ideas sometimes take time . . ."

"Ooh! I've got an idea!"

"More questions . . . we think some more . . ."

"Now, what sort of story might be made up out of these three props together?"

More ideas come now . . .

"We divide into groups . . . we talk and plan . . ."

"We decide who's going to be who . . ."

"And who's going to wear what . . ."

"I'm ready but nobody else is!"

One group has a story about going shopping.

"Oh, boy, it's our turn!"

"And everybody dies but me!"

FOR THE COLLEGE STUDENT

1. In groups, brainstorm for ideas for dialogue scenes and skits based on literature or other curricular areas. Keep a file of these materials.
2. Select one of your dialogue scenes and play it with your group. Take turns being the initiator and practice asking narrow and broad questions.
3. Set up a dialogue scene with your group and play the role of moderator.
4. Select one of the skit ideas presented in this chapter and plan it out with your group. Share your skits with the rest of your class.

LITERATURE FOR DIALOGUE SCENES

The following poems and stories involve pair and group encounters and offer interesting possibilities for creating dialogue. They are arranged in alphabetical order according to title. The following symbols are used to indicate the age level they might be best suited for:

Y   young children in kindergarten, first, and second grades

M   middle-grade children in third and fourth grades

O   older children in fifth and sixth grades

M—O   "Barter," Sara Teasdale.   (1)
"Life has loveliness to sell . . ." What would Life as a salesperson have to sell? What would Life say trying to convince someone to buy? What would you trade for Life's loveliness?

M—O   "The Builders," Sara Henderson Hay.   (31)
A person speaks critically of someone's lack of building capabilities. There is a strong reference to the story of the "Three Pigs." To whom is the person speaking, and what might the other person say in return?

Y—M   "Doorbells," Rachel Field.   (4) (35)
You never know who might be ringing your doorbell.

M   "The Hare and the Bear," Yasue Maiyagawa.   (21)
A bear accidentally injures a hare and tries to nurse him back to health. But the hare takes advantage of the situation.

M   "How Wihio Made a Trade," Grace Jackson Penney.   (37)
Wihio tricks some rabbits into his bag. Then he bargains with Coyote for a bigger bag, which turns out to have buffalo bones in it.

M   *Just Say Hic!* Barbara K. Walker. Chicago: Follet, 1965.
Hasan, a simple fellow, is told to repeat the word salt (hic) to remember what to buy. He is overheard to say the word and there begins a series of misunderstandings as each person he meets tells him to say a different word.

M—O   *The King's Fountain,* Lloyd Alexander. New York: Dutton, 1971.
A king wants to build a fountain that would cut off the water supply to the people. A poor man tries to find someone to persuade the king not to build the fountain. Each has his excuse, and the poor man is left to speak to the king himself.

M   "Mean Song," Eve Merriam.   (40)
Mean things are said in nonsense words. Who is the speaker, and why are they so angry? What does the other person say?

M   "Mrs. Peterkin Puts Salt in Her Coffee," Lucretia Hale.   (35)
The chemist tries a variety of chemicals, the old woman tries herbs, but no one can get rid of the salty taste.

M   *Not This Bear!* Bernice Myers. New York: Four Winds, 1967.
A little boy in a furry coat and hat has to convince a bear family that he is not one of them.

Y—M   "Overheard on a Saltmarsh," Harold Monro.   (31)
A goblin and a nymph argue over some green glass beads. What reasons do they have for wanting them?

M—O   "Phizzog," Carl Sandburg.   (4)
Create a dialogue scene in which you receive your newly made face and you want to exchange it.

M—O   "The Princess Who Always Believed What She Heard," Mary C. Hatch. (42)
A contest is held to see who can tell a story big enough so that the Princess will say, "It's a lie!"

Y—M   "The Rabbit, the Bear and the Zinniga-Zanniga," Dr. Seuss. Boston: Houghton Mifflin Reader, *Bright Peaks.*
A rabbit outsmarts a bear by convincing him he's sick.

M—O   "The Short Horse," Ellis Credle.   (38)
Uncle Bridger teaches Jess how to talk his way out of renting a horse.

M—O   "Southbound on the Freeway," May Swenson.   (31)
A visitor from "Orbitville" mistakes cars for Earth creatures and gives an interesting description of them. To whom is he reporting?

M—O   "Summons," Robert Francis.   (31)
What would be something important to summon a person to? How will the summoned person react?

M   "The Three Wishes," Olive Beaupré Miller.   (35)
The old tale of the husband and wife who wish foolishly for pudding, then for the pudding to be on the wife's nose, leaving the final wish to remove it.

M   *The Tiger in the Teapot,* Betty Yurdin. New York: Holt Owlet, 1968.
A family tries to entice the tiger out of the teapot before teatime. The little sister succeeds.

Y—M   "The Tiger, the Brahman, and the Jackal," Flora Annie Steel. A Brahman enlists the aid of a clever jackal to help him outwit a tiger who wants to eat him.

O   "A Travelled Narrative," Charles M. Skinner.   (51)
Ichabod, a "shiftless fellow," tries to sneak out of the general store with butter hidden under his hat. The other customers try to detain him with conversation so the butter will melt and give him away.

M—O   "Two Friends," David Ignatow.   (33)
It seems that two friends who pass each other and talk hurriedly really don't listen to each other's comments.

M   "The Zax," Dr. Seuss.   (32)
Two Zax meet and neither will give way for the other—ever. Why?

Chapter Eleven

Story
Dramatization

We have already referred to a number of stories and to various ways of dramatizing them. Some of the stories were essentially pantomime; others were essentially dialogue encounters. But there are also many stories, some simple and some more complex, which are a mixture of both pantomime and dialogue and need other techniques for dramatizing them. In this chapter, we will examine some additional ways of approaching story dramatization.

Story dramatization generally refers to the process of making an informal play improvisationally from a story. The dramatization is created by the group, facilitated by the leader, after much interchanging of roles and experimentation of ideas. The playing and experimenting may take place during one class period or may extend over days' or even weeks' time.

Our definition of story dramatization goes further to include using story material as a stimulus for creating a number of drama activities without necessarily performing the story as an improvised play. The many aspects of the story, the characters, the setting, the situations, are all explored and extended through multiple activities.

First we shall look at story dramatization which culminates in improvised playing and then at story dramatization which uses story material as a basis for exploratory work.

STORIES INTO PLAYS

Selecting the Story

Several considerations should be made in selecting a story for dramatization. Assuming that the literature is of good quality, the story should also have appeal for both the leader and the children. In addition, there should be interesting action in the story that can be played satisfactorily without elaborate stagings. The dialogue should be interesting, but not so complicated that the children are frustrated in their attempts to improvise from it. The characters should be believable and in sufficient number (or capable of being expanded) so that the entire class can be involved in the playing, should this be desirable.

Presenting the Story

Stories may be presented in a variety of ways. They may be read or told in the leader's own words. Some stories are available on excellent recordings. Illustrations may be shared if the leader feels they will help the dramatization rather than stifling it. Some leaders might even consider showing films of stories. Whatever method of presentation is used, the focus should be on helping the children understand both the action of the story and the interaction of the characters so that they can recreate it and expand upon it.

Dialogue

An important part of the presentation of the story is the dialogue. Children usually listen very carefully to the dialogue in the stories that are read or told to them. Much of that dialogue is repeated in their playings and improvised upon. If the dialogue is too complicated, it should be simplified.

Sometimes the addition of dialogue to the storytelling helps the children see verbalizing possibilities. Often leaders change indirect dialogue to direct dialogue for this reason. For example, a line might read,

> As the young man went down the road he met an old woodcutter. He asked the old man if he knew the way to town. The old man told him to follow his nose.

Here is the result of adding direct dialogue to the above passage:

> As the young man went down the road, he met an old woodcutter. He said to the old man, "Excuse me, sir, I wonder if you could tell me the way to town?"
> The old man answered, "Follow your nose, follow your nose. You can get to almost anywhere you want if you follow your nose!"

Casting the Story

For first playings the leader may need to play the main role. If the leader prefers not to do this, he or she should try to cast the children who will be the most successful in order to establish the model for the rest of the class to build on.

Double (or even triple) casting remains a useful technique in aiding the children with both action and dialogue. And it allows more children the opportunity to play the various parts with fewer replayings.

Organization through Narration and Character Role

Generally a teacher's main concern with story dramatization is planning and facilitating in the most efficient manner. Two techniques the leader will find indispensable in organizing the dramatization have already been discussed several times: narration and playing a character role. In narration, the leader guides from outside the dramatization whenever it is needed, while with a character role, the guiding is from within. Both techniques can even be used in the same dramatization.

The leader can use narration to

1. open the story.
    "Once upon a time there was . . ."
2. guide the story if it lags or if the children forget the sequence of events.
    "And then the bear started off down the road . . ."
3. control the action if problems arise.
    "Finally the people decided to stop arguing and do something about the situation . . . "
4. add pantomime ideas if the children need suggestions.
    "The rabbit looked at himself in the mirror and admired his new clothes."
5. provide transitions for scenes, indicating passage of time or change of environment.
    "The next morning the old lady went out to the smokehouse . . ."
6. close the story.
    "and he never went looking for trouble again."

The leader can use the playing of a character role in story dramatization in the following ways:

1. As the main character, the leader can carry the dialogue, if necessary, and become the pylon around which the children organize themselves and play their parts. This is most helpful in stories with younger children.
2. In a secondary role, such as a king's prime minister or a friend to the central character, the leader can offer advice and suggestions in character which help the story along.
3. The leader can step into a scene in a spontaneously invented role and help progress the story along if the sequence of events is forgotten.
4. The leader can step into a scene in a spontaneously invented role and reactivate the children's involvement if the playing is becoming perfunctory.
5. The leader can step into a scene in a spontaneously invented role and offer new situations for the children to react to and new challenges for the children to solve.

Additional Aids for Organization

Although narration and playing a character role help immensely in organizing and guiding the playing, there are other techniques the leader can use.

First is the careful organization of space. The dramatization can take place in a number of areas of the classroom. Usually the front of the classroom is used as the "stage." But scenes may also be set in various areas around the classroom. It is also helpful to place the scenes around the room in chronological order of their appearance in the story.

The leader should decide ahead of time where the scenes will be played. The plan is explained to the children and perhaps mapped out on the chalkboard. By separating and grouping the children in various parts of the classroom, it is clearer both to the leader and to the children what parts they are playing and where their part in the story occurs. Sometimes the children can help in these decisions.

Secondly, the leader should use the desks whenever possible. Desks can be "homes" for townspeople, "pens" for animals, "stores" for shopkeepers, and so forth. Whenever possible, large groups should remain at their desks until it is time for their scene. These children can also be the audience which will be needed for evaluation.

Thirdly, the leader can look for the natural controls within the story itself. Sometimes characters are rendered immobile in frozen positions because they are enchanted (as in "Sleeping Beauty") or for other reasons. Some characters may logically go to sleep or take a rest. Often characters can "return to their homes" or desks. Such controls should be capitalized upon so that not all children are moving and/or talking at the same time. They are quieted but still feel as if they are involved in the story. If these controls are not explicit in the story, the leader may add them in the telling of the story or in the narration.

SIMPLE STORY DRAMATIZATION

The Cat and the Parrot

The leader will find that there are some stories that are so easily dramatized that they can be gone through immediately. More ideas may be added to the story in subsequent playings. The following is an example of this approach using Sara Cone Bryant's story "The Cat and the Parrot" (3).*

> Synopsis: A parrot is the dinner guest in the home of a cat. A meager meal is served, but the parrot returns the invitation to the cat and serves a feast. The cat eats everything, including his host, and casually sets out for home. On the way he meets, one by one, an old woman; an old man with a cart and a donkey; a wedding procession including a newly married prince, his wife, his soldiers, and many elephants walking two by two. The cat tells everyone he meets to get out of his

---

* Another version of this story is Jack Kent's picture book *Fat Cat* (Parents', 1971).

way. When they refuse he eats them: "Slip! slop! gobble!" He finally eats two land crabs who pinch a hole in his stomach, and everyone escapes. The cat is left to sew up his coat.

The leader can play the main character and be in a legitimate position to make the story line progress and to give orders and directions. Because there are numerous other characters in the story, the entire class can play seated in a circle. The playing can begin when the cat leaves the parrot's house. All the characters can be seated according to the order of their appearance in the scene.

To designate that they have been eaten, the characters can line up behind the leader and continue on the journey with the cat in follow-the-leader fashion. The leader might pretend to experience a bit of queasiness and slow his or her pace as the stomach gets fuller. The cat might also laboriously try climbing up a hill or crossing a swinging bridge. Of course, all of the children who have been "eaten" must imitate the movements of the cat, since they are all one entity!

After the cat falls asleep under a tree and the children escape from the stomach, they can tiptoe back to their "homes" or seats. The leader may even assume a narrator's voice and direct this part if control is needed. Then the leader as the cat wakes up and finishes off the story by sewing up the hole in his or her coat, much to the cat's dismay and the children's delight.

If the leader wishes to spend more time with the story, other activities can be added. In a separate activity, the various characters can be pantomimed moving and acting as the children think they might: the prince's walk is stately, the donkey trots, or the old woman hobbles angrily. The children also might like to think of specific tasks the characters could be doing as the cat travels along his way. The old man with the donkey and cart, for example, might be trying to mend a broken wheel.

Once the leader "carries" the children through such a story, there are usually a few who would like to play the main part. The leader may then cast one or two children as the cat, while continuing to play the character in a subordinate manner if it seems necessary. By the time the story is played a third time, the role of the cat can be left entirely to the children.

Bartholomew and the Oobleck

Other stories can be engineered to fit the previous pattern. For example, the basic action in Seuss's *Bartholomew and the Oobleck* (Random House, 1949) is fairly simple. It is a story that can be played by any elementary grade. With younger children, the leader will probably need to play the role of Bartholomew the first time.

In simplifying this story, the leader may decide to tell it rather than read it. Later, if the leader and the children wish to work with the story further, the original version may be shared.

In the opening scene, the King complains to Bartholomew about how

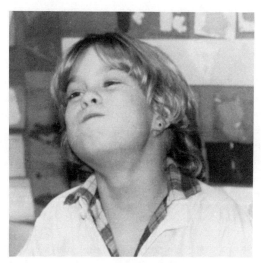

The Captain of the Guard in a Seuss story gets his mouth stuck when he tries to eat oobleck.

boring all weather conditions are. Each of these roles could be double cast. The Magicians (three/five) are summoned in spite of Bartholomew's warning, and they go off to their cave (corner of the room) to make the oobleck. They work far into the night while Bartholomew, the King, and the entire kingdom go to sleep (at the desks). By morning, the Magicians finish their task and fall exhausted into bed.

When Bartholomew sees the green, sticky oobleck falling from the sky the next morning, he goes off to the Bellringer, the Trumpet Blower, and the Captain of the Guard for their help in warning the people. But in the process, each becomes stuck in some manner in oobleck. These parts can all be triple cast and grouped in the three remaining corners of the room.

As Bartholomew swings back through the center of the classroom, he passes the various townspeople (at their desks) all stuck in oobleck. He decides to return to the palace, and here he finds the palace personnel in the same sticky predicament. In his frustration, Bartholomew demands that the King apologize for his unwise behavior. After the King apologizes, the oobleck slowly melts and everyone becomes unstuck. The story ends with a rousing cheer for King Derwin, who has decided that the natural elements are much better than oobleck.

EXTENDED STORY DRAMATIZATION

Sometimes story dramatization is given a more thorough treatment than has just been described. The story may have a variety of characters, or an involved plot, or may require extensive dialogue to forward the action. Some stories, though simply written, can be made more elaborate by adding more characters, scenes, and plot embellishment.

Programming

With extended dramatization a programmed approach is often used. Programming means analyzing and dividing the story into all the separate activities it offers. The scenes are played one at a time, usually according to their level of difficulty. For example, movement or action scenes might be played before dialogue scenes are attempted. Or, scenes that can be narrated might precede those that require more creative interpretation. Activities that can be enacted by all the children simultaneously are played first. To dramatize the entire story, the "rehearsed" scenes are then played in the appropriate sequence.

Space

Usually it is best to have the children play initial activities at their desks or in limited space. As a start the leader may focus on the main character and narrate some action from the story or develop some pantomime activities related to the story for all to play. In this way, the children can all begin to identify with the characters immediately and can participate in at least part of the story right away.

Once the children move away from their desks, however, they aren't usually anxious to return to them. Therefore, the leader should program the playing to move gradually from the desk to the larger playing areas.

With all of the above in mind, some leaders begin with activities related to a story even before telling it. For example, they might have the children play some pantomimes such as pretending to eat food, knocking on a strange door, peeking in a window, sleeping on a hard surface and then on very soft pillows, even before the story of "The Three Bears" is introduced for dramatization.

Discussing the Story

Although children are usually satisfied with playing the action in many materials, depth of characterization and meaning usually cannot be reached without some discussion and analysis.

While there may be many interpretations of meaning in stories, the leader may need to devote some thought to the theme to be focused on, as one leader discovered when he used the book, *Horton Hatches the Egg* (p. 209), by Dr. Seuss. In this story, an elephant does a favor for a runaway bird, agreeing to sit on her egg for a day. The bird does not return, and Horton feels obligated to wait a year until it hatches. In spite of the many difficulties he encounters, he remains "faithful 100 percent."

In introducing this story the leader focused on the following question:

T: Have you ever made a promise and then wished you hadn't?

This question caused the children to think of many unpleasant experiences they had had and didn't wish to repeat. The leader ignored Horton's faithfulness, and the more the children discussed the story, the stronger their conviction became that anyone who would go through such an experience would have to be stupid. Eventually they lost all interest in the story.

An introduction that focuses more clearly on the theme of the story might be the question, "Did you ever do a very nice favor for someone, even though it took a great deal of work on your part?"

Sometimes children have difficulties understanding the motivations of characters. One leader discovered this in a discussion prior to a story from *Tom Sawyer* (138). When she asked, "What kind of person is Aunt Polly and how does Tom feel about her?" she was deluged with responses such as, "She's a witch and rides a broom." One child, in all seriousness, said "Tom would like to take her out behind the barn and beat the crap out of her." The interpretation was that Aunt Polly was sadistic and extremely cruel to Tom.

By examining the evidence in the book, the leader guided the children to see that Aunt Polly did care for Tom but often had difficulty accepting the very natural inclinations of boys his age, and that Aunt Polly also made comparisons between Tom and Sid, who was considered a sissy by most of the children but a model child by Aunt Polly's standards. The children came to realize that her demands of Tom were no more or less than those for many boys of his day. Tom knew and accepted Aunt Polly's demands, although he was not above trying to get around them whenever he thought he could get away with it.

There are times when there can be leeway for interpretations. For example, when one leader asked, "How do you suppose Little Red Riding Hood felt as she skipped down the path on the way to Grandma's house for a visit?" one little girl doggedly replied, "Awful." When the teacher asked, "Why?" the little girl's understandable response was, "Because her mother made her go."

One six-year-old boy felt that the Little Billy Goat in "The Three Billy Goats Gruff" would run away rather than talk to the Troll. "*I'd* run away," he said. "I wouldn't stop to talk! I'd be too scared!"

In these latter two cases, there is no reason why the children could not play the roles as they saw them. As long as the overall interpretation of the story is not affected adversely, various insights into the characters can add richness and new meaning for everyone.

Rehearsing the Scene

As the children continue to work with the story, the leader may cast only a part of the class at a time in the scenes while the rest of the class observes. Then the scene is recast and replayed in order to give all the children a chance to play as many characters as possible.

For older children, the leader might discuss a scene and then divide the

Pairs of sixth graders practice moving the dead body in "Old Dry Frye."

children into groups. Each group can work out its ideas for the scene, rehearse it briefly, and then share it with the class.

Playing the Story

When the entire story is played without interruption, the children may still need assistance in remembering the sequence of events. There are several ways to help. As mentioned before, the leader may serve as a narrator, may step into the playing in a character role, or may line up the characters in the order of their appearance. Another possibility may be to write a simple outline of the story on the board.

Evaluation

Evaluation of the dramatization can be made after each scene is played. To evaluate pantomime scenes as objectively as possible, several individual children or pairs may enact a scene at the same time. One leader chose this method for a serious scene in "The Legend of the Moor's Legacy" (35). Several children were paired to play the scene in which the water carrier meets the dying Moor and takes him home with him. As the leader side-coached, some children played the scene with deep feeling and involvement, while others had difficulty. The audience readily saw which actions were convincing, and no comment was necessary for the unconvincing ones.

The points to consider in the evaluation center on whether the story is understandable. The action should be clear. The characters should be believable, both in their actions and in their dialogue.

When the evaluation is made, it is important to use the characters' names rather than the children's names. This practice can be encouraged both in self-evaluation and in audience evaluation.

T: The King really seemed to care about his subjects.
C: I spoke the Captain's orders in a gruff voice, but I tried to show that he was a kind person by smiling just a little.

Replaying the Story

As the children replay the story, often additional characters and scenes are created. The leader and the class together may also think of ways to include sound effects, lighting, music, or other additions the children can operate for themselves. These additions should grow out of the group creative process, facilitated rather than imposed by the leader.

CREATING A PLAY FROM A SIMPLE STORY

"Why the Bear Is Stumpy Tailed"

The following extended illustration demonstrates one way of analyzing and playing the story, "Why the Bear Is Stumpy Tailed" (4). In this story, which is usually enjoyed by young children, a bear is told by a sly fox that he can catch fish if he will just put his tail down in the water and wait for the fish to bite. Since it is winter time, the bear cuts a hole in the ice and begins to fish. He waits patiently, but in the meantime the water freezes over. When he gets up, he discovers his tail is caught fast. As he struggles to free himself, he pulls off his tail, and that is why today bears have short tails instead of long ones.

Narrating

The leader may choose to narrate the story the first time through. Everyone can play the part of the bear, and the action can begin with his decision to go and fish.

T: . . . So the bear decides he will try catching fish the way the fox said *he* did. The bear goes off toward the pond. He feels very hungry and can hardly wait to catch a long string of fish.

Although the action scene in which the bear loses his tail is an exciting one, there is a minimum of movement during the bear's long wait. The leader's narration here will be most important in making the story interesting and exciting.

T: The bear settled himself down and waited for the fish to begin to bite. His coat was thick and heavy and he felt snug and warm, even though his tail was in the ice water. He looked around at all the sights. Some animals were scampering nearby and he waved to them. He thought he could see some fish under the ice darting to and fro. Soon he began to get a little bit chilled, so he breathed on his paws to warm them. . . .

The narration could include additional characters. One group of second-graders suggested that skaters could be skating on the pond just before the bear got there. They also wanted trees, a sun, and snowflakes falling as night approached. In order to give the trees and sun action to perform, the leader narrated, "The wind blew as it got colder and the trees bowed and waved and danced in the wind." It was decided that the sun would be in the background but should make a slow, arcing path to indicate rising and setting while the bear fished.

Creative Pantomime

The same scene of the bear fishing could be played as a creative pantomime. The children could be questioned about the equipment they would use and what they could think of to do in order to pass the time waiting.

> **T:** What do you think the bear takes with him in order to fish? How does he cut the hole in the ice?
>
> **C:** The pond is covered with snow, and the bear has to shovel it away before he can cut the hole.
>
> **C:** The bear cuts a hole with his sharp claws.
>
> **C:** He has an ice cutter and a tiny ice house and a small heater.
>
> **T:** When the bear had to sit there for such a long time, he must have gotten tired. I wonder what he does to pass the time?
>
> **C:** He gets cold and wraps his muffler around his ears and he twiddles his thumbs and then he hums a song about the summertime to himself.
>
> **C:** He reads a book.
>
> **C:** He keeps looking for someone to come and talk to him, but no one's there but the trees; so he counts all the trees he can see.
>
> **T:** When I play the music, you start pretending to be the bear when he goes to the pond. When you think you've got enough fish, you pull your tail until it pops off. If some of you finish your ideas before other people do, just sit down where you are and wait.

Now the leader may side-coach and remind the children of some of their ideas.

Dialogue

In order to help the children play the dialogue scene in the beginning of the story, the leader could be the fox and then the bear briefly, with the children at their desks.

> **T:** Let's pretend I'm the fox and you're the bear. What might you say to me when you see me with a long string of fish? Remember how you like fish. (Leader pantomimes holding fish and looking at them admiringly, licking chops.)

C: Those are good-looking fish. Where'd you get them?
C: I want some fish like that. I'm hungry.
C: Hello, Fox. Where'd you get those fish? I'll buy some from you.
T: Good. Now let's pretend I'm the Bear and you're the Fox. What would you say to me? (As the Bear) Hey, Fox, where'd you get those fish?
C: Uh, well, see, you cut a hole in the ice and put your tail in it. They'll bite and you'll get some.
C: It's real easy. You just cut a hole in the ice.
C: You put your tail in the water, but you have to wait a long time. But it's really fun to do. And these fish are delicious.

If the leader wants to encourage more dialogue, he or she can pretend to be unconvinced and add, "Aw, I don't believe that. You just made up that story." Now the Foxes will have to work a little harder to convince the Bear of their fishing method.

Another way of playing the dialogue scene is to pair up four verbal volunteers, double cast as the Bear and the Fox, and try out the scene in front of the class. The leader may step in as either another bear or another fox if additional help is needed.

Additional Scenes

For further creative work the group may elaborate on the story. The following are some suggestions.

Additional pantomime scenes may be created:

T: The story doesn't tell us, but what do you think the fox would be doing before he meets the bear?
C: He's planning on how he's going to trick the bear. He's writing all his ideas in a notebook.
C: He's down at the market buying fish. That's where he really got them.
C: He's really ice-fishing, but he's doing it with a real fishing pole.

A similar pantomime scene might be made up about the bear:

T: What do you think the bear is doing before he meets the fox?
C: He's combing his beautiful tail.
C: He's searching for a good breakfast.
C: Sleeping. He loves to sleep.

These pantomimes may be played by half of the class sharing their ideas with the other half. Or a count-freeze pantomime (See Chapter Eight) may be arranged.

An additional dialogue scene might be created:

T: Let's suppose that the bear has suddenly discovered that he has been tricked by the fox and that he is stuck in the ice. But he doesn't want to admit what has happened because he's embarrassed.

Now, there might be a number of animals who come by and see him there. Each has a reason for wanting the bear to leave, and they try to coax him away.
Because he doesn't want them to see him stuck there, he has to make up a story. Who do you suppose might pass by? What might be their reason for asking the bear to leave? What reason would the bear give for having to stay where he is?
C: His mother wants him to come home to dinner, but he says he isn't hungry.
C: A friend comes by and wants him to play but he says he would rather ice-fish.
C: Some little animals come by and wonder why he doesn't chase them like he usually does, and he tells them he is getting too old for that.

For a final scene, the leader might play a Tail Salesperson who has heard about the bear's problem and has arrived from out of town to sell the bear a new tail. There is a complete sample case of all sorts of tails the bear might be interested in. Color, style, size, and price are all considered. The tails can be tried on and viewed in the salesperson's full-length mirror.

The leader might play the salesperson's role first and then divide the children into pairs, using the techniques discussed in Chapter Eleven.

STORY MATERIAL
AS A STIMULUS FOR DRAMA ACTIVITIES

At the beginning of this chapter we stated that our definition of story dramatization also included using story material as a stimulus for a number of activities which do not necessarily culminate in an improvised play. For such experiences we generally divide the material into pantomime and dialogue scenes and then further subdivide those categories into individual and group playing. After such an outline of activities is made, it is fairly easy to select the activities which might be meaningful for a group to explore.

If it is desirable, various activities in such a listing can be used as rehearsal units and then spliced into a full-length dramatization. The following is one such plan.

The Emperor's New Clothes
Hans Christian Andersen

I. Pantomime Activities
    A. Individual Pantomime
        1. You are the Emperor who loves clothes and you are posing for your latest portrait. How will you pose to show off all the new garments you're wearing?
        2. You are the Emperor, proudly walking in the procession, listening to all the appreciative comments of the admiring crowd. Then you hear the voice of the child saying you have no clothes on. You freeze. How will you look? (Leader plays processional music and then says the child's line.)
        3. The rogues wove their cloth at night by candlelight. Be one of the candles

slowly melting and then burning out as daybreak approaches. (This could serve as a quieting activity.)

4. When the Emperor doesn't get his way, he throws a temper tantrum. Demonstrate one of his temper tantrums—silently and in slow motion.

5. The Emperor returns to his palace after the procession. Think of three things he might do. As I count, pantomime each of your three ideas.

B. Pair and Group Pantomime

1. You are the two swindlers setting up your loom. You're unpacking it and setting it up carefully for this special job. The court is watching you, so look professional.

2. In groups of eight-ten, create the special loom on which the marvelous fabric is to be woven.

3. You are the swindlers putting on a good show of how diligently and carefully you work at weaving, cutting out and sewing these garments. (Music background)

4. You are the rogues when you are certain that no one is watching you work. What will you do to pass the time and to entertain yourself, locked up in the workroom?

5. The Emperor is being dressed for the great procession by the two rogues. Mirror this activity.

6. In groups of ten, create a frozen picture of the procession.

7. The band is rehearsing for the procession. A conductor leads as you play. Use groups of six. (Use march music such as Elgar's "Pomp and Circumstance.")

II. Verbal Activities

A. Solo

1. You're the Emperor's young son or daughter. Tell us what Christmas present you're getting for your dad this year. How do you know he'll like it?

2. You're the Emperor's mother. How did your son get so interested in clothes? Has he always been like this?

3. You're the parade marshall, planning the procession. Who will be in it, what will be the parade route, and what will be the order of people in the procession?

B. Pairs and Groups

1. The Emperor has learned his lesson about listening to clothes swindlers. But today new swindlers come to town. What will they try to sell to the Emperor? Will it have unusual qualities as the special cloth did? Remember that the Emperor may be harder to convince than last time. Groups of three.

2. You are the old Minister visiting the rogues. What are your excuses for having trouble seeing the material?

3. You are an official who is to visit the weavers and see how the work is coming along. You don't trust them and you don't really believe their story, but you don't want to say so to the Emperor. What else will you use as your excuse to him to get out of going on this mission?

4. You are the Emperor's wife, who has a meager supply of funds for clothes. You'd like a new gown and you're trying to get money from the Minister of Finance. Show him your wardrobe as evidence that you need a bigger clothes allowance.

5. You are the citizens of the kingdom where the Emperor spends huge sums on his clothes. There are a number of building projects, community funds, and so forth that need tending to. You go as a committee to the Emperor to present your case on behalf of the kingdom. The Emperor and his advisors reluctantly decide to fund one of the projects. Let's play the scene and find out how the Emperor decides which project will be funded.

6. You are the rogues rehearsing your description of the fabric you have woven. The description might include comments on the lovely patterns, the careful attention to detail, the unusual color combinations.

7. The rogues have received an order of knighthood to wear in their buttonholes and the title of ''Gentlemen Weavers.'' Now that they have left the kingdom, they would like to sell this prize. Bargain with a merchant for the best price you can get for this medal.

8. The Emperor has spent the entire kingdom's treasury on clothes for himself. Now he must go to the bank for a loan. He must try to convince the bank president that he will be a good credit risk. The bank president is a shrewd operator.

9. The King's garment workers are exhausted from trying to keep up with all the new clothes orders the Emperor demands. We hear them complaining as they work. The scene ends when they decide to go on strike.

10. You are a clothing designer who has just designed a new outfit for the Emperor to wear. It is the most unusual design the Emperor has ever seen. Convince the Emperor to order this outfit from you, even though the Emperor is not sure it's suited to him.

11. The Emperor holds a press conference some time after the incident with the rogues. Reporters still have questions about what happened, but they must be careful in asking them so as not to rouse the Emperor's anger. The Emperor may enlist the aid of his Minister in answering the questions.

PRESENTATION OF
STORY DRAMATIZATIONS

Usually story dramatizations are played in the classroom, and only for that group's viewing. However, if the children's interest remains high throughout their work and they are satisfied with their efforts, they may want to share their work with other classes or with relatives and friends.

The presentation of any creative drama experiences should remain improvised. If the class has spent time with the project and it has been a meaningful experience, the children will probably be thoroughly familiar with their ideas and how they want to present them. They will have no need to recite memorized lines because the experience will have become a part of them.

Presentations can easily be given in an informal style right in the classroom. Elaborate costuming, scenery, and props are not necessary; the story and the people in it are more important than any embellishments. If any additions are used they should be kept to a minimum so that they do not dominate the presentation.

College students enact a frozen picture from "Snow White and the
Seven Dwarfs."

In presenting creative drama experiences, the children are selecting the
ideas and the materials that have appealed to them to share with an audience.
Such experiences can be more enjoyable and more educationally beneficial than
the presentation of a scripted play because the children have created a project
uniquely theirs.

FOR THE COLLEGE STUDENT

1. Select a simple story suitable for dramatization. Plan out its dramatization in
   the simplified form used for "The Cat and the Parrot" or *Bartholomew and the
   Oobleck* in this chapter. Present the story to your classmates and lead them in
   the dramatization of it. Discuss afterwards with your classmates the effectiveness of the entire activity.

2. Select a story suitable for more elaborate dramatization. Plan out the dramatization in the form used for "Why the Bear is Stumpy-Tailed" or "The Emperor's New Clothes" in this chapter. Present the story to your classmates and
   lead them in the dramatization of it. Discuss afterwards with your classmates
   the effectiveness of the entire activity.

3. Read some of the stories suggested in the bibliography at the end of this
   chapter. Choose your favorites and be prepared to discuss why you think they
   are good choices. Give special thought to their themes.

4. Select other stories suitable for dramatization and keep a file of them.

STORIES TO DRAMATIZE

The materials are arranged in alphabetical order. The following symbols are used to indicate the age level they might be best for:

Y young children in kindergarten, first, and second grades
M middle-grade children in third and fourth grades
O older children in fifth and sixth grades

Y "The Adventure of Three Little Rabbits," author untraced. (35)
Three little rabbits get stuck in some spilled syrup and almost become rabbit stew.

O "All Summer in a Day," Ray Bradbury. Chicago: Follett, 1970, *The World of Language, Book 6.*
Children on Venus anxiously wait for the sun, which shines one hour every seven years. Minutes before the sun appears, they lock Margot into the closet and forget about her during their hour in the outdoors.

O "Anansi and the Crabs," Philip Sherlock. (2)
Anansi wants to be a preacher but can't find a congregation.

M "Anansi and the Fish Country." Philip Sherlock. (2)
Anansi tries to trick fish by playing doctor.

M "Anansi Plays Dead," Harold Courlander and Albert Kofi Prempeh. (20)
Anansi pretends to die so that he will not have to be prosecuted for a crime, but the villagers trick him.

M "Anansi's Hat-Shaking Dance," Harold Courlander and Albert Kofi Prempeh. (20)
Anansi fasts and becomes so hungry he has to sneak food.

M *Anatole and the Cat,* Eve Titus. New York: McGraw-Hill, 1957.
A French mouse is a cheese taster in Duval's cheese factory. Other *Anatole* stories may also be of interest.

Y *Ask Mr. Bear,* Marjorie Flack. New York: Macmillan, 1932. (35)
Danny wants a birthday gift for his mother and goes to the animals for advice.

M *Bartholomew and the Oobleck,* Dr. Seuss. New York: Random House, 1949.
King Derwin of Didd gets tired of all the things that fall from the sky and orders oobleck to be substituted.

M *The Bigger Giant,* Nancy Green. Chicago: Follett, 1963.
Fin McCool, a giant, is afraid of a bigger giant. Fin's little wife outwits the bigger giant.

M *Bunya the Witch,* Robert Kraus and Mischa Richter. New York: Dutton, 1971.
Bunya discovers she's a witch when she accidentally turns children into frogs and their parents into pigs.

O "The Case of the Sensational Scent," Robert McCloskey. (94)
Robbers, a suitcase with $2,000, a skunk and after-shave lotion create an unusual adventure for Homer Price.

M "The Cat and the Parrot," Sara Cone Bryant. (3)
A cat with an insatiable appetite eats everyone he meets.

M—O "Clever Manka," Parker Fillmore. (4)
Czech folk tale about a girl who proves her intelligence on more than one occasion.

O   *The Clown of God,* Thomas Anthony DePaola. Harcourt Brace Jovanovich, 1978.
     A once-famous juggler gives his final performance before the statue of Mary and the Child. For mature groups.

M   "The Conjure Wives," Frances G. Wickes.   (35)
     Selfish witches are turned into owls.

M   *The Cuckoo's Reward,* Daisy Kouzel and Earl Thollander. New York: Doubleday, 1977.
     A cuckoo helps save the grain from fire in this Mexican folktale.

O   *The Devil's Bridge,* Charles Scribner, Jr. New York: Scribner's, 1978.
     The Devil promises a French town that he will build them a bridge for the price of a human soul.

M—O "The Doughnuts," Robert McCloskey.   (94)
     An adventure with a doughnut machine that just won't quit making doughnuts.

M   *The Dragon Takes a Wife,* Walter Dean Myers. Indianapolis: Bobbs-Merrill, 1972.
     Delightful story of a dragon who needs to win a battle with a knight so that he can get a wife. A fairy tries to help him, but nothing works until she turns herself into a lady dragon! Told in the black idiom.

O   *Duffy and the Devil,* Harve Zemach. New York: Farrar, Straus & Giroux, 1973.
     The Devil, like Rumplestiltskin, helps Duffy with her chores.

M   "The Elephant's Child," Rudyard Kipling. New York: Walker, 1970 and (4)
     The elephant's child, who has " 'satiable curtiosity," finds out some answers to his questions but gets a long nose doing it. After he discovers all of the advantages a long nose has, his relatives decide they want one also.

M   "The Emperor's New Clothes," Hans Christian Andersen.   (4) (35)
     A vain Emperor is swindled by rogues posing as weavers of a fabric invisible to those unworthy of the office they hold.

M   *Fat Cat,* Jack Kent. New York: Parents', 1971.
     Another version of "The Cat and the Parrot."

M   *The Fence,* Jan Balet. New York: Delacorte, 1969.
     A poor family in Mexico is taken to court by a rich family because the former sniffed the delicious aromas from the kitchen of the rich family's house.

Y—M *Gillespie and the Guards,* Benjamin Elkin. New York: Viking, 1956.
     Three brothers with powerful eyes become guards of the kingdom. The King offers a reward to anyone who can get past them. Gillespie, a young boy, tricks the guards.

M   "The Golden Touch," Nathaniel Hawthorne.   (35)
     The tale of a greedy king who wishes that everything he touches could be turned to gold.

O   *The Golem: A Jewish Legend,* Beverly McDermott. Philadelphia: Lippincott, 1976.
     A rabbi in Prague creates a clay figure to help suppress an uprising against the Jewish community.

M—O *Granny and the Desperadoes,* Peggy Parish. New York: Macmillan, 1970.
     Granny captures some desperadoes and turns them over to the sheriff, but not before she gets them to do chores for her.

Y—M *Horton Hatches the Egg,* Dr. Seuss. New York: Random House, 1940.
     Horton, the elephant, hatches an egg for lazy Maizie.

M   "How Jahdu Took Care of Trouble," Virginia Hamilton.   (45)
     Jahdu tricks Trouble and frees everyone from the huge barrel they have been
     caught in. One of the lovely tales a grandmother tells to instill black pride in her
     grandson.

M—O "How Pa Learned to Grow Hot Peppers," Ellis Credle   (38)
     Pa is too easygoing to be able to raise peppers with zip in them, so the family
     has to find a way to get him fired up.

M   "How the Animals Got Their Fur Coats," Hilda Mary Hooke.   (43)
     All the animals get lovely new coats except Moose, who gets the leftovers.
     Charming characters in a Canadian Indian legend.

M   "How the Birds Got Their Colors," Hilda Mary Hooke.   (43)
     Delightfully funny tale of how all the birds get colorful feathers except the
     Sapsucker. Canadian Indian legend.

M   "How the Little Owl's Name Was Changed," Charles E. Gillham.   (5)
     Brave Little Owl takes fire away from evil men in this Alaskan Eskimo
     folktale.

M   *How the Sun Made a Promise and Kept It,* Margery Bernstein. New York:
     Scribner's, 1974.
     In this retelling of a Canadian myth, the sun is captured and the animals attempt
     to free it.

O   *It Could Always Be Worse,* Margot Zemach. New York: Farrar, Straus &
     Giroux, 1976.
     Rabbi advises crowded, irritable family to keep taking animals into their house.
     Then, when he finally advises taking the animals out, the house seems spacious.
     Freeze the mayhem in the house each time the man goes to the rabbi.

M   *Is Milton Missing?* Steven Kroll. New York: Holiday House, 1975.
     A girl discovers her missing dog in a television studio starring in a commercial.

M—O *Jim and the Beanstalk,* Raymond Briggs. Reading, Mass.: Addison-Wesley,
     1970.
     New version of an old tale.

O   *Joco and the Fishbone,* William Wiesner. New York: Viking, 1966.
     Joco the Hunchback chokes on a fishbone and everyone tries to get rid of the
     body. Joco eventually coughs up the bone. A retelling of a tale from *The
     Arabian Nights.* Compare with "Old Dry Frye" in this bibliography.

Y   *Journal Cake Ho!* Ruth Sawyer. New York: Viking, 1953.
     The Journey Cake escapes Johnny as well as a variety of animals.

M—O *Kassim's Shoes,* Harold Berson. New York: Crown Publishers, 1977.
     Kassim finally agrees to throw out his old shoes, but then has trouble getting rid
     of them.

O   *King Orville and the Bullfrogs,* Kathleen Abell. Boston: Little, Brown, 1974.
     King loses a bagpipe-playing contest to his future sons-in-law but his problems
     only begin. Much detailed narration.

Y—M *King Rooster, Queen Hen,* Anita Lobel. New York: Morrow, 1975.
     Rooster and Hen decide to become King and Queen and gain their servants
     along the way in this Danish folktale.

M—O *The King's Stilts,* Dr. Seuss. New York: Random House, 1939.
     When the King's stilts are stolen, he becomes too depressed to protect the
     kingdom from its main enemy: large birds called Nizzards.

O   "Knights of the Silver Shield."   (49)
     A young man carries out his commander's orders in spite of his disappointment.

O   "The Legend of the Moor's Legacy," Washington Irving.   (35)
A water carrier inherits a secret passport to a cave of riches.

M—O   *Lentil,* Robert McCloskey. New York: Viking, 1940.
A boy saves the day for a small, Midwestern town with his harmonica.

Y   *The Little Engine That Could,* retold by Watty Piper. New York: Platt & Munk, 1954.
A little engine is able to take the stalled train over the mountain to deliver Christmas toys.

Y   "The Little House," Valery Carrick.   (34)
A group of little animals make their home in a jar until a Bear comes along.

Y—M   *The Little Rabbit Who Wanted Red Wings,* Carolyn S. Bailey. New York: Platt & Munk, 1978.
A rabbit gets his wish, but then finds that there are disadvantages.

Y—M   *Loudmouse,* Richard Wilbur. New York: Macmillan, 1968.
A mouse with a very loud voice turns out to be an effective burglar alarm.

M   *Lyle, Lyle, the Crocodile,* Bernard Waber. New York: Houghton Mifflin, 1965.
A crocodile who is more human than animal has remarkable adventures. Other *Lyle* stories may be of interest.

M   *The Magician Who Lost His Magic,* David McKee. New York: Abelard-Schuman, 1970.
Melric loses his magic because he misused it by helping people to do things they should do for themselves. He gets the magic back in time to save the day for the King.

M—O   *Many Moons,* James Thurber, New York: Viking, 1943.
A princess wishes for the moon and finally gets it.

Y—M   *Millions of Cats,* Wanda Gag. New York: Coward, McCann, & Geoghegan, 1938.
A little old man discovers many more cats than he expected to.

Y   *Mushroom in the Rain,* Mirra Ginsburg. New York: Macmillan, 1974.
A mushroom expands when numerous animals seek shelter under it.

O   *The Nightingale,* Eva Le Gallienne, trans. New York: Harper & Row, Pub., 1965.
The Emperor of China hears the nightingale's beautiful song and orders him to stay in court and sing. When he receives a gift from Japan of a mechanical bird that sings very well, the nightingale is banished, but returns when the Emperor becomes ill.

M—O   *Of Cobblers and Kings,* Aure Sheldon, New York: Parents', 1978.
Because of his common sense a cobbler rises from one important position to another until he becomes Grand Chancellor. Then he notices that the people of the kingdom have no shoes.

O   "Old Dry Frye," Richard Chase.   (18)
An old preacher accidently dies and everyone tries to get rid of the body, afraid they will be arrested for his murder. Compare with *Joco and the Fishbone* in this bibliography.

M   *Once Upon a Dinkelshühl,* Patricia Lee Gauch. New York: Putnam's, 1977.
The gatekeeper's daughter and her friends save their town from being burned by foreign invaders. Medieval setting.

Y—M   "The Peddler and His Caps," Geraldine Brain Siks.   (35)
This version of an old tale has been elaborated to include more characters and dialogue.

O   *Petronella,* Jay Williams. New York: Parents', 1973.
     A princess rescues a prince in this turnabout tale.

Y—M *Petunia,* Roger Duvosin. New York: Knopf, 1950.
     Petunia, a goose, thinks she has knowledge because she owns a book.

M—O *The Pied Piper of Hamelin,* Tony Ross. New York: Lothrop, Lee & Shepard,
     1977.
     Robert Browning's poem retold.

M—O *Pitidoe the Color Maker,* Glen Dines. New York: Macmillan, 1959.
     Pitidoe is the lazy apprentice of a color maker who ignores the recipes for color
     and turns everything purple. All the color fades and is returned only when
     Pitidoe discovers color in his tears.

M—O "A Portrait Which Suited Everyone and Pleased No One," M. A. Jagen-
     dorf.   (35)
     Tyll is commissioned to paint the court portrait, but each member wants a
     flattering picture of himself. One of the many tales about this legendary German
     prankster.

M—O *Princess Rosetta and the Popcorn Man,* retold by Ellin Greene. New York:
     Lothrop, Lee & Shepard, 1971.
     When the Princess Rosetta of Romalia is stolen by a neighboring kingdom, only
     the popcorn man's solution works.

Y—M "The Princess Who Could Not Cry," Rose Fyleman   (35)
     A peasant girl solves the princess's problem with an onion.

O   *The Rabbi and the Twenty-Nine Witches: A Talmudic Legend,* Marilyn Hirsh.
     New York: Holiday House, 1976.
     A rabbi notices that troublesome witches don't appear on rainy days. When he
     tricks them out into the rain, they shrink into nothing.

Y—M *The Reluctant Dragon,* Kenneth Grahame. New York: Holiday House, 1953.
     A peaceable dragon doesn't want to fight with a knight.

O   "Rip Van Winkle," Washington Irving.   (35)
     The American tale of a man who falls asleep for twenty years to return to a
     world that has forgotten him.

O   "Robin Hood's Merry Adventure with the Miller," Howard Pyle.   (35)
     Robin Hood and the Miller fight for the right of way on a log.

M—O "Salting the Pudding," B. A. Botkin.   (51)
     Ma doesn't have time to salt the pudding, so everyone else in the family does.

M—O *Six Companions Find Fortune,* Katya Sheppard, trans. New York: Doubleday,
     1969.
     Retired soldier finds a strong man, a hunter, a blower, a runner, and a frost
     maker. They win a race. The King does not want to reward them, so he tries to
     get rid of them in various ways, each of which is foiled by the specific skills of
     each man.

M   *Sparrow Socks,* George Selden. New York: Harper & Row, Pub., 1965.
     A family's sock business falls off until the son makes socks for sparrows. All
     who see the socks decide they want a pair just like them. Scotch setting.

O   *The Squire's Bride,* P. C. Asbjornsen. New York: Atheneum, 1975 and (35)
     An old squire decides to marry a young woman who has other ideas.

Y—M *The Star Thief,* Andrea di Noto. New York: Macmillan, 1971.
     A thief raids the night's sky and hides all of the stars in his cellar.

M—O   "Stone in the Road," traditional.   (35)
A Duke, as a lesson to his lazy people, places a stone in the road with gold underneath. Whoever removes the stone will be rewarded.

M—O   *Stone Soup,* Marcia Brown. New York: Scribner's, 1947.
Three soldiers return from the war and stop in a village. The villagers are tired of feeding soldiers, and they hide all their food. The soldiers teach them how to make stone soup, with vegetables and meat added for flavor.

M   *A Story—A Story,* Gail E. Haley. New York: Atheneum, 1970.
The African tale of how all stories came to be Anansi's, the spider man. Anansi must capture and give to the Sky God a leopard, hornets, and a dancing fairy whom men never see.

Y—M   *Tale of a Crocodile,* Ann Kim. New York: W. W. Norton, 1968.
A rabbit enlists the aid of his children to get rid of the crocodile.

M   "Taper Tom," Thorne-Thomsen.   (35)
Tom, a magic goose, and a string of people stuck to it make a sad Princess laugh.

O   *Three Strong Women,* Claus Stamm, trans. New York: Viking, 1962.
A wrestler meets his match with strong family of women. They train him and he becomes the champion. A Japanese tall tale.

Y—M   "Ticky-Picky-Boom-Boom," Philip Sherlock.   (2)
Tiger is chased by yams from Anansi's fields and tries to find hiding places with his friends.

M   "The Ugly Duckling," Hans Christian Andersen.   (3) (4)
The sensitive story of a "duckling" who is rejected by all other animals. He happily discovers that he is actually a swan.

O   "Urashima Taro and the Princess of the Sea," Yoshiko Uchida, ed.   (4) (12)
Urashima is enticed to live in the sea and spends much more time there than he imagines. When he returns home, he finds how much has lapsed. A Japanese folktale.

M—O   *The Wave,* Margaret Hodges. New York: Houghton Mifflin, 1964.
There is a small earthquake, and Grandfather knows a tidal wave will follow. The villagers are unaware of the danger, and Grandfather must burn his rice fields to warn them. Japanese setting.

M   *When the Drum Sang,* Anne Rockwell. New York: Parents', 1970.
A little girl is stolen by a man who hides her in a drum in this African folktale.

Y—M   *Where the Wild Things Are,* Maurice Sendak. New York: Harper & Row, Pub., 1963.
Max is sent to his room for punishment and imagines that he goes off to a land where wild things live.

Y—M   "Why the Bear is Stumpy Tailed," George Webbe Dasent.   (4)
The Bear is tricked into fishing in the ice with his tail and loses it.

Y—M   "Why the Evergreen Trees Keep Their Leaves in Winter," Sara Cone Bryant.   (35)
Kindly evergreens help a wounded bird and win reward.

O   *The Woodcutter's Duck,* Krystyna Turska. New York: Macmillan, 1972.
Bartek outwits the army commander who wants the young man's pet duck. A Polish folktale.

O   "The Youth Who Wanted to Shiver," Eric Carle.   (14)
Young man wonders what shivering is and goes through some harrowing ex-

periences to find out. But only when he is doused with minnows and cold water in his warm bed does he understand!

The following is a list of traditional and well-known fairy tales that children enjoy dramatizing. Look at the many versions of each, particularly the illustrated ones.

M   "Beauty and the Beast"

M   "Cinderella"

Y   "The Elves and the Shoemaker"

Y   "The Gingerbread Boy"

Y   "Goldilocks and the Three Bears"

Y—M   "Hansel and Gretel"

Y—M   "Jack and the Beanstalk"

Y   "Little Red Riding Hood"

Y—M   "The Musicians of Bremen"

M   "Rapunzel"

M   "Rumpelstiltskin"

M   "Sleeping Beauty"

M   "Snow White and the Seven Dwarfs"

Y   "The Three Billy Goats Gruff"

Y   "The Three Little Pigs"

Y—M   "The History of Tom Thumb"

Chapter Twelve

Planning Drama Lessons

Throughout this book we have focused on various kinds of drama activities, leading the reader through a progression of ideas which advance from the simpler to the more complex. Many of these individual activities can be incorporated into regular classroom teaching at any time the teacher chooses. If, however, a leader can work for extended periods of time—anywhere from a half hour to an hour, and at regular intervals—one will want to design a lesson that is more than just a series of activities. This chapter is designed to help the leader discover ways to plan drama lessons.

PRELIMINARY CONSIDERATIONS

Although some leaders may find themselves in teaching situations where the attainment of drama goals outlined in Chapter One is the predominant focus, more often than not the teacher will be expected to combine drama with other areas of the curriculum. For this reason, it is usually best to select an appropriate curricular topic, such as pilgrim life, westward movement, seasons, or current events, which then becomes the theme of the lesson and ties the activities together.

As the curricular objectives are being planned, the leader also considers the drama goals. Perhaps the group needs encouragement in verbal communication and then verbal games or dialogue scenes are the choice. Perhaps the children need assistance in listening to one another and the leader will decide to use pantomime activities as a way of focusing their attention. Perhaps they need work in small groups to develop their socialization skills. Once both sets of goals are decided, the leader then designs appropriate activities to fit the theme.

Generally, anywhere from three to five activities are planned. Sometimes "backup" material or alternatives to the activities are also included. Most leaders prefer to be overprepared in order to have more flexibility.

The first activity may be considered a warm-up activity. This may be a crucial activity for the special teacher who works with a classroom only for drama lessons. Warm-up material should not be too difficult for the children to do and should put everyone in a relaxed mood, ready to work together. If the leader must work with a class that is already "high" at the beginning of the period, it might be more appropriate to work with material that will expend their excess energy and calm them down. In this case, it should also be highly structured, highly controlled.

As the activities progress, they should become more challenging for the children. The lesson should be built just as the structure of a story or a play takes shape. One piece should be used as the core of the lesson; generally this is the most challenging activity. Then the lesson should begin to taper off and end with a quieting activity.

The leader always needs to determine (perhaps even as the lesson is progressing) just how much time and effort should be put into a given activity. It may take more than one playing to achieve the depth of involvement desired. At the same time, if the children are not responding to the material and the leader cannot see a way of combating this problem, then the activity should probably be dropped.

Sometimes an activity will be played as a run-through. Other times the leader will want to challenge the children further. Concentration will be encouraged and the leader will push for better work. This may also mean that the material will have to be broken down into smaller, more workable units.

Whenever an activity is repeated, a new challenge should be added. Otherwise there is the danger that an activity can "plateau" and begin to get stale. Ultimately, an activity with numerous repetitions and no new challenges simply becomes boring.

The end of the drama lesson should have a relaxing and calming effect on the group. The children should have a chance to think about the experience they have just had and absorb it. Particularly if the class is to move on to seat-work after the drama lesson, a quieting activity is almost demanded.

Following are two sample lesson ideas for two different grade levels. They are presented as one approach to lesson planning. There are five activities in each, with alternative suggestions for some. It is not intended that all the material could be covered in a one-hour session. Rather the plans provide the leader with flexibility and the opportunity to make decisions according to the group's responses during the playing. Some leaders may even use such lesson plans over a week's time, spending perhaps twenty minutes each day on an activity.

Winter (Snow)

Grade Level: K–3

Objectives: Gaining an understanding of the snowy season and the various activities connected with it.

Experiencing creative movement in enacting winter activities.

Practicing nonverbal communication and interpretation of nonverbal communication through pantomimes for guessing.

Dramatizing a folktale with opportunities for pantomime and verbal interaction. Experiencing characterization of selfish and generous qualities in the trees; helplessness of wounded bird.

1. Warm-up Activity: *Snowy Day,* by Ezra Jack Keats (Viking, 1962).

    Leader opens session with comments about snow appropriate to the experiences of the particular group of children.

    Presents picture book, a narrative pantomime story about a small boy who has his first memorable experience in the snow.

    After sharing the story and pictures with the children, the leader guides them through a pantomime of the various activities in the book, including dressing for snowy weather, building a snowman, making a snow angel, being a mountain climber. The ending is the return indoors, taking off outdoor clothing, going to bed, and dreaming of a wonderful day in the snow.

    (Played at desk area.)

2. Team Pantomime: Snow Activities

    Now that the children have experienced in solo pantomime several kinds of snow activities, the leader discusses with them other snow activities not mentioned in *Snowy Day.* Pictures are shown of people who are engaged in winter activities such as shoveling snow, sledding, ice skating, feeding birds, skiing, and so forth. Children add their own ideas to the list.

    Class is divided in half. One team will perform a winter activity for the other team to guess. Depending on the maturity of the children, the leader may let them decide which topic they want, or they may draw from one of the pictures as from a deck of cards and pantomime that idea.

    (Pantomimers may be in front of the classroom; audience in its seats.)

3. "Why the Evergreen Trees Keep Their Leaves in Winter" by Florence Holbrook (35).

    The leader tells a simplified version of the folktale of the little bird with a broken wing who cannot fly south with its friends. When it seeks shelter in the trees, it is shunned. Only the evergreens offer assistance. When the wind blows in the winter, the Frost King tells the wind to spare the leaves of the evergreen trees because of their kindness to the little bird.

    Preview pantomime. All the children act out the following pantomimes in unison, with side-coaching from the leader, to try some of the pantomime and verbal ideas in the story.

    a. Be birds flying south for winter. In side-coaching, the leader may mention various

The birds fly south for winter.
(Photo courtesy of Jon Vander Meer.)

kinds of birds, the flapping of wings for takeoff, and soaring at higher altitudes. Might also include a circling back one more time for the little bird.

b. Be the little bird with a broken wing trying to fly, looking sadly at your friends flying away. You feel the cold and puff out your feathers to protect yourself from the winds.

c. You are the trees, the birch, oak, or the willow, standing proudly, feeling very stately, yet very cautious of strangers.

Leader now plays the bird with the broken wing and approaches some of the children with the request to make a home in their branches. If some children forget that these trees say ''no'' to the little bird (some children may feel very sorry for the bird, especially if the leader is convincing), the leader may say, ''Oh, you must be one of the friendly evergreen trees.''

d. Now the leader narrates the children through the experience of having the cold and wind touch their leaves, making them fall. The leader might want to pretend to be the wind who touches each tree and makes the leaves fall. This is a nice control feature as the trees must wait until the leader comes to them. (Note: little children may literally fall to signify the leaves falling. Leader may need to side-coach a slow motion fall.)

e. Be the friendly evergreen trees who offer their branches, their protection from the north wind, and even berries to eat. If the children do not offer these ideas mentioned in the story, the leader, as the little bird, may comment on them.

(All of these activities can be played at the desk area. If a larger area is used, the children may be in a circle to facilitate leader's interaction with them.)

4. Now the leader may wish to put the simple story together as a small play. Groups of threes can be the various trees in the forest. The leader may decide to play the little

The wounded bird asks the trees for shelter.

bird the first time through, in order to help with the dialogue. If there are verbal children in the classroom, the leader may choose to narrate from the sidelines. The part of the bird may be double or even triple cast. A child may be the wind. If the leader narrates, he or she may play the Frost King.

In an evaluation of the playing afterward, the leader might ask, "Could we see a difference in the two kinds of trees—selfish and generous?" "How many different tree shapes, or kinds of trees, did we see?" "How could we tell the bird was wounded?"

The children and the leader might also discuss changes and/or additions they want to make in the playing of the story. If the story is played seveal times, there should be extensions in the dialogue and deepening of involvement and understanding of the story. The children might be encouraged to think of other extensions of the story: a scene between the birds at the beginning of the story when they discover the wounded bird's problem; perhaps a return of the birds in the spring who find the young bird well again. These additions will take more time than just one period.

(The dramatization may take place in the front of the classroom, or if the circle arrangement was used earlier, it may be continued.)

5. Quieting Activity. Melting Snowman.

Be a snowman melting in the warm sun. "Your right arm melts the fastest and starts to slide down your round body. Now your left arm starts to go. The sun gets higher in the sky and starts to melt your head. Your face starts to run and your head begins to roll off. Then your shoulders begin to slump and your back begins to curve. You're only about half as tall as you once were. The sun is getting warmer and now you're beginning to melt faster. You sink into a large lump. Now the lump starts to spread out until you are just a puddle."

After a moment of relaxation, the Frost King (leader) touches the children as signal to return to their desks.

(This activity should be done, if at all possible, where the children are at the end of the story dramatization.)

Abraham Lincoln

Grade Level: 4-6

Objectives: Gaining an understanding of some of the events in the life of an important American historical figure, recalling information previously studied.

Experiencing pantomiming and interpreting pantomime of occupations of Lincoln's time.

Enacting dialogue situations appropriate to circumstances of Lincoln's presidency.

Dramatizing in groups an interpretation of an episode in Lincoln's life demonstrating personal characteristic of honesty.

1.   Warmup Activity: "Nancy Hanks"

This poem, by Rosemary Carr and Stephen Vincent Benet (4), suggests that Nancy Hanks, Abe Lincoln's mother, might come back as a ghost and wonder how her son made out in the world.

The poem is read as sensitively as possible, as if Nancy Hanks herself is speaking. Then the leader plays the role of Nancy Hanks, joined perhaps by two other students as Nancy also. (The leader may also let children take over the role entirely and moderate the discussion instead.) The class is asked to convince Nancy that her son did, indeed, "get on." To encourage verbalization, Nancy should pretend to find it difficult to believe all the information about Lincoln. Her objections might be:

"But when I died, Abe and his pa were barely making it in that log cabin in Indiana. How could he have become a president?"

"But we were so poor, Abe couldn't even go to school more than just a few days. Where'd he learn to read and write?"

Other points of information she might ask: "What happened to Tom, Abe's father?" "What did Abe grow up to look like? Was he tall? Do you have a picture of him?" "How is it that you know so much about him?" And so on.

(Activity can take place at the desks.)

2.   Ten-Count Freeze: Jobs Held by Lincoln

During his lifetime, Lincoln held a number of jobs: rail splitter, postmaster, carpenter, peddler, surveyor, sawmiller, lawyer, storekeeper, farmer, riverboat driver, in addition to being president.

Several children at a time will pantomime one of these occupations of Lincoln.

(Pantomimers use the front of the classroom.)

3.   Abraham Lincoln felt that everyone should have a right to talk to the president. There were always crowds of people to see him, and Lincoln made every effort to see as many as possible.

Discuss: What kinds of people would try to see the president—young, old, men, women, and children? What reasons would people have to see a president? How would Lincoln try to handle so many people at a time?

Set the scene in the White House with Lincoln's office and a waiting room. Children decide who they are and what their reason for seeing the president might be. People may come to see Lincoln individually, but pairs and small groups will give more children a chance to participate.

Alternative plan: Select certain situations for the children to enact. State role and person's reason on cards and distribute.

To assist in playing the scene, the leader could play Lincoln in order to establish a model. As Lincoln, the leader could also introduce others into the scene: "Mrs. Lincoln, who'll want to meet you since you've come all the way from Illinois . . ." or "My son Tad, who's just about your age . . . "

The leader might play a presidential aide and be on hand to assist when needed. As presidential aide, the leader can also monitor the crowd and perhaps introduce those who are waiting to see the president. Again, others could be added to the scene, such as a photographer who wants to get a picture of the many people who come to see the president. (May need to assist with information about cameras of the period.)

In order to establish tension in the scene, the leader might enter unannounced as the secretary of state and say that Lincoln is late for the Cabinet meeting. The secretary could be upset over Lincoln's spending so much time with people. Child playing Lincoln will be in position of having to defend his policy.

A time limit on the length of each person's visit may have to be established. Some interviews may also have to be "postponed" to a later date if the period ends before everyone has had a chance to play his or her idea.

(Scene in front of the classroom. Waiting room could be the desks.)

4. Group Scenes: "Honest Abe"

Read to the class the short story of how Lincoln got his name, "Honest Abe." The class may divide in groups and enact its version of the story of how Abe walked six miles to return six pennies a woman overpaid him for some cloth.

Alternative: Have children create a scene of their own in which Lincoln does an honest deed. What sort of situation might have occurred in one of Lincoln's other jobs in which he would have an opportunity to live up to his name of "Honest Abe"?

(Groups form in various areas of the classroom for discussing and planning. Scenes are shared in front of the classroom.)

5. Quieting Activity: Lincoln Statue

Show the class a picture of the Lincoln Memorial or other statue. On a slow count of ten, the children become the statue.

Variation: Class could slowly become a statue of Lincoln at any stage of his life in an important scene. As the children are frozen, the leader could quietly comment on the various positions the children are in and possibly identify some of the scenes.

(Could be done at desk area.)

FOR THE COLLEGE STUDENT

1. Select a curricular theme or topic and then brainstorm the many drama activities the theme suggests. Then select five activities for a drama lesson, sequencing them appropriately. Specify curricular and drama objectives.

2. Design and teach a lesson plan to your classmates or to a group of children. Analyze afterward your successes and ways you could improve. What changes did you make in the lesson plan as a result of the group's responses?

Chapter Thirteen

The Leader
and
the Group

The previous chapters have been devoted to guiding children in the varied experiences of creative drama. An important part of this process must include guiding children to be self-seeking, self-directed, authenticated individuals capable of integrating themselves into a democratic, cohesive group. In this chapter we shall explore some of the basic concepts of group interaction as applied to the classroom setting.

THE NATURE OF THE CLASSROOM GROUP

Every classroom is composed of a group, including the teacher, organized for the express purpose of education. To most effectively accomplish this, a high degree of cohesive interaction is required. Effective group interaction also depends on each member's (including the teacher's) unique and honest contributions.

The methods of achieving group interaction cannot be specifically described because of the variables involved in the nature of groups themselves. No two children, leaders, or groups are alike. Neither do they remain consistent in their differences from day to day or even minute to minute. As every teacher knows, variations in demeanor and attitude can be caused by such things as weather, time of day and year, physical aspects of the environment, material presented, presence or absence of individual members, and age, sex ratio, and size of the group. Furthermore, every individual in the group, including the teacher, is a constantly growing and evolving human being—never static. The leader must recognize these variables in order to guide the group most effectively.

Each person in the group is unique because of different experiences and background. Yet each member in a group is equally important because one's individuality makes its special contribution.

Leaders must also recognize their role as group members and should be honest and objective about themselves. We should acknowledge that our background with its unique experiences has contributed to the self we presently are. We will try to examine the source of our ideas, values, feelings, and behaviors. We will recognize that we favor certain curricular subjects; that we enjoy working on particular pet projects; that we like or dislike certain personalities; that we have a personality that can be labeled "jovial," "sensitive," "demanding," and the like; or that we value certain ideas above others.

In all classroom learning, the leader's total personality will probably influence the children more than any subject matter taught. Especially in experiences dealing with human emotions and interpersonal relationships, the leader's own behaviors will serve as a strong example. We will need to examine and understand our own sensitivities as human beings in order to teach human interaction to children with honesty and relevance.

POSITIVE CLASSROOM CLIMATE

The climate in the classroom is determined by the overall feelings experienced by the group members. In a positive climate, the students and the teacher have a mutual trust and respect for each other which facilitates the development of self-esteem and optimal learning.

Individuals make their best contributions when they feel confident and possess a positive self-image. This attitude develops in a climate of acceptance, psychological freedom, and open communication.

Acceptance is the belief that all people are worthy individuals. They are accepted as they are, although certain behaviors and actions may be disapproved. Acceptance forms the very foundation for successful group interaction, which creative drama attempts to foster.

The teacher initiates acceptance and becomes the model for it. Each child is accepted as a human being with important feelings and ideas. The leader's guidance reflects an understanding of children's various stages of growth and development as well as their interests, needs, and concerns. The right of every child to be treated with equality is respected, and this attitude is taught to the group by example and practice.

Psychological freedom means that a person is secure enough in the social, physical, and emotional environment to operate with ease. Everyone has known the feelings of fear and anxiety in uncomfortable and tense situations. At such times, all the eyes of the world appear to be staring at us and making impossible demands. Our insecurity with the situation may cause us to become shy and withdrawn, or hostile and aggressive. We are unable to operate with maximum effectiveness.

The leader must be responsible for establishing an atmosphere of psychological freedom. We must create the secure climate in which children can express themselves freely, without fear of reprisal. Not only is this climate important for positive self-growth, it is crucial for encouraging the risk-taking that creativity demands.

Creative drama is a natural medium for the free expression of ideas, feelings, and attitudes. Fostering open communication becomes fundamental and paramount in the leader's successful guidance of creative drama. We must value and respect the sincere, open, and honest communication that creative drama can engender. Furthermore, we should be sensitive to our obligation to communicate our own thoughts and feelings with equal sincerity.

ACCEPTANCE

Conveying acceptance to children is one of the most important factors in fostering their self-growth. We convey acceptance by our general attitudes, our nonverbal behaviors and by our verbal comments.

A first step in being able to accept another person is to accept oneself. Essentially when we recognize our own humanness, we are more accepting of others. Teachers who expect perfection from themselves and from their students will continually be frustrated and will become more unaccepting. Unaccepting behaviors are then translated into negativism which pervades the entire classroom.

When we are aware of our own selves and our feelings, we can more easily reflect them in our verbal comments. For example, the teacher who says, "I get really frustrated when I see all this clutter in the room," rather than "You are the messiest kids I've ever seen," has owned up to personal feelings and has taken responsibility for them. These so-called "I-Messages" help the teacher and the children see where the feelings lie. The "You-Message" frequently places blame and negative judgment on the students, causing guilt and resentment rather than the change of behavior which the teacher had hoped for.

Acceptance of Ideas and Behaviors

Students assess their worth as human beings by the verbal and nonverbal statements communicated to them. In fact, we all appreciate acceptance as it is demonstrated by a nod, a pat on the back, a smile, a kind word about our efforts and our ideas, and an understanding of our feelings.

In accepting children's ideas and behaviors, the leader might say:

"That's a good idea."
"Nice work!"
"I think all this noise means you're excited."

Because the leader becomes an accepting person, the children will often pick up on this model and begin to express acceptance and appreciation also.

Teacher, what music were you playing when we were pretending? It's neat.
I liked watching Jim when he pretended he was that stubborn donkey and he rolled on his back.
You were good, Annette.

While it is important to accept the ideas of children, there is no need to claim creative genius for a rather ordinary idea. Children have an awareness of what is pretty good and what is outstanding, and exaggerated praise is usually recognized as phoney.

One leader discovered this fact from the children themselves. She had the habit of being overly enthusiastic with everyone and everything. When a group of children spontaneously praised one child for his ideas in playing a scene, the child expressed delight and was very pleased. The children reminded him that the teacher often praised his work, but his response was, "Oh, she says everything's good."

Acceptance of Creativity and Imitation

Beginning teachers are often so concerned about evoking creativity in children that they expect immediate and outstanding results. However, it is frequently the case that children's ideas are rather ordinary at first until they have had the chance to experiment further and probe deeper into an idea. Some beginning teachers express their disappointment openly or with thinly disguised forlorn facial expressions. However, the leader should be accepting of these initial attempts at creative thinking and continue to be enthusiastic in order to keep the flow of ideas coming.

Often in creative drama activities children will imitate each other or even repeat a previous response, particularly if the teacher has praised it. This is normal and natural; imitation is a basic mode of learning. Yet, some teachers feel that imitating is similar to cheating and convey this attitude to children. Sometimes children express considerable concern about imitative behaviors in classmates:

Mary's doing *my* idea!

Tom's copying!

In response to these protestations, the leader must communicate an acceptance of imitation in such a way that protects the child who is imitating yet reassures the child who has originated the idea.

> When people see an idea that they like, they enjoy using it. Tom must have liked your idea. . . .

Throughout all drama experiences, the leader is encouraging the sincere and honest expression of ideas and feelings. If for any reason we reject a sincere and honest response, we risk closing the channels of communication. The following examples demonstrate this point.

> A group of fourth graders were pretending to be robots. In the first playing they were robots working hard all day long, performing a variety of tasks. For the second playing, the leader suggested that they be robots entertaining themselves on a night off. In the discussion that followed the playing, one boy said, "I had a fight with my wife and went to the gasoline station and got oil and got drunk."

The child's answer was logical, and most importantly, delivered in a sincere way. The answer was accepted with a nod of the head. If the leader had given a shocked look or rejected the answer as inappropriate, he would have given reproof to a child's honest expression. From a pragmatic point of view, he could also have triggered other children into creating "drunken robots," too, if they thought it would get attention.

> One six-year-old, pretending to be a witch casting an evil spell, said fervently that he was "turning all the parents in the world into furniture." The teacher, playing the "oldest and wisest" witch, merely cackled and said, "I see."

If the teacher had remarked something to the effect, "Are you sure that's what you'd like to do to parents?" or "You shouldn't say things like that," she would have rejected the child's strong feelings, which apparently he felt secure enough to express in a safe environment.

Acceptance through Leader Participation

Acceptance can also be demonstrated when the leader participates and plays with the children. Of course, not all teachers will feel equally disposed toward participation. Each teacher must decide what is comfortable. There are other techniques one can use to compensate, and one should feel more comfortable with participation as time goes on.

The leader need not be skilled in playing; in fact, one could intimidate some children by being too accomplished. Participation should, instead, em-

Acceptance can be demonstrated when the teacher plays with the children.
(Photo courtesy of Jon Vander Meer.)

phasize the spirit of play rather than the skill. If one is enthusiastic and appears to enjoy the experience, the children are encouraged to participate and to relax and enjoy themselves also.

For example, as a child pretends to walk a tightrope, the leader may join her, walking the child's imaginary rope. These actions say to the child, "Your idea looks like fun. I'd like to pretend it with you."

If teachers play with the children, the communication is stronger than if the teacher simply observed from the sidelines. One becomes a stronger member of the group and establishes a meaningful, working relationship with it. As a result, we learn about ourselves and the other members more clearly. This insight can be valuable in assisting effective classroom interrelationships in all learning activities.

Feelings

Every experienced teacher knows the importance of a positive emotional climate in the classroom and of a learner's healthy emotional outlook. Without a feeling of well-being, learning is not possible. If for no other reason, emotions must be dealt with because of their effect on learning.

Many children have a great many problems related to emotional feelings. Realistically the teacher will not be able to solve many of the child's problems. Neither can we assume the responsibilities of a therapist or a counselor who diagnoses and treats specific emotional problems. But simply in the number of waking hours spent together, perhaps the teacher, of all the people in the children's world, is in an ideal position to help them understand and cope with human emotions.

Creative drama, as an enjoyable, active experience, creates by itself a positive emotional atmosphere. The strong movement of marching around the room to a bouncy rhythm can help a child achieve a fresh and renewed outlook on the rest of the day; or pretending to be on a raft with Tom Sawyer floating down the Mississippi may help a child forget, if only temporarily, one's own struggles with life.

Leaders can deal even more directly with the subject of emotion. They can help the children understand what emotions are, how they are expressed, why people behave as they do, and how emotional responses differ. Such questions are also a part of other curricular areas such as social studies, literature, or health.

The subject of emotions is dealt with every time the leader guides the children in a discussion of the characters in stories and the motivations behind their behaviors. Children readily identify with certain characters. Often these are the ones they choose to play, and through those characters the children have the opportunity to release strong feelings.

We will want children to understand that people all over the world share emotions of fear, love, hate, and joy. When students hear someone expressing understanding of their emotions, they know their feelings are normal.

For some children it can be particularly helpful for the teacher to identify with them in the experiencing of common human emotions.

I know how you feel.
I can understand how you must have felt.
I felt the same way when I was in that situation.

We will want children to understand that even though feelings are neither good nor bad in themselves, some can be troublesome or painful.

No one likes to be called names.
Yes, you can feel hurt if everyone else is invited to a party and you aren't.

Learning to cope with emotions may mean learning to understand that feelings are normal and have a reason for existing. Instead of rejecting feelings, we try to understand why they occur and what causes them.

Differences of emotional expression are influenced by the concepts and values held by various cultures. No doubt it will be surprising for some children to learn that in some parts of the world, the men greet each other by kissing; or that fistfighting in some cultures would be a shameful way to express anger. Even within the classroom community there may be some dissimilar values. Children may be surprised to find that a classmate doesn't like ice cream— something they think is universally liked. Or they may find it curious that some children say they like the sound of thunder and are not afraid of it.

Understanding and appreciating these differences is a valuable learning experience. The common respect people must have for one another's feelings begins with the teacher and children.

> One of the authors was guiding a class of third graders in creative drama. The leader noticed one boy's negative response to physical contact when she took his hand to form a circle and when she unthinkingly gave him a friendly pat on the head. She made a mental note that Tom did not like contact and that she would not touch him.
>
> But the very next time she met the children, she forgot her intentions. This time she was playing with the children, pretending to be smoke rising from the floor. The mood was quiet, mysterious, but it was quickly broken for Tom when the teacher's smoke movements accidentally touched him.
>
> The teacher stopped playing and said quietly to Tom, "Tom, I know you don't like for me to touch you. I'm sorry that I did just now. I've told myself not to do it, but I seem to be having a hard time making myself mind."
>
> There was a moment of absolute silence. By now everyone was aware of what had happened. Tom's face changed from one of real disgust to one of surprise. Then the eight-year-old said, "That's all right, I understand." Tom appreciated her concern for his feelings and at that moment a bond of understanding was formed between them.

Often a child is denied normal emotional feelings with such statements as, "Big boys don't cry," or "It's silly to be afraid of the dark." But rejection of feelings only causes us to question our perceptions of the world.

Rather than rejecting feelings, it is more helpful to acknowledge that the feelings are normal, allowable, and have a reason for being. "Sometimes crying helps us feel better," or "We're sometimes afraid of the dark because we can't see what's there" are statements that encourage positive emotional growth.

Accepting Self

Sometimes children have a difficult time accepting themselves. Often these are the feelings the teacher is most tempted to reject.

> "That's a pretty sweater you have on, Mark," said the teacher at the beginning of the session.
>
> "I don't like it, I hate myself in it," said chubby Mark, who had not yet played with his classmates in creative drama although he had been attending the sessions regularly.

The teacher was tempted to say, "Well, I don't know why you don't like it. It is really a pretty sweater." Or "You shouldn't hate anyone, not even yourself." But she knew that these statements would have been rejecting ones. She recognized that Mark's weight problem may have caused his concern, so she made no further comment at all. As it turned out, Mark played that day for the first time; and he continued to participate on succeeding days.

Accepting statements may be hard to give when the teacher appears to be under direct attack.

One seven-year-old boy in an early session in creative drama said to the teacher, "You're stupid."
The teacher, although stunned, asked, "Why do you think so, Rocky?
"Because you pretend and make up things. That's stupid," was his reply.
The teacher reflected his feelings: "It's true that I do like to pretend and make up things. You feel that pretending is stupid."

Possibly Rocky had heard something similar before. He wasn't going to risk pretending if someone might call *him* "stupid" for doing it. He didn't want the label, so in defense he applied it to someone else before it was applied to him.

The teacher did not reject Rocky's statement but let him know that she understood his feelings. In being allowed to express his concerns, and in knowing that someone understood them, his anxiety had been relieved. Interestingly, he continued to attend the volunteer sessions and in time participated very freely.

Accepting Mistakes

The process of learning also involves experimenting, often accompanied by uncertainty and mistakes. Many children have never been helped to realize that mistakes are natural and normal for everyone. Often they become distressed by mistakes; they have learned a societal attitude that says mistakes indicate failure and failure cannot be tolerated.

One of the most effective ways leaders can communicate acceptance of mistakes is to acknowledge their own.

Boy, I seemed to goof that time. Let me try another idea. . . .

And just as we can stop and acknowledge our own difficulties, we can also guide the children to do the same.

Some people didn't follow the rules. Perhaps they forgot them. Let's try it again, and remember that you can use only the space at the side of your desk for this activity.
I sensed that some of you had second thoughts about the way your scene was going. Would you like to try again?

REJECTION

Even though leaders accept ideas and feelings, they must set limits on negative behaviors. It would be ridiculous for any teacher to allow children to fight with each other, hurt others' feelings, shout obscenities, or refuse to follow rules.

The children need to learn that the specific things that people do with their emotions and feelings influence their ability to be a part of society. A person may feel angry, but if you kick someone, you are likely to be avoided or even kicked in return.

Rejecting statements must be made with care and not cause children to feel disgraced or to lose self-respect. "You're a bad boy," "Naughty girls like you..." "That's a mean thing to do..." are not helpful, but destructive.

Children's self-concepts are formed on the basis of the opinions expressed about them. They are susceptible to fulfilling or living up to both the negative as well as the positive statements made about them. In addition, negative statements close off communication. Often the statements are simply ignored. Or worse yet, a feeling of rebellion sets in and in the long run, little is gained.

It is possible to disapprove of behaviors and actions without rejecting the individual. It is important that the children feel *they* are not being rejected; it is what they are *doing* that needs to be controlled. Notice how the following statements acknowledge the children's feelings but reject the behavior accompanying them.

> I know that you're angry, but fighting is not allowed in the classroom.
> All your talking lets me know you're excited. But you know the rules. We can't begin playing until everyone settles down. I'll know that you're ready when everything is quiet. . . .
> I know you're disappointed that you all can't play this first time. But in just a few moments we'll be repeating it, and everyone will have a chance.

There may be times when children's behaviors become disruptive to the rest of the class. When this happens, rules for participating should be reinforced as objectively as possible.

It is helpful to speak to children privately so they are able to "save-face."

> Please sit down. When you feel that you can follow the rules to remain by yourself and not disturb others, you may rejoin the group.

Sometimes children's behavior is such that the teacher cannot allow them to participate with the group at all.

> I'm sorry. I know you are disappointed. But I cannot allow you to poke and pinch other people who are trying to do their work. Perhaps it will be easier for you to follow the rules in class tomorrow.

Whenever children are removed from the group, they should be allowed to watch if they wish. Some children will quietly watch the others play; some prefer to read or rest privately. Although the participating children enjoy playing activities in a quieter setting, the aggressive child needs the activity as much as anyone else, and should be returned to it as soon as possible.

Sometimes children will demand attention. In their attempts, they will sometimes do the opposite of what the teacher requests. Ignoring these behaviors may be helpful in convincing them that this is not the best way to gain recognition. In the following example, the child was unusually loud and aggressive. He needed much attention and found that contradicting the teacher or doing the opposite of the directions would draw attention to himself. The leader, who often gave in to his demands, decided to change tactics.

> **T:** I'll be the North Wind that blows all of the Snow People inside the house. Here we go!
> **C:** I'm not going inside.
> **T:** OK. The rest of us will go inside and David, you can stay outside.
> **C:** I'm coming! I'm coming!

GROUP INVOLVEMENT

While creative drama emphasizes the value of individual expression, it also emphasizes the value of group involvement. Learning to function in a democratic society is a high educational priority. While we encourage each child to develop individual potential, we also emphasize the importance of sensitive interrelationships with others. Ultimately the leader guides the group to learn that it functions best when everyone contributes. Organization, cooperation, group problem solving and decision making thus become an integral part of the group experience.

The group experience is an interesting one. Although a group may be composed of a wide range of individuals, it has a personality all its own—as if it were one huge individual embodying the separate individuals. The group is capable of growing and changing, just as individuals are.

Creative drama encourages group interaction, and sometimes the power of the group creates difficulty for both the children and the teacher. If the children have not had much experience with group work, and the leader does not understand how to guide it, a great many problems may occur. When the group is given the opportunity to work on its own, it begins to have a life of its own. Beginning teachers may panic at this power, especially if they see their own contact and control diminishing. Even the experienced leader finds these moments traumatic.

When the teacher plans the activities carefully, instructs clearly, and when the group knows what is expected of it, group work should pose few problems. Strong direction as well as support may be required from the leader for beginning groups until the children experience success and feel confident in group work.

Some children have an easy time cooperating and integrating themselves within almost any group. For them democratic involvement is natural. The children demonstrate their maturity and readiness to accept each other and enjoy working together.

A.

Maria and I have an idea. Can we do it together?

Creating a group idea requires careful planning and social cooperation.
(Photo courtesy of Jon Vander Meer.)

B.

John and I are going to be the ticket men and those guys are going to come and buy a ticket from us. What are you girls going to do?

They also have ideas for facilitating organization and interaction.

A.

I think we should put our hand up if we want to say something.

B.

I think each group should have a corner of the room to plan our skits so we're not bothered.

C.

Oh, I know how we can do this story, teacher. You be the old lady and we'll be the rabbits.

They listen to each other and empathize with feelings.

A.

Leslie: I know how the boy in that story felt. The saddest time for me was when my dog died. He was run over by a car.
Michael: That's sad.

B.

Sue: Robby was really funny when he pretended to come in the palace door and was singing that funny song.

They are interested in each other and spontaneously comment on and question further the ideas of their peers.

A.

Owen: I wanted a horse.
Teacher: Did you get one?
Owen: I'm too little. If I rode it, I'd fall off.
Eric: Oh, you're crazy. You can't have a horse because you gotta have a ranch to have a horse and you gotta have a saddle and you gotta have a bridle and you gotta have horseshoes and you gotta have a lot of food to feed 'em.
Owen: Oh, no! You don't have to have all that stuff for the horse.
Eric: Well, maybe you're right.

There are some children who have difficulties in group interaction. Some choose to avoid any group. They are hesitant to participate, to contribute an idea or an opinion. Still others demand attention from the group; they refuse to listen to others and have difficulties compromising and cooperating. Their personal ego needs interfere with their ability to interact successfully with the group.

Democratic living is not easy! Cooperative interaction takes time, and as we have noted previously, social maturation is not necessarily contingent on chronological age. Furthermore, while group cohesiveness steadily grows, the group is dynamic and changing. There will invariably be days when the leader and the children wonder how they can ever get together or why in the world they would ever want to! These seemingly backward steps are a natural part of the group process. The children are constantly growing in awareness of themselves as individuals and as a part of the group.

Yet the group is powerful. The need to belong to a group is strong, and the leader can count on this need to be the motivation for children to continue to make attempts to integrate themselves. For children who do have difficulties, the teacher will need to give special understanding, help, and support.

The leader may need to guide children to formulate the specifics of how to get along with each other. One class listed the following:

Because I like to have people listen to me, I will listen to others.
Because I wouldn't want anyone to call my ideas "stupid" or "dumb," I don't say that about anyone's idea.

We enjoy seeing our classmates' ideas take shape.

Because I don't want anyone to make fun of the way I feel, I won't make fun of anyone else's feelings.

I can have my own ideas as long as what I do doesn't bother anybody else.

If I don't like the idea that the group has, I don't have to play, but I should not disturb the others.

Because I don't like being disturbed, I will not purposely disturb others.

Because there are times when I want people to be a good audience for me, I'll be a good audience for them.

General discussions about group cooperation and compromise can help.

When people cooperate, what do they have to do?

How can a group decide what ideas it will use?

How can a group make certain that everyone has a chance to speak and contribute?

Sometimes in a group only a few members do all the talking. When this happens, how do the other members feel? What can they do?

The subject of group cooperation and compromise can be the basis for drama experiences.

T: What examples can you think of to show why groups must compromise and cooperate?

C: Every summer my family decides where we'll spend our vacation. My mom and dad tell how much money we can spend and how far that would take us, and then we vote. Before we voted we used to argue a lot. My sister always screamed about going to the lake because she had a boyfriend there. I always vote for camping.

C: Well, this isn't about compromise; just the opposite. My brother's in Mr. Bender's class and when the art teacher wanted groups to make a mural they couldn't do it. They couldn't agree on anything. One of the kids even ripped up the paper. My brother said Mr. Bender just flipped and really got mad at them.

C: Our committee had a hard time planning the class Halloween party. Not to mention names, but *someone* wanted to bring in *real* eyeballs and guts for kids to touch when they had their blindfolds on. He was going to get them from the butcher. Some kids said we'd be sick so we made him take a vote.

T: I can see you have a lot of ideas. Let's divide into groups of five. Each group will plan a scene on the importance of cooperation and compromise. Everyone should have a part.

Before groups organize themselves, it is helpful if the leader reminds them of their challenge to cooperate and compromise.

T: Before your group can plan the building of your version of a "Wonder of the World," you'll have to decide what "Wonder" you will build. You may not like the idea that your group decides on. But remember that you are a part of a group, and people in groups help each other when they compromise.

It is important to a democratic society and to the growth and development of individuals that children learn to handle their own problems and make their own decisions. The decisions the children make may not always be the ones the leader would have made, but the process of thinking through an idea and experimenting with trial and error is a necessary learning experience.

The teacher can grant the children the opportunities to be self-directed in many ways.

Let's see, how can we do this? Does anyone have a suggestion?

We've been playing this story for quite a while. Are you still interested in it or should we go on to something else?

Do we need a preview playing this time?

Do you think everyone can play all at the same time, or should we start out with just a few people first?

How much space do you think we can handle today?

Of course, whenever the children make their own decisions they must also accept the consequences. If things don't work out, then stopping the playing to reanalyze the situation is inevitable. Just as the teacher can make mistakes and miscalculations about what a group is ready to do, so can the children in managing themselves. The important point is that they have had a hand in the decision making.

In addition, the leader can help the group deal with its own problems of human interaction. Often these situations occur in regular day-to-day classroom living. In the example below, the teacher uses a teachable moment to help a group of second graders see alternatives in handling a particular behavior problem. The teacher and the children had just begun a discussion when a rather constant and irritating problem reoccurred.

George: Troy's hitting me again.

Teacher: Troy seems to be a problem for you, George. What are you going to do about it?

George: What am *I* going to do about it?

Teacher: Yes, how are you going to solve your problem?

George: Well . . . I'll . . . (shouts to Troy) STOP DOING THAT!!!!

Teacher: That's one way that might work. Is there anything else you could do?

George: I'd hit him too.

Teacher: That's another possibility. Do you think it will work?

Angela: Troy would hit you back, wouldn't you, Troy? (Troy doesn't respond.)

Cindy: Ask him nice to leave you alone.

Teacher: If you did ask nicely and it still didn't work, what else might you do?

Jimmy: Just don't play with him any more.

Rusty: Go sit by somebody else.

Teacher: Let's take a few minutes to imagine that someone keeps hitting you but you have a plan for solving this problem. I'll count to ten and all of you act out by yourselves what you would do or say if someone had just hit you again. One . . . two . . . three . . . I saw different solutions. Let's talk about them. (The children discuss what they did.)

In a previous chapter we suggested that a group usually works best when the members are free to choose their coworkers. Because planning and sharing with others can be difficult, many children find it more comfortable talking and working with their selected friends.

Yet for the sake of class unity and cohesiveness as well as the children's social growth, the leader will want to widen their experiences in interacting with various groupings. We will want them to have the opportunity to learn that everyone can contribute to a group relationship.

When the leader plans to break up the usual groupings or cliques, it is best to explain the reasoning:

T: For this activity we're going to form new groups. I know that it is enjoyable to work with people you particularly like. But I'm concerned that we are all able to be flexible and to recognize the contributions that every single person in our class can make. You may discover that the unfamiliar ideas that new people have can stimulate new ideas in you. So just for today, and for all those reasons, we're going to experiment.

Throughout all experiences in creative drama, the goal is to help children understand and empathize with others; to learn to put themselves into other people's shoes. We want them to discover their common bond of feelings with people they know, people they read about, historical figures, famous personalities, people of other countries. We want them to know each other better and appreciate themselves as viable human beings. This understanding is important to drama. And it is this understanding and awareness that frees us from alienation in a world whose future ultimately depends on sensitive human interrelationships.

FOR THE COLLEGE STUDENT

1. Consider your own individual uniqueness. What are your values, feelings, likes, dislikes, and so on?

2. Discuss with your classmates those specific incidents during your elementary years when a teacher demonstrated acceptance of you. Recall specific incidents when you felt rejected.

3. Practice verbally accepting ideas. Brainstorm with your classmates the verbal feedback a teacher can give to accept ideas.

4. Practice verbally accepting feelings. Use the procedure suggested above.

5. Practice rejecting behaviors without rejecting the child. Brainstorm with a partner behaviors that can be rejected; take turns verbally rejecting them. Check each other to see that the language does not inadvertently reject the individual. Books suggested in the bibliography can help you.

6. Make a list of situations that can be dramatized focusing on democratic living in the classroom.

7. Read Chapter nine of Elizabeth George Speare's *The Witch of Blackbird Pond* (149), in which Kit leads children in a dramatization of "The Good Samaritan." Also read the episode beginning in Chapter seven of Louise Fitzhugh's *Harriet the Spy* (90), in which the gym teacher attempts an enactment of a Christmas dinner. Analyze the problems each teacher faced. What solutions can you offer?

8. There are many books for children that deal with emotions. The following are only a few. Read some of them and discuss their themes.

   Brooks, Gwendolyn, *Bronzeville Boys and Girls*. New York: Harper & Row, Pub., 1956.

   Cohen, Miriam, *The New Teacher*. New York: Macmillan, 1972.

   Cohen, Miriam, *Will I Have a Friend?* New York: Macmillan, 1967.

   Feelings, Tom and Nikki Grimes, *Something On My Mind*. New York: Dial Press, 1978.

   Hoban, Russell, *The Sorely Trying Day*. New York: Harper & Row, Pub., 1964.

   Lewis, Richard (ed.), *Miracles: Poems by Children of the English Speaking World*. New York: Simon and Schuster, 1966.

   Preston, Mitchell Edna, *The Temper Tantrum Book*. New York: Viking, 1969.

   Viorst, Judith, *I'll Fix Anthony*. New York: Harper & Row, Pub., 1969.

   Viorst, Judith, *Alexander and the Terrible, Horrible, No Good, Very Bad Day*. New York: Atheneum, 1972.

   Wondriska, William, *All the Animals Were Angry*. New York: Holt, Rinehart & Winston, 1970.

Yashima, Taro, *Crow Boy*. New York: Viking, 1955.

Zolotow, Charlotte, *The Quarreling Book*. New York: Harper & Row, Pub., 1963.

9. Collect stories, poems, books, and articles that can help children understand emotions.

TEACHER-AID MATERIALS

AMIDON, EDMUND, AND ELIZABETH HUNTER, *Improving Teaching*. New York: Holt, Rinehart & Winston, 1966. A valuable text for making teachers aware of their specific verbal behaviors and their consequences.

AXLINE, VIRGINIA M., *Play Therapy*. New York: Ballantine, 1969. Discussion of play therapy techniques, including special attention to uses for the classroom teacher.

BERGER, TERRY, *I Have Feelings*. New York: Behavioral Publications, 1971. Situations and pictures covering seventeen different feelings and an explanation of them.

BORTON, TERRY, *Reach, Touch, and Teach*. New York: McGraw-Hill, 1970. A book devoted to the importance of understanding feeling and expanding self-awareness as a significant part of the educational process.

CARROLL, ANNE WELCH, *Personalizing Education in the Classroom*. Denver: Love Publishing Co., 1975. Although this book addresses itself to the special education teacher, the material is applicable to a wide variety of situations. Contains special chapters on communication in the classroom and on groups.

FISK, LORI AND HENRY CLAY LINDGREN, *A Survival Guide for Teachers*. New York: John Wiley, 1973. A thoroughly practical guide to classroom management written by a young, successful teacher.

GINOTT, HAIM G., *Between Parent and Child*. New York: Avon, 1965. A best-seller by a noted educator and therapist with practical suggestions for developing meaningful relationships.

GINOTT, HAIM G., *Between Teacher and Child*. New York: Macmillan, 1972. Helpful suggestions for strengthening interpersonal relationships in the classroom and at home.

GORDON, THOMAS, *T. E. T. Teacher Effectiveness Training*. New York: Peter H. Wyden, Publisher, 1974. A psychotherapist applies his knowledge to the classroom setting and discusses such topics as communication, active listening, and conflict resolution.

GRAMBS, JEAN DRESDEN, *Intergroup Education Methods and Materials*. Englewood Cliffs, N.J.: Prentice-Hall, 1968. A useful source for the teacher who wishes to focus on human relations activities in the classroom. Extensive bibliography included.

GREENBERG, HERBERT M., *Teaching With Feeling*. New York: Macmillan, 1969. An exploration of teachers' feelings toward themselves as well as children, supervisors, parents, and colleagues.

JONES, RICHARD M., *Fantasy and Feeling In Education*. New York: New York University Press, 1968. Deals with the importance of including a consideration of the emotions, cultural values, and feelings in certain curricular topics.

LeShan, Eda, *What Makes Me Feel This Way?* New York: Macmillan, 1972. A noted educator, writer, and family counselor explores the emotional feelings common to us all. Written for children but helpful for adults as well.

Lederman, Janet, *Anger and the Rocking Chair.* New York: McGraw-Hill, 1969. One teacher's approach in dealing with children's emotions in the classroom, based on Gestalt psychology.

Limbacher, Walter J., *Here I Am.* Dayton, Oh.: George A. Pflaum, 1969.

—————, *I'm Not Alone.* Dayton, Oh.: George A. Pflaum, 1970.

—————, *Becoming Myself.* Dayton, Oh.: George A. Pflaum, 1970. Text Books for a mental health program in grades four, five, and six, written by a psychologist. The books deal with feelings and growing up.

Marshall, Hermine H., *Positive Discipline and Classroom Interaction.* Springfield, Ill.: Charles C Thomas, Publisher, 1972. The author's approach is that discipline problems are to be seen and solved as an integral part of the teaching-learning process.

McCroskey, J. C. *Quiet Children and the Classroom Teacher.* Falls Church, Va.: Speech Communication Association, 1977. Special consideration given to the problem of reticence.

Moustakas, Clark, *The Authentic Teacher: Sensitivity and Awareness in the Classroom.* Cambridge, Mass.: Doyle, 1966. A helpful text in inviting awareness of the importance of a meaningful relationship between teacher and child.

Rogers, Carl R., *Freedom to Learn.* Columbus, Oh.: Charles E. Merrill, 1969. A psychotherapist and teacher discusses his approach to education based on his theory of personality.

Schmuck, Richard A. and Patricia A., *Group Process in the Classroom* 2nd ed. Dubuque, Iowa: William C Brown Co., Publishers, 1975. The focus of this text is that much of the learning in the classroom is the result of interpersonal and group interaction.

Shaftel, Fannie, and George Shaftel, *Role Playing for Social Values.* Englewood Cliffs, N.J.: Prentice-Hall, 1967. Explanation of techniques in role playing. Includes story situations to dramatize.

Tester, Sylvia, *Moods and Emotions.* Elgin, Ill.: David C. Cook, 1970. A booklet discussing various ways to teach the subject of emotions in the classroom. Includes sixteen large photos illustrating emotions.

Bibliography
of Story and Poetry
Anthologies and Books
for Dramatization

(1) *All the Silver Pennies,* Blanche Jennings Thompson. New York: Macmillan, 1967.

(2) *Anansi, the Spider Man,* Philip M. Sherlock. New York: Thomas Y. Crowell, 1954.

(3) *Anthology of Children's Literature.* (5th ed.), Edna Johnson, Evelyn R. Sickels, Frances Clarke Sayers, and Carolyn Horovitz. Boston: Houghton Mifflin Company, 1977.

(4) *The Arbuthnot Anthology of Children's Literature* (4th ed.), May Hill Arbuthnot, rev. by Zena Sutherland. Glenview, Ill.: Scott, Foresman, 1976.

(5) *Beyond the Clapping Mountains,* Charles E. Gillham. New York: Macmillan, 1964.

(6) *The Blackbird in the Lilac,* James Reeves, New York: Dutton, 1959.

(7) *Catch a Little Rhyme,* Eve Merriam. New York: Atheneum, 1966.

(8) *Catch Me a Wind,* Patricia Hubbell. New York: Atheneum, 1968.

(9) *Children's Literature for Dramatization: An Anthology,* Geraldine Brain Siks. New York: Harper & Row, Pub., 1964.

(10) *Cinnamon Seed,* John T. Moore. Boston: Houghton Mifflin Company, 1967.

(11) *The Crack in the Wall and Other Terribly Weird Tales,* George Mendoza. New York: Dial Press, 1968.

(12) *The Dancing Kettle and Other Japanese Folk Tales.* Yoshiko Uchida (ed.). New York: Harcourt Brace Jovanovich, 1949.

(13) *Eleanor Farjeon's Poems for Children.* Philadelphia: Lippincott, 1951.

(14) *Eric Carle's Story Book; Seven Tales by the Brothers Grimm.* Franklin Watts, 1976.

(15) *Favorite Stories Old and New*, selected by Sidonie Matsner Gruenberg. Garden City, N.Y.: Doubleday, 1955.

(16) *Fingers Are Always Bringing Me News*, Mary O'Neill. Garden City, N.Y.: Doubleday, 1969.

(17) *Fire On the Mountain and Other Ethiopian Stories*, Harold Courlander and Wolf Leslau. New York: Holt, Rinehart & Winston, 1950.

(18) *Grandfather Tales*, Richard Chase. Boston: Houghton Mifflin Company, 1948.

(19) *Gwot! Horribly Funny Hairticklers*, George Mendoza. New York: Harper & Row, Pub., 1967.

(20) *The Hat-Shaking Dance and Other Tales from the Gold Coast*, Harold Courlander and Albert Kofi Prempeh. New York: Harcourt Brace Jovanovich, 1957.

(21) *The Hare and the Bear and Other Stories*, Yasue Maiyagawa. New York: Parents' Magazine Press, 1971.

(22) *I Feel the Same Way*, Lilian Moore. New York: Atheneum, 1967.

(23) *Little Bear's Visit*, Else Holmelund Minarik. New York: Harper & Row, Pub., 1961.

(24) *The Martian Chronicles*, Ray Bradbury. Garden City, N.Y.: Doubleday, 1958.

(25) *Mouse Tales*, Arnold Lobel. New York: Harper & Row, Pub., 1972.

(26) *Nobody is Perfick*, Bernard Waber. Boston: Houghton Mifflin Company, 1971.

(27) *Now We Are Six*, A. A. Milne. New York: Dutton, 1927.

(28) *Oh, What Nonsense!* selected by William Cole. New York: Viking, 1966.

(29) *Once the Hodja*, Alice Geer Kelsey. New York: Longmans, Green, 1943.

(30) *On City Streets*, Nancy Larrick (ed.). New York: M. Evans and Co., Inc., 1968.

(31) *Reflections on a Gift of Watermelon Pickle*, Stephen Dunning, Edward Lueders, Hugh Smith (eds.). Glenview, Ill.: Scott, Foresman, 1966.

(32) *The Sneetches and Other Stories*, Dr. Seuss. New York: Random House, 1961.

(33) *Some Haystacks Don't Even Have Any Needle*, compiled by Stephen Dunning, Edward Lueders, Hugh Smith. Glenview, Ill.: Scott, Foresman, 1969.

(34) *Storytelling*, Ruth Tooze. Englewood Cliffs, N.J.: Prentice-Hall, 1959.

(35) *Stories to Dramatize*, Winifred Ward. New Orleans, La.: Anchorage Press, 1952.

(36) *Take Sky*, David McCord. Boston: Atlantic-Little, Brown, 1962.

(37) *Tales of the Cheyennes*, Grace Jackson Penney. Boston: Houghton Mifflin Company, 1953.

(38) *Tall Tales from the High Hills*, Ellis Credle. Camden, N.J.: Thom. Nelson, 1957.

(39) *That's Why*, Aileen Fisher. Camden, N.J.: Thom. Nelson, 1946.

(40) *There Is No Rhyme for Silver*, Eve Merriam. New York: Atheneum, 1962.

(41) *The Thing At the Foot of the Bed and Other Scary Tales*, Maria Leach. New York: The World Publishing Company, 1959.

(42) *Thirteen Danish Tales*, Mary C. Hatch. New York: Harcourt Brace Jovanovich, 1947.

(43) *Thunder in the Mountains: Legends of Canada*, Hilda Mary Hooke. Toronto: Oxford University Press, 1947.

(44) *The Tiger and the Rabbit and Other Tales*, Pura Belpré. Philadelphia: Lippincott, 1965.

(45) *The Time-Ago Tales of Jahdu*, Virginia Hamilton. New York: Macmillan, 1969.

(46) *Time for Poetry* (rev. ed.), May Hill Arbuthnot. Glenview, Ill.: Scott, Foresman, 1959.

(47) *The Wandering Moon,* James Reeves. New York: Dutton, 1960.

(48) *Where the Sidewalk Ends,* Shel Silverstein. New York: Harper & Row, Pub., 1974.

(49) *Why the Chimes Rang,* Raymond Macdonald Alden. Indianapolis, Ind.: Bobbs-Merrill, 1954.

(50) *Windsong,* Carl Sandburg. New York: Harcourt Brace Jovanovich, 1960.

(51) *World Tales for Creative Dramatics and Storytelling,* Burdett S. Fitzgerald. Englewood Cliffs, N.J.: Prentice-Hall, 1962.

(52) *Yertle the Turtle and Other Stories,* Dr. Seuss. New York: Random House, 1958.

BOOKS FOR DRAMATIZATION

The following books have been referred to throughout the text. They are listed here alphabetically according to title. The books are only a representative sampling. Some are literary classics. Others have been selected for their historical and geographical settings, social themes, and variety of heroes and heroines. They contain many situations and episodes for dramatization with both pantomime and dialogue scenes.

The following symbols are used to indicate the age level it might be best suited for:

Y   young children in kindergarten, first, and second grades

M   middle-grade children in third and fourth grades

O   older children in fifth and sixth grades

(53)   O   *Adam of the Road,* Elizabeth Janet Gray. New York: Viking, 1942. A minstrel and his son are separated when the boy goes off in search of his stolen dog. His search leads him to many exciting adventures. Thirteenth-century English setting.

(54)   M—O   *Alice in Wonderland* and *Through the Looking Glass,* Lewis Carroll. Many editions. The classic stories of Alice's unusual adventures.

(55)   M   *All Alone,* Claire Huchet Bishop. New York: Viking, 1953. Two boys who are in charge of the herds in the French Alps violate the rule of constant vigil.

(56)   O   *Amos Fortune, Free Man,* Elizabeth Yates. New York: Dutton, 1950. The biography of a slave who struggles for and gains his freedom.

(57)   M—O   *... And Now Miguel,* Joseph Krumgold. New York: Crowell, 1953. The story of a sheepherding family in New Mexico.

(58)   M—O   *The Apple and the Arrow,* Mary and Conrad Buff. Boston: Houghton Mifflin, 1951. The legendary William Tell leads the people of Switzerland in their revolt against Austria. Middle Ages.

(59)   Y—M   *A Bear Called Paddington,* Michael Bond. Boston: Houghton Mifflin, 1958. A charming humanlike bear arrives in London and is adopted by a family. Life becomes full of adventures that border on the disastrous.

(60)   M   *Ben and Me,* Robert Lawson. Boston: Little Brown, 1939. The amusing story of how a mouse helped Benjamin Franklin with his achievements.

(61)   M—O   *The Black Cauldron,* Lloyd Alexander. New York: Holt, Rinehart & Winston, 1965. Taran and his friends must find and destroy the evil Black Cauldron.

(62)   M   *The Borrowers,* Mary Norton. New York: Harcourt Brace Jovanovich, 1953. The adventures of the little people who live under the floorboards of the house and borrow small objects to furnish their home.

(63)   O   *The Bronze Bow,* Elizabeth George Speare. Boston: Houghton Mifflin, 1961. The setting is Israel during the time of Jesus. Daniel desires to play a part in driving the Romans from his land. His hate and revenge dissolve in understanding.

(64)   M—O   *By the Great Horn Spoon!* Sid Fleischman. Boston: Little, Brown, 1963. A young boy and his aunt's butler stow away on a ship headed for California gold in this humorous historical fiction adventure.

(65)   M   *Caddie Woodlawn,* Carol Ryrie Brink. New York: Macmillan, 1935. The adventures of Wisconsin pioneers.

(66)   M   *Carolina's Courage,* Elizabeth Yates. New York: Dutton, 1964. Carolina, a pioneer girl on a wagon train, is able to assist in the advance through Indian territory.

(67)   M—O   *Centerburg Tales,* Robert McCloskey. New York: Viking, 1951. The further adventures of Homer Price and the people in his small town.

(68)   M   *Charlie and the Chocolate Factory,* Roald Dahl. New York: Knopf, 1964. A young boy wins the opportunity to tour a famous and unusual chocolate factory. English setting.

(69)   M   *Charlotte's Web,* E. B. White. New York: Harper & Row, Pub., 1952. Wilbur the pig, with the help of his barnyard friends and most particularly Charlotte the spider, develops into a most unique pig.

(70)   O   *A Christmas Carol,* Charles Dickens. New York: Macmillan, 1950. The classic story of Scrooge and the Cratchit family.

(71)   Y—M   *Christmas on the Mayflower,* Wilma P. Hays. New York: Coward, McCann & Geoghegan, 1956. A dramatic conflict is presented when the crew of the *Mayflower* wants to return to England before the safety of the pilgrims is assured.

(72)   O   *The Count of Monte Cristo,* Alexandre Dumas. Many editions. Dantes's adventures during the revolutionary period in France.

(73)   Y—M   *The Courage of Sarah Noble,* Alice Dalgliesh. New York: Scribner's, 1954. The true story of a little girl who bravely accompanies her father into the Connecticut territory in the early 1700s.

(74)   M   *The Cricket in Times Square,* George Selden. New York: Farrar, Straus & Giroux, 1960. A cricket brings music, happiness, and some prosperity to a family in New York City. There are two stories in one. One story centers on the animals and insects; the other on the family's struggle with their newsstand business.

(75)   O   *The Crimson Moccasins,* Wayne Dyre Doughty. New York: Harper & Row, Pub., 1966. The story of a half-white Indian who painfully learns that he must be a bridge between his peoples.

(76)   M—O   *The Door in the Wall,* Marguerite de Angeli. New York: Doubleday,

1949. The story of Robin, son of a great lord, who is left crippled after an illness. He proves his courage and is rewarded. Fourteenth-century England.

(77)   Y—M   *The Drinking Gourd,* F. N. Monjo. New York: Harper & Row, Pub., 1969. A New England boy learns of the Underground Railroad in the 1850s.

(78)   M   *The Enormous Egg,* Oliver Butterworth. Boston: Little, Brown, 1956. A dinosaur is hatched, and the scientific world is astounded.

(79)   M—O   *The Family Under the Bridge,* Natalie Savage Carlson. New York: Harper & Row, Pub., 1958. Armand, a hobo who lives under one of the bridges of Paris, "adopts" a family during the housing shortage after WW II.

(80)   O   *Farmer in the Sky,* Robert A. Heinlein. New York: Scribner's, 1950. The realities and adventures of living on another planet.

(81)   O   *The Forgotten Door,* Alexander Key. Philadelphia: Westminster, 1965. In this science fiction story, Jon, a boy from another world, falls through a forgotten door into this world. Because he's different, both he and the family who befriends him are in danger.

(82)   O   *Friedrich,* Hans Peter Richter. New York: Holt, Rinehart & Winston, 1970. A Jewish family finds its world slowly falling apart as its members struggle to survive in Germany during the rise of Hitler and the Third Reich. A powerfully moving story.

(83)   M—O   *From the Mixed Up Files of Mrs. Basil E. Frankweiler,* Elaine L. Konigsberg. New York: Atheneum, 1967. Claudia and her brother run away to live for a week in New York City's Metropolitan Museum of Art. A modern adventure.

(84)   M—O   *The Good Master,* Kate Seredy. New York: Viking, 1935. Kate, a mischievous child, is understood and helped by her uncle. Hungarian setting.

(85)   M   *The Great Cheese Conspiracy,* Jean Van Leeuwen. New York: Random House, 1969. A gang of mice, who have learned about burglaries from old gangster movies, decide to rob a cheese store.

(86)   M   *The Great Quillow,* James Thurber. New York: Harcourt Brace Jovanovich, 1944. Quillow outwits a giant and saves his town.

(87)   M   *Hah-Nee of the Cliff Dwellers,* Mary and Conrad Buff. Boston: Houghton Mifflin, 1956. A terrible drought has made the Cliff Dwellers afraid. They blame Hah-Nee, an adopted boy.

(88)   M   *The Half-Pint Jinni,* Maurice Dolbier. New York: Random House, 1948. The adventures of a small jinni who can only grant half a wish.

(89)   M   *The Happy Orpheline,* Natalie Savage Carlson. New York: Harper & Row, Pub., 1957. A happy orphan is afraid she will be adopted by a woman who claims to be the Queen of France.

(90)   M   *Harriet the Spy,* Louise Fitzhugh. New York: Harper & Row, Pub., 1964. To counteract the loneliness caused by affluent and indifferent parents, Harriet keeps a notebook on her observations of people.

(91)   M—O   *Harriet Tubman: Conductor on the Underground Railway,* Ann Petry. New York: Thomas Y. Crowell, 1955. The story of a famous slave.

(92)   M—O   *The Helen Keller Story,* Catherine Owens Peare. New York: Thomas Y. Crowell, 1959. The biography of a great American woman.

(93) M—O *The Hobbit,* J. R. R. Tolkien. Boston: Houghton Mifflin Company, 1938. Home-loving Bilbo Baggins is pressed into service to seek out and kill the dragon, Smaug.

(94) M—O *Homer Price,* Robert McCloskey. New York: Viking, 1943. Humorous adventures of a boy in a small town.

(95) O *The House of Dies Drear,* Virginia Hamilton. New York: Macmillan, 1970. A family moves into a house that was once a station on the Underground Railroad. The house is full of memories, which make for a fascinating, suspenseful story.

(96) O *The House of Sixty Fathers,* Meindert DeJong. New York: Harper & Row, Pub., 1956. The story of a young Chinese boy who gets separated from his family and finds himself in Japanese occupied territory during World War II.

(97) M *The Hundred Dresses,* Eleanor Estes. New York: Harcourt Brace, Jovanovich, 1944. Wanda, a daughter of an immigrant family, is rejected by her classmates.

(98) M *James and the Giant Peach,* Roald Dahl. New York: Knopf, 1961. Inside the magic peach, James finds many insect friends, and together they have a fantastic journey across the ocean.

(99) Y—M *John Billington,* Clyde Robert Bulla. New York: Thomas Y. Crowell, 1956. Historic fiction account of a young boy who was one of the passengers on the *Mayflower.*

(100) M *John John Twilliger,* William Wondriska. New York: Holt, Rinehart & Winston, 1966. A young boy and his dog discover the secret of the mean, mysterious stranger who has taken over a town.

(101) O *Johnny Tremain,* Esther Forbes. Boston: Houghton Mifflin Company, 1943. Johnny, a young silver apprentice in Boston, struggles to maturity during the 1770s.

(102) O *Journey Outside,* Mary Q. Steele. New York: Viking, 1969. Dilar leaves the dark world of the Raft People to search for the Better Place. He learns a great deal about ignorance and wisdom. It is both an adventure and an allegory.

(103) M *J. T.,* Jane Wagner. New York: Dell, 1969. Taken from the television play, *J. T.* is the story of a boy growing up in the crowded city. He finds an old battered cat, and through his love for the animal begins to find himself.

(104) M *The Little House in the Big Woods,* Laura Ingalls Wilder. New York: Harper & Row, Pub., 1959. The true story of an American pioneer family in Wisconsin.

(105) Y *Little Pear,* Eleanor Frances Lattimore. New York: Harcourt Brace Jovanovich, 1931. The amusing adventures of a little Chinese boy.

(106) M—O *The Lotus Caves,* John Christopher. New York: Macmillan, 1969. A science fiction story of two boys who live on the moon. They leave their community to explore one day and become entrapped underground in a plant which possesses superintelligence.

(107) M—O *Magic at Wychwood,* Sally Watson. New York: Knopf, 1970. Elaine does not conform to the stereotype of a princess. Her undaunted nature is the cause of conflict in this satire on chivalry.

(108)   M   *Mary Jemison: Seneca Captive,* Jeanne Le Monnier Gardner. New York: Harcourt Brace Jovanovich, 1966. The exciting biography of a courageous white girl who was captured and adopted by Indians in the late 1700s.

(109)   M   *Mary Poppins,* P. L. Travers. Harcourt Brace Jovanovich, 1962. Mary, a nanny for Michael and Jane, entertains them with many magical adventures.

(110)   M   *Matchlock Gun,* Walter D. Edmonds. New York: Dodd, Mead, 1941. A young boy defends his home while his father is off fighting in the French and Indian Wars.

(111) Y—M   *The Mouse and the Motorcycle,* Beverly Cleary. William Morrow, 1965. A mouse has interesting adventures with a toy motorcycle.

(112) M—O   *Mrs. Frisby and the Rats of NIMH,* Robert C. O'Brien. New York: Atheneum, 1971. Laboratory rats seek to make a better world for themselves.

(113)   O   *My Brother Sam Is Dead,* James Lincoln and Christopher Collier. New York: Four Winds, 1974. The moving story of a Connecticut family during the Revolutionary War.

(114)   M   *Mystery of the Musical Umbrella,* Friedrich Feld. New York: Random House, 1962. A brother and sister help a gentleman find his stolen invention—a musical umbrella. English setting.

(115)   O   *Penn,* Elizabeth Janet Gray. New York: Viking, 1938. The story of William Penn, who became a convert to the Quaker way of life. He suffers religious persecution as well as his father's wrath.

(116) Y—M   *Peter Pan,* Sir James Barrie. New York: Scribner's, 1950. The classic story of a boy who doesn't want to grow up.

(117) M—O   *The Phantom Tollbooth,* Norman Juster. New York: Random House, 1961. Milo has many adventures in a fantastical land. He tries to be the mediator between two kings who are having a dispute over the importance of mathematics and language.

(118) Y—M   *Pinocchio,* C. Collodi (pseud.). New York: Macmillan, 1951. The adventures of a puppet who wants to become a real boy.

(119)   M   *Pippi Longstocking,* Astrid Lindgren. New York: Viking, 1950. Pippi, a superhuman girl, lives by herself and is independent. Her adventures are unorthodox.

(120)   O   *The Pushcart War,* Jean Merrill. Reading, Mass.: Addison-Wesley, 1964. A humorous spoof on the traffic problems in New York City in the year 1976. Push cart vendors and truck drivers start a war with pea shooters.

(121) M—O   *Queenie Peavy,* Robert Burch. New York: Viking, 1966. Queenie's father is in jail and her mother works hard at a factory. She is always in trouble but gradually learns to control her actions, attitudes, and destiny. Depression years in Georgia.

(122) Y—M   *Quiet on Account of Dinosaur,* Jane Thayer. New York: Morrow, 1964. Mary Ann finds a dinosaur and takes him to school. A problem arises when the dinosaur is frightened by noise.

(123) Y—M   *Rabbit Hill,* Robert Lawson. New York: Viking, 1944. The small animals are concerned about the "new folks" who are moving into the empty house.

(124)   O   *(The Merry Adventures of) Robin Hood*, Howard Pyle. New York: Scribner's, 1946. The legendary adventures of the outlaw-hero of England.

(125)   M   *Roosevelt Grady*, Louisa R. Shotwell. New York: Grosset & Dunlap, 1963. A nine-year-old boy wants to live in one place and stop migrating from fruit crop to fruit crop.

(126) Y—M   *Sam, Bangs and Moonshine*, Evaline Ness. New York: Holt, Rinehart & Winston, 1966. Sam, a fisherman's daughter, makes up fanciful stories. Trouble begins when she tells her friend Thomas about her mermaid mother.

(127) Y—M   *Sarah Whitcher's Story*, Elizabeth Yates. New York: Dutton, 1971. Based on a true account, this story is of a little pioneer girl in New Hampshire who becomes lost in the woods for four days.

(128)   O   *Secret of the Andes*, Ann Nolan Clark. New York: Viking, 1952. Cusi, an Indian boy, lives with the Inca llama herder and helps him tend the sacred flock. The young boy leaves to search for his heart's desire, but returns to learn the secret of the Andes and to take the vow to be the Inca llama herder.

(129)   O   *Shadow of a Bull*, Maia Wojciechowska. New York: Atheneum, 1964. Everyone expected Manolo to be a great Spanish bullfighter like his father, but he has many fears.

(130) M—O   *Shan's Lucky Knife*, Jean Merrill. Reading, Mass.: Addison-Wesley, 1960. Shan, a country boy from the hills of Burma, is taken advantage of by the sly boatmaster he works for. In the end Shan outwits him and gains great wealth.

(131)   O   *Sing Down the Moon*, Scott O'Dell. Boston: Houghton Mifflin, 1900. A fourteen-year-old Navaho girl tells her story of slavery and forced migration. Mid 1860s setting.

(132) M—O   *Sounder*, William H. Armstrong. New York: Harper & Row, Pub., 1969. A young sharecropper's son sets off to find his father who has been imprisoned.

(133) Y—M   *Squaps, the Moonling*, Artemis Verlag. New York: Atheneum, 1969. A shy moonling hangs on the suit of an astronaut and is taken back to earth. He can only say "squaps," he likes the rain, and he can float when there's a full moon.

(134)   M   *Strawberry Girl*, Lois Lenski. Philadelphia: Lippincott, 1945. A story, set in Florida in the early 1900s, of two quarreling families. Eventually the women serve as peacemakers.

(135) Y—M   *Sumi's Prize*, Yoshiko Uchida. New York: Scribner's, 1964. Sumi, a little Japanese girl, is the only girl to enter a kite-flying contest.

(136) Y—M   *Thy Friend, Obadiah*, Brinton Turkle. New York: Viking, 1972. A young early-American Quaker boy tries to reject a friendly seagull.

(137)   O   *Tituba of Salem Village*. Ann Petry. New York: Thomas Y. Crowell, 1964. Tituba, a slave from Barbados, is slowly drawn into the Salem witch hunts and is herself accused of witchcraft.

(138) M—O   *(The Adventures of) Tom Sawyer*, Mark Twain. Many editions. The American classic of a Missouri boy's adventures on the Mississippi River in the 1800s.

(139)   O   *Tomás Takes Charge,* Charlene Joy Talbot. New York: Lothrop, Lee & Shepard, 1966. When his father disappears, Tomás must find shelter and food for his sister in the tenements of New York City.

(140)   O   *Treasure Island,* Robert Louis Stevenson. Many editions. Young Jim Hawkins and the villainous rogue, Long John Silver, sail to a tropic isle and become involved in a climactic battle for treasure.

(141)   O   *Tuck Everlasting,* Natalie Babbitt. New York: Farrar, Straus & Giroux, 1975. The Tuck family discovers they are incapable of dying. Winnie Foster, a young girl who runs away from home and falls in love with Jesse Tuck, must choose between mortality and immortality.

(142)   M   *Venture for Freedom,* Ruby Zagoren. New York: Dell, 1969. The son of an African king, Venture, was sold into slavery in America in the 1700s. This account is based on his autobiography.

(143)   O   *Walk the World's Rim,* Betty Baker. New York: Harper & Row, Pub., 1965. Three Spaniards and a Negro slave, the survivors of an expedition of 1527, befriend a young Indian boy and take him to Mexico with them. The boy's friendship with the slave teaches him greater meaning in life.

(144) M—O   *"What Then, Raman?"* Shirley L. Arora. Chicago: Follett Publishing Company, 1960. Raman, a boy of India, is the first in his village to learn to read. From his teacher he learns of the responsibility that education carries with it.

(145) M—O   *The Wheel on the School,* Meindert De Jong. New York: Harper & Row, Pub., 1954. The children of Shora, a little Dutch fishing village, involve the whole town in their project to get the storks to return.

(146)   M   *While the Horses Galloped to London,* Mabel Watts. New York: Parents', 1973. On his carriage ride to London, Sherman guards a cooking pot which he uses to outwit the outlaw, Rough Roger.

(147)   M   *Wind in the Willows,* Kenneth Grahame. New York: Scribner's, 1935. The charming adventures of Mole, Rat, Badger, and Toad.

(148) Y—M   *Winnie the Pooh,* A. A. Milne. New York: Dutton, 1954. Winnie, a stuffed bear, and his animal friends have many delightful days.

(149)   O   *The Witch of Blackbird Pond,* Elizabeth George Speare. Boston: Houghton Mifflin, 1958. After leaving her home in Barbados, Kit Tyler feels out of place in a Puritan community in Connecticut. Her spirited personality arouses suspicion, and she finds herself accused of witchcraft.

(150) M—O   *A Wrinkle in Time,* Madeline d'Engle. New York: Farrar, Straus & Giroux, 1962. Children's search for their missing father in outer space.

(151) M—O   *Zeely,* Virginia Hamilton. New York: Macmillan, 1967. A sensitive story about Geeder, a girl who fantasizes that an older girl, Zeely, is a Watusi queen.

Index